SPECTRUM

Math

Grade 7

Columbus, Ohio

Send all inquiries to:
School Specialty Publishing
8720 Orion Place
Columbus, OH 43240-2111

ISBN 0-7696-3707-8

2 3 4 5 6 7 8 9 10 POH 11 10 09 08 07

Table of Contents Grade 7

Table of Contents, continued

Chapter 9 Probability and Statistics

Chapter 10 Geometry

Chapter 11 Perimeter, Area, and Volume

Chapter 12 Preparing for Algebra

NAME ____________________

Check What You Know

Whole Numbers

Add, subtract, multiply, or divide.

	a	b	c	d	e
1.	24 + 68 + 53	326 + 479 + 194	7036 + 1428 + 311	37924 + 18657 + 93214	114738 + 506247 + 382011
2.	74 − 8	325 − 47	8804 − 7963	57264 − 19896	402685 − 237418
3.	17 × 28	473 × 57	3862 × 9	7043 × 6	5877 × 43
4.	43 × 37	648 × 209	829 × 634	2189 × 615	1724 × 568
5.	8)56	3)743	5)3807	66)794	28)596
6.	71)934	19)6118	42)9527	36)10379	53)74891

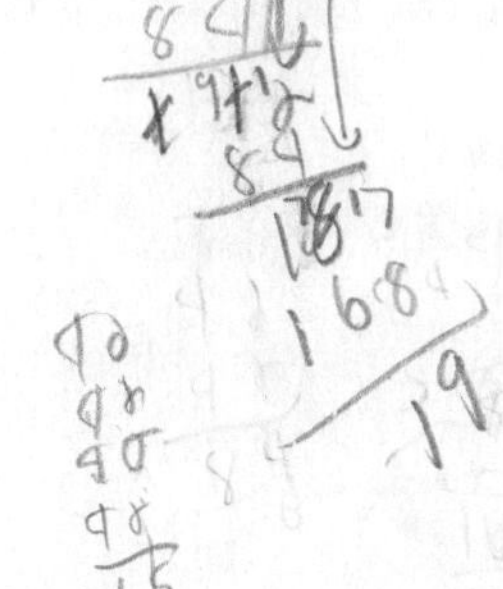

CHAPTER 1 PRETEST

NAME ______________________

Check What You Know

Whole Numbers

SHOW YOUR WORK

Solve each problem.

7. Manuel read 58 pages on Sunday, 37 pages on Monday, and 43 pages on Tuesday. How many total pages did he read? Manuel read ______ pages.	**7.**
8. If a car travels at an average speed of 48 miles per hour, how long will it take to go 1,776 miles? It will take ______ hours.	**8.**
9. Kendra earns $63 dollars a week at her part-time job. She plans to work 28 weeks this year. How much money will she earn? She will earn ______.	**9.**
10. A factory produced 593,257 calculators. However, 5,728 of them were defective. How many were good? Of all the calculators, ______ were good.	**10.**
11. Mr. Fallows bought 3,560 square feet of land. It cost $33 for each square foot. How much did Mr. Fallows spend? Mr. Fallows spent ______.	**11.**
12. Mr. Fallows divided his 3,560 square feet of land into 23 equal plots, and he used the rest for a compost pile. How large was each plot? How large was the compost pile? Each plot was ______ square feet. The compost pile was ______ square feet.	**12.**

NAME ______________________

Lesson 1.1 Adding through 6 Digits

	Add ones.	Add tens.	Add hundreds.
addend addend + addend sum	1 324138 407317 + 62332 7	1 324138 407317 + 62332 87	1 324138 407317 + 62332 787

	Add thousands.	Add ten thousands.	Add hundred thousands.
	1 1 324138 407317 + 62332 3787	1 1 324138 407317 + 62332 93787	1 1 324138 407317 + 62332 793787

Add.

	a	b	c	d	e
1.	375 + 17	42 + 136	526 + 417	2248 + 13271	642371 + 115238
2.	78 + 49	341 + 406	5583 + 2473	78426 + 1381	113471 + 207369
3.	53 + 928	620 + 620	3865 + 927	55371 + 40693	849380 + 20618
4.	43 27 + 108	126 403 + 369	4287 3500 + 1124	38257 4126 + 5310	586203 102479 + 130592
5.	33 12 60 + 14	441 302 124 + 113	3121 1407 2242 + 1158	13112 20841 33072 + 11825	135276 213401 106592 + 321145

NAME ______________________

Lesson 1.2 Subtracting through 6 Digits

	Subtract ones.	Subtract tens.	Subtract hundreds.
	7 14	7 14	6 15 7 14
minuend	8 3 7 5 ~~8~~ ~~4~~	8 3 7 5 ~~8~~ ~~4~~	8 3 ~~7~~ ~~5~~ ~~8~~ ~~4~~
− subtrahend	− 6 4 5 7 3 6	− 6 4 5 7 3 6	− 6 4 5 7 3 6
difference	8	4 8	8 4 8

	Subtract thousands.	Subtract ten thousands.	Subtract hundred thousands.
	6 15 7 14	7 13 6 15 7 14	7 13 6 15 7 14
minuend	8 3 ~~7~~ ~~5~~ ~~8~~ ~~4~~	~~8~~ ~~3~~ ~~7~~ ~~5~~ ~~8~~ ~~4~~	~~8~~ ~~3~~ ~~7~~ ~~5~~ ~~8~~ ~~4~~
− subtrahend	− 6 4 5 7 3 6	− 6 4 5 7 3 6	− 6 4 5 7 3 6
difference	1 8 4 8	9 1 8 4 8	1 9 1 8 4 8

Subtract.

	a	b	c	d	e
1.	38 − 7	629 − 35	4224 − 115	55243 − 34127	203798 − 121471
2.	44 − 28	708 − 521	8974 − 2187	38719 − 16423	932487 − 350378
3.	93 − 8	392 − 98	5936 − 2852	77259 − 39648	832945 − 41858
4.	34 − 26	842 − 551	7734 − 2817	98327 − 9415	438721 − 394632
5.	88 − 29	487 − 338	3381 − 2465	64238 − 7156	704632 − 464651
6.	62 − 39	530 − 267	6642 − 3951	87403 − 29312	384723 − 66905

NAME ______________________

Lesson 1.3 Problem Solving

SHOW YOUR WORK

Solve each problem.

1. Stu bought a book for $17. He paid with a $20 bill. How much change did he receive?

   Stu received __________ in change.

2. The populations of Pottsville, Middleton, and Swain are 38,247; 42,635; and 1,324. What is the total population of these cities?

   The total population is __________.

3. Rosa's car is due for its next service at 150,000 miles. So far she has driven 138,271 miles. How many more miles can she drive until her car needs service?

   She can drive __________ more miles.

4. A girl's club had a car wash to raise money. The girls made $224 on Friday, $392 on Saturday, and $434 on Sunday. In the three days, how much money did they raise?

   They raised __________.

5. The stadium has 35,867 seats. Only 26,437 people attended last night's game. How many seats were empty?

   There were __________ empty seats.

6. In the first four games of the season, the Muskrat basketball team scored 77, 88, 93, and 101 points. How many points did they score in the first 4 games?

   They scored __________ points.

7. At Gainesville Middle School, there are 327 students in the sixth grade, 463 students in the seventh grade, and 308 students in the eighth grade. How many students are there at Gainesville Middle School?

   There are __________ students at Gainesville Middle School.

1.

2.

3.

4.

5.

6.

7.

NAME ____________________

Lesson 1.4 Multiplying through 4 Digits

Multiply 5824 by 7 ones.	Multiply 5824 by 4 tens.	Multiply 5824 by 1 hundred. Then add.
$\begin{array}{r} \overset{5\,1\,2}{5824} \\ \times\ 147 \\ \hline 40768 \end{array}$	$\begin{array}{r} \overset{3\ \ 1\ }{5824} \\ \times\ 147 \\ \hline 40768 \\ 232960 \end{array}$	$\begin{array}{r} 5824 \\ \times\ 147 \\ \hline 40768 \\ 232960 \\ +\ 582400 \\ \hline 856128 \end{array}$ Add

Multiply.

	a	b	c	d
1.	$\begin{array}{r} 37 \\ \times\ 4 \\ \hline \end{array}$	$\begin{array}{r} 682 \\ \times\ 7 \\ \hline \end{array}$	$\begin{array}{r} 526 \\ \times\ 3 \\ \hline \end{array}$	$\begin{array}{r} 2173 \\ \times\ 5 \\ \hline \end{array}$
2.	$\begin{array}{r} 46 \\ \times 53 \\ \hline \end{array}$	$\begin{array}{r} 376 \\ \times\ 49 \\ \hline \end{array}$	$\begin{array}{r} 423 \\ \times\ 64 \\ \hline \end{array}$	$\begin{array}{r} 5833 \\ \times\ 71 \\ \hline \end{array}$
3.	$\begin{array}{r} 68 \\ \times 29 \\ \hline \end{array}$	$\begin{array}{r} 287 \\ \times 423 \\ \hline \end{array}$	$\begin{array}{r} 323 \\ \times 605 \\ \hline \end{array}$	$\begin{array}{r} 4827 \\ \times\ 356 \\ \hline \end{array}$
4.	$\begin{array}{r} 37 \\ \times 468 \\ \hline \end{array}$	$\begin{array}{r} 732 \\ \times 268 \\ \hline \end{array}$	$\begin{array}{r} 3371 \\ \times\ 340 \\ \hline \end{array}$	$\begin{array}{r} 2479 \\ \times\ 236 \\ \hline \end{array}$

NAME ____________________

Lesson 1.5 Dividing by 1 Digit

Divide 275 by 8.

$$\begin{array}{r} 3 \\ 8\overline{)275} \\ -240 \\ \hline 35 \end{array}$$

30 × 8 = 240

subtract.

Divide 35 by 8.

$$\begin{array}{r} 34\text{ r}3 \\ 8\overline{)275} \\ -240 \\ \hline 35 \\ -32 \\ \hline 3 \end{array}$$

4 × 8 = 32

subtract.

3 < 8, so it is a remainder.

Divide.

	a	b	c	d	e
1.	7)43	3)87	4)215	6)408	3)2334
2.	9)83	2)75	5)427	7)3804	6)1037
3.	4)56	7)123	3)526	2)4129	4)7723

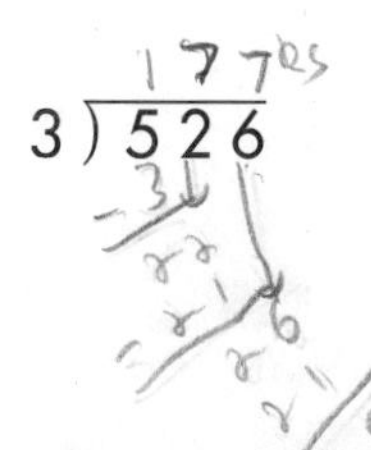

NAME ____________________

Lesson 1.6 Dividing by 2 Digits

Divide 39 by 17.

```
      2
17)392
  -340   20 × 17 = 340
    52   subtract.
```

Divide 52 by 17.

```
     23 r1
17)392
  -340
    52
   -51   3 × 17 = 51
     1   subtract.
```

1 < 17, so it is a remainder.

Divide.

	a	b	c	d	e
1.	12)409	26)722	43)159	72)518	63)741
2.	37)984	51)348	16)614	83)265	98)686
3.	44)820	14)322	54)329	28)937	31)835

NAME ______________________________

Lesson 1.6 Dividing by 2 Digits

Divide 78 by 23.	Divide 94 by 23.	Divide 24 by 23.
3 23)78443 − 69 3 × 23 = 69 9443 subtract.	34 23)78443 − 69 9443 − 92 4 × 23 = 92 243 subtract.	3410 r13 23)78443 − 69 9443 − 92 243 − 23 1 × 23 = 23 13 subtract. 13 < 23, so the ones digit is 0 and 13 is a remainder.

Divide.

	a	b	c	d	e
1.	$14\overline{)3827}$	$72\overline{)6839}$	$35\overline{)21210}$	$49\overline{)61738}$	$62\overline{)39426}$
2.	$25\overline{)4417}$	$41\overline{)9717}$	$53\overline{)11208}$	$26\overline{)59324}$	$12\overline{)77139}$
3.	$38\overline{)9462}$	$54\overline{)5831}$	$81\overline{)30498}$	$97\overline{)98417}$	$73\overline{)32631}$

NAME ____________________

Lesson 1.7 Problem Solving

SHOW YOUR WORK

Solve each problem.

1. Jackie expects 327 people at her banquet. She noticed that there are 48 napkins in a package. How many full packages of napkins will she need? How many napkins will be left?

Jackie will need ________ full packages and ________ napkins will be left.

1.

2. The auditorium has 175 rows of seats. Each row has 54 seats. How many seats are there in the auditorium?

There are ____________ seats in the auditorium.

2.

3. The school collected 48,251 box tops. If each student brought in exactly 113 box tops, how many students are in the school?

There are ____________ students in the school.

3.

4. An average of 326 cars drive over the Rollins Bridge every day. How many cars drive over the bridge each year (365 days)?

Each year, ____________ cars drive over the bridge.

4.

5. Luisa's car goes 24 miles on a gallon of gas. How many gallons of gas will she need to drive 1,128 miles?

Luisa will need ____________ gallons of gas.

5.

6. There are 5,280 feet in a mile. If it is 127 miles from Danville to Center City, how many feet apart are the two cities?

The two cities are ____________ feet apart.

6.

7. Marcus needs 448 bricks for a construction project. He can buy bricks in cases of 72. How many cases does he need to buy? How many extra bricks will he have?

He needs to buy ______ cases, and he will have ______ extra bricks.

7.

NAME ______________________

Check What You Learned

Whole Numbers

Add, subtract, multiply, or divide.

	a	b	c	d	e
1.	39 + 46 + 88	527 + 650 + 396	6824 + 5173 + 2051	33623 + 97046 + 81997	732448 + 196823 + 243599
2.	91 − 7	539 − 96	3510 − 1906	74237 − 58246	656043 − 278126
3.	44 × 68	731 × 96	1328 × 6	5744 × 3	2108 × 18
4.	83 × 91	632 × 570	812 × 348	2436 × 291	1509 × 854
5.	$6\overline{)73}$	$4\overline{)891}$	$3\overline{)5752}$	$23\overline{)560}$	$49\overline{)642}$
6.	$63\overline{)5927}$	$26\overline{)7244}$	$37\overline{)4128}$	$94\overline{)38249}$	$78\overline{)27378}$

CHAPTER 1 POSTTEST

NAME ____________________

Check What You Learned

SHOW YOUR WORK

Whole Numbers

Solve each problem.

7. There were 343 men, 427 women, and 856 children at the carnival. What was the total attendance?

There were __________ people in attendance.

8. Olivia and Steve baked 22 batches of cookies for the bake sale. Each batch had 36 cookies. How many cookies did they bake?

They baked __________ cookies.

9. Maria needed to send out 237 invitations. She bought stamps in books of 20 and then bought extra stamps individually. How many books of stamps did she buy? How many extra stamps did she have to buy?

She had to buy __________ books and __________ extra stamps.

10. It is 4,382 feet around the lower walking track at the park. It is 2,747 feet around the upper track. How much longer is the lower track than the upper track?

The lower track is __________ feet longer.

11. A team of 5 runners competed in a relay race. Each runner had to run 730 yards. How long was the race?

The race was __________ yards long.

12. A factory manufactures 68,424 parts a day. The factory operates 24 hours a day and makes the same number of parts each hour. How many parts does it make in an hour?

It makes __________ parts in an hour.

7.

8.

9.

10.

11.

12.

CHAPTER 1 POSTTEST

NAME ____________

Check What You Know

Fractions

CHAPTER 2 PRETEST

Add, subtract, multiply, or divide. Write each answer in simplest form.

	a	b	c	d
1.	$2\frac{1}{4} + 2\frac{2}{3}$	$3\frac{1}{2} + 2\frac{1}{7}$	$2\frac{1}{8} + 4\frac{2}{3}$	$1\frac{5}{7} + 2\frac{4}{5}$
2.	$6\frac{1}{3} - 2\frac{1}{4}$	$\frac{3}{8} - \frac{1}{4}$	$5\frac{3}{10} - 2\frac{4}{5}$	$3\frac{4}{7} - 1\frac{1}{2}$
3.	$\frac{3}{4} \times \frac{1}{6}$	$\frac{5}{7} \times \frac{2}{3}$	$\frac{1}{2} \times \frac{4}{9}$	$\frac{7}{10} \times \frac{3}{8} \times \frac{1}{4}$
4.	$2\frac{1}{3} \times 1\frac{3}{8}$	$5\frac{1}{2} \times 1\frac{1}{4}$	$3\frac{3}{7} \times 1\frac{5}{6}$	$3\frac{1}{4} \times 1\frac{1}{3} \times \frac{1}{2}$
5.	$5\frac{1}{4} \div 1\frac{3}{8}$	$6\frac{4}{7} \div 12$	$1\frac{1}{2} \div \frac{3}{5}$	$2\frac{2}{3} \div 3\frac{1}{6}$

NAME ____________________

Check What You Know

Fractions

SHOW YOUR WORK

Solve each problem.

6. One box of clips weighs $4\frac{2}{3}$ ounces. Another box weighs $5\frac{3}{8}$ ounces. What is the total weight of the two boxes?

   The total weight is ____________ ounces.

7. Luggage on a certain airline is limited to 2 pieces per person. Together the 2 pieces can weigh no more than $58\frac{1}{2}$ pounds. If a passenger has one piece of luggage that weighs $32\frac{1}{3}$ pounds, what is the most the second piece can weigh?

   The second piece can weigh ____________ pounds.

8. Mavis spends $1\frac{1}{4}$ hours on the bus every weekday (Monday through Friday). How many hours is she on the bus each week?

   She is on the bus ____________ hours each week.

9. A bucket that holds $5\frac{1}{4}$ gallons of water is being used to fill a tub that can hold $34\frac{1}{8}$ gallons. How many buckets will be needed to fill the tub?

   ____________ buckets are needed to fill the tub.

10. A black piece of pipe is $8\frac{1}{3}$ centimeters long. A silver piece of pipe is $2\frac{3}{5}$ times longer. How long is the silver piece of pipe?

    The silver piece is ____________ centimeters long.

11. One section of wood is $3\frac{5}{8}$ meters long. Another section is $5\frac{2}{3}$ meters. When the two pieces are put together to make a single piece, how long is the piece of wood?

    The piece of wood is ____________ meters long.

6.
7.
8.
9.
10.
11.

NAME ____________________

Lesson 2.1 Finding the Greatest Common Factor

16 = 1×16, 2 × 8, 4 × 4 — (1), (2), (4), (8), and 16 are factors.

24 = 1 × 24, 2 × 12, 3 × 8, 4 × 6 — (1), (2), 3, (4), 6, (8), 12, 24 are factors.

The common factors of **16** and **24** are circled.

The greatest common factor is **8**.

List the factors of each number shown below.
Then, list the common factors and greatest common factor.

		Factors	Common Factor(s)	Greatest Common Factor
1.	14	1, 2, 7, 14		
	21	1, 3, 7, 21	1, 7	7
2.	12	____		
	20	____	____	____
3.	10	____		
	12	____	____	____
4.	24	____		
	36	____	____	____
5.	9	____		
	15	____	____	____
6.	6	____		
	8	____	____	____
7.	18	____		
	20	____	____	____

NAME ______________________

Lesson 2.2 Reducing to Simplest Form

A fraction is in simplest form when the greatest common factor of the numerator and denominator is 1. A mixed numeral is in simplest form when its fraction is in simplest form and has a value between 0 and 1. Divide the numerator and denominator by their greatest common factor.

$$\frac{6}{12} = \frac{6 \div 6}{12 \div 6} = \frac{1}{2} \qquad 7\frac{14}{21} = \frac{14 \div 7}{21 \div 7} = 7\frac{2}{3}$$

Write each of the following in simplest form.

	a	b	c
1.	$\frac{18}{20}$ ________	$3\frac{18}{24}$ ________	$\frac{25}{95}$ ________
2.	$\frac{14}{28}$ ________	$\frac{36}{40}$ ________	$9\frac{8}{12}$ ________
3.	$\frac{36}{48}$ ________	$7\frac{4}{12}$ ________	$\frac{27}{36}$ ________
4.	$8\frac{9}{12}$ ________	$6\frac{5}{20}$ ________	$4\frac{50}{70}$ ________
5.	$4\frac{3}{15}$ ________	$\frac{16}{32}$ ________	$2\frac{12}{52}$ ________

NAME ____________________

Lesson 2.3 Finding Common Denominators

The **least common multiple (LCM)** is the smallest multiple that is shared by two numbers. Rename fractions so they have common denominators by finding the LCM of the denominators.

$\frac{1}{2}$ and $\frac{2}{3}$ do not have common denominators. The LCM of 2 and 3 is 6.

$\frac{1}{2} \times \frac{3}{3} = \frac{3}{6}$ $\frac{2}{3} \times \frac{2}{2} = \frac{4}{6}$

$\frac{3}{6}$ and $\frac{4}{6}$ do have common denominators.

Find the LCM and rename each pair of fractions with common denominators.

	a		b	
1.	$\frac{1}{6}$ and $\frac{2}{5}$	______________	$\frac{3}{8}$ and $\frac{1}{3}$	______________
2.	$\frac{3}{4}$ and $\frac{1}{7}$	______________	$\frac{1}{6}$ and $\frac{3}{4}$	______________
3.	$\frac{1}{2}$ and $\frac{5}{8}$	______________	$\frac{1}{4}$ and $\frac{3}{10}$	______________
4.	$\frac{1}{5}$ and $\frac{4}{9}$	______________	$\frac{2}{5}$ and $\frac{1}{4}$	______________
5.	$\frac{1}{3}$ and $\frac{3}{5}$	______________	$\frac{1}{6}$ and $\frac{2}{9}$	______________

NAME ______________________

Lesson 2.4 Renaming Fractions and Mixed Numerals

Every whole number can be written as a fraction with a denominator of 1.

$3 = \frac{3}{1} \quad 10 = \frac{10}{1} \quad 25 = \frac{25}{1}$

Change $2\frac{3}{4}$ to a fraction.

$$2\frac{3}{4} = \frac{2}{1} + \frac{3}{4} = \frac{2 \times 4}{4} + \frac{3}{4}$$
$$= \frac{8 + 3}{4} = \frac{11}{4}$$

Change $\frac{15}{6}$ to a mixed numeral.

$$\frac{15}{6} = 6\overline{)15} \to 2 \text{ R } 3 \;(15 - 12 = 3) = 2\frac{3}{6} = 2\frac{1}{2}$$

Change each of the following to a fraction. Reduce to simplest form.

	a	b	c	d
1.	$3\frac{5}{8}$ ______	9 ______	$2\frac{3}{7}$ ______	$5\frac{1}{2}$ ______
2.	$1\frac{2}{16}$ ______	$8\frac{3}{12}$ ______	14 ______	$3\frac{5}{6}$ ______
3.	$4\frac{1}{3}$ ______	$4\frac{7}{9}$ ______	$1\frac{2}{5}$ ______	47 ______

Change each of the following to a mixed numeral in simplest form.

	a	b	c	d
4.	$\frac{10}{3}$ ______	$\frac{23}{8}$ ______	$\frac{9}{6}$ ______	$\frac{39}{7}$ ______
5.	$\frac{15}{4}$ ______	$3\frac{8}{3}$ ______	$\frac{18}{12}$ ______	$5\frac{5}{3}$ ______
6.	$\frac{19}{11}$ ______	$\frac{42}{10}$ ______	$7\frac{12}{5}$ ______	$\frac{52}{11}$ ______

NAME ____________________

Lesson 2.5 Adding and Subtracting Fractions

To add or subtract when the denominators are different, rename the fractions so the denominators are the same.

$$\begin{array}{r} \frac{2}{3} \\ +\ \frac{3}{7} \\ \hline \end{array} = \begin{array}{r} \frac{2}{3} \times \frac{7}{7} \\ +\ \frac{3}{7} \times \frac{3}{3} \\ \hline \end{array} = \begin{array}{r} \frac{14}{21} \\ +\ \frac{9}{21} \\ \hline \frac{23}{21} \end{array} = 1\frac{2}{21}$$

$$\begin{array}{r} \frac{4}{5} \\ -\ \frac{1}{10} \\ \hline \end{array} = \begin{array}{r} \frac{4}{5} \times \frac{2}{2} \\ -\ \frac{1}{10} \\ \hline \end{array} = \begin{array}{r} \frac{8}{10} \\ -\ \frac{1}{10} \\ \hline \frac{7}{10} \end{array}$$

Write each answer in simplest form.

	a	b	c	d
1.	$\frac{3}{4} + \frac{5}{8}$	$\frac{1}{2} + \frac{1}{3}$	$\frac{3}{4} + \frac{2}{5}$	$\frac{1}{6} + \frac{1}{3}$
2.	$\frac{3}{8} + \frac{4}{5}$	$\frac{1}{2} + \frac{3}{10}$	$\frac{2}{3} + \frac{3}{12}$	$\frac{3}{4} + \frac{7}{10}$
3.	$\frac{1}{4} + \frac{3}{8}$	$\frac{2}{5} + \frac{3}{7}$	$\frac{1}{7} + \frac{7}{8}$	$\frac{2}{3} + \frac{1}{5}$
4.	$\frac{3}{5} - \frac{1}{4}$	$\frac{1}{2} - \frac{3}{10}$	$\frac{7}{8} - \frac{1}{2}$	$\frac{4}{5} - \frac{1}{3}$
5.	$\frac{5}{6} - \frac{1}{3}$	$\frac{2}{3} - \frac{1}{5}$	$\frac{5}{8} - \frac{1}{6}$	$\frac{7}{10} - \frac{1}{2}$
6.	$\frac{3}{4} - \frac{2}{3}$	$\frac{5}{9} - \frac{1}{2}$	$\frac{1}{2} - \frac{1}{3}$	$\frac{7}{11} - \frac{2}{9}$

NAME ______________________

Lesson 2.6 Adding and Subtracting Mixed Numerals

To add or subtract mixed numerals when the denominators of the fractions are different, find a common denominator and rename the fractions.

$$\begin{array}{r} 3\frac{1}{2} \\ +2\frac{2}{3} \\ \hline \end{array} = \begin{array}{r} 3\frac{3}{6} \\ +2\frac{4}{6} \\ \hline 5\frac{7}{6} \end{array} = 6\frac{1}{6}$$

$$\begin{array}{r} 4\frac{1}{4} \\ -2\frac{1}{2} \\ \hline \end{array} = \begin{array}{r} 4\frac{1}{4} \\ -2\frac{2}{4} \\ \hline \end{array} = \begin{array}{r} 3\frac{5}{4} \\ -2\frac{2}{4} \\ \hline 1\frac{3}{4} \end{array}$$

Write each answer in simplest form.

	a	b	c	d
1.	$1\frac{1}{3} + 2\frac{1}{4}$	$3\frac{3}{8} + 7\frac{1}{2}$	$4\frac{2}{7} + 2\frac{1}{3}$	$1\frac{2}{5} + 3\frac{3}{10}$
2.	$4\frac{4}{9} + 3\frac{1}{3}$	$1\frac{1}{8} + 1\frac{7}{10}$	$2\frac{1}{6} + 3\frac{5}{8}$	$1\frac{3}{7} + 2\frac{1}{5}$
3.	$3\frac{1}{2} + 2\frac{1}{4}$	$2\frac{5}{6} + 1\frac{5}{9}$	$3\frac{4}{7} + 1\frac{1}{10}$	$4\frac{1}{3} + 2\frac{1}{2}$
4.	$2\frac{3}{8} - 1\frac{2}{9}$	$3\frac{1}{4} - 1\frac{1}{3}$	$4\frac{1}{2} - 3\frac{3}{4}$	$6\frac{5}{8} - 4\frac{6}{7}$
5.	$3\frac{2}{11} - 1\frac{5}{8}$	$7\frac{2}{3} - 3\frac{2}{5}$	$5\frac{1}{3} - 2\frac{1}{2}$	$2\frac{5}{6} - 1\frac{2}{7}$
6.	$4\frac{7}{9} - 2\frac{2}{3}$	$3\frac{1}{5} - 1\frac{3}{4}$	$4\frac{5}{6} - 2\frac{1}{8}$	$3\frac{1}{8} - 1\frac{3}{4}$

NAME ____________________

Lesson 2.7 Problem Solving

SHOW YOUR WORK

Solve each problem.

1. At closing time, the bakery had $2\frac{1}{4}$ apple pies and $1\frac{1}{2}$ cherry pies left. How much more apple pie than cherry pie was left?

There was __________ more of an apple pie than cherry.

2. The hardware store sold $6\frac{3}{8}$ boxes of large nails and $7\frac{2}{5}$ boxes of small nails. In total, how many boxes of nails did the store sell?

The store sold __________ boxes of nails.

3. Nita studied $4\frac{1}{3}$ hours on Saturday and $5\frac{1}{4}$ hours on Sunday. How many hours did she spend studying?

She spent __________ hours studying.

4. Kwan is $5\frac{2}{3}$ feet tall. Mary is $4\frac{11}{12}$ feet tall. How much taller is Kwan?

Kwan is __________ foot taller.

5. This week, Jim practiced the piano $1\frac{1}{8}$ hours on Monday and $2\frac{3}{7}$ hours on Tuesday. How many hours did he practice this week? How much longer did Jim practice on Tuesday than on Monday?

Jim practiced __________ hours this week.

Jim practiced __________ hours longer on Tuesday.

6. Oscar caught a fish that weighed $4\frac{1}{6}$ pounds and then caught another that weighed $6\frac{5}{8}$ pounds. How much more did the second fish weigh?

The second fish weighed __________ pounds more.

1.

2.

3.

4.

5.

6.

NAME ____________________

Lesson 2.8 Multiplying Fractions

Reduce to simplest form if possible. Then, multiply the numerators and multiply the denominators.

$$\frac{3}{8} \times \frac{5}{6} \times \frac{1}{7} = \frac{\overset{1}{\cancel{3}} \times 5 \times 1}{8 \times \underset{2}{\cancel{6}} \times 7} = \frac{1 \times 5 \times 1}{8 \times 2 \times 7} = \frac{5}{112}$$

Write each answer in simplest form.

	a	b	c	d
1.	$\frac{1}{2} \times \frac{3}{4}$	$\frac{2}{3} \times \frac{4}{5}$	$\frac{3}{4} \times \frac{3}{4}$	$\frac{4}{5} \times \frac{1}{8}$
2.	$\frac{3}{5} \times \frac{7}{8}$	$\frac{1}{3} \times \frac{3}{5}$	$\frac{3}{7} \times \frac{1}{5}$	$\frac{3}{10} \times \frac{4}{5}$
3.	$\frac{5}{8} \times \frac{3}{8}$	$\frac{2}{3} \times \frac{1}{2}$	$\frac{5}{6} \times \frac{2}{3}$	$\frac{4}{7} \times \frac{1}{3}$
4.	$\frac{1}{2} \times \frac{1}{3} \times \frac{2}{3}$	$\frac{2}{3} \times \frac{3}{5} \times \frac{1}{2}$	$\frac{2}{3} \times \frac{4}{5} \times \frac{2}{7}$	$\frac{1}{3} \times \frac{5}{8} \times \frac{1}{2}$
5.	$\frac{1}{4} \times \frac{3}{4} \times \frac{1}{2}$	$\frac{1}{3} \times \frac{3}{4} \times \frac{1}{2}$	$\frac{3}{7} \times \frac{2}{3} \times \frac{3}{4}$	$\frac{5}{8} \times \frac{2}{3} \times \frac{1}{5}$
6.	$\frac{3}{7} \times \frac{1}{2} \times \frac{2}{5}$	$\frac{4}{9} \times \frac{3}{5} \times \frac{1}{8}$	$\frac{7}{8} \times \frac{2}{5} \times \frac{1}{3}$	$\frac{4}{5} \times \frac{3}{4} \times \frac{5}{8}$

NAME ____________________

Lesson 2.9 Multiplying Mixed Numerals

Rename the numbers as fractions. Reduce to simplest form. Multiply the numerators and denominators. Simplify.

$$3\frac{1}{5} \times 2\frac{2}{3} \times 1\frac{1}{8} = \frac{16 \times \overset{1}{\cancel{8}} \times \overset{3}{\cancel{9}}}{5 \times \underset{1}{\cancel{3}} \times \underset{1}{\cancel{8}}} = \frac{16 \times 1 \times 3}{5 \times 1 \times 1} = \frac{48}{5} = 9\frac{3}{5}$$

Write each answer in simplest form.

	a	b	c
1.	$3 \times 1\frac{2}{7}$	$2\frac{1}{4} \times 3\frac{1}{3}$	$1\frac{1}{9} \times 3\frac{1}{4}$
2.	$2\frac{1}{4} \times 6$	$1\frac{2}{3} \times 3\frac{7}{8}$	$2\frac{1}{7} \times 1\frac{1}{3}$
3.	$4\frac{1}{2} \times 2\frac{1}{3} \times 3$	$5\frac{1}{4} \times 2\frac{1}{2} \times 1\frac{1}{3}$	$4\frac{1}{8} \times 3\frac{2}{7} \times 7$
4.	$\frac{5}{6} \times 1\frac{1}{3} \times 2$	$\frac{2}{3} \times 1\frac{5}{8} \times 3\frac{1}{4}$	$1\frac{1}{2} \times 2\frac{2}{3} \times 1\frac{1}{8}$
5.	$2\frac{1}{4} \times 1\frac{1}{8} \times \frac{2}{3}$	$\frac{5}{6} \times 1\frac{3}{8} \times 2\frac{2}{3}$	$2\frac{1}{4} \times 1\frac{1}{3} \times 1\frac{2}{9}$
6.	$5 \times 1\frac{1}{7} \times 2\frac{1}{5}$	$1\frac{1}{7} \times \frac{5}{8} \times 2\frac{1}{3}$	$1\frac{1}{9} \times \frac{3}{8} \times 2\frac{1}{3}$

NAME ______________________________

Lesson 2.10 Reciprocals

Any two numbers with a product of 1 are reciprocals.

$\frac{3}{4} \times \frac{4}{3} = \frac{12}{12} = 1$	$1\frac{3}{4} \times \frac{4}{7} = \frac{7}{4} \times \frac{4}{7} = \frac{28}{28} = 1$
$\frac{3}{4}$ and $\frac{4}{3}$ are reciprocals.	$1\frac{3}{4}$ (or $\frac{7}{4}$) and $\frac{4}{7}$ are reciprocals.

Write the reciprocal.

	a	b	c	d	e	f
1.	$\frac{2}{3}$ ______	$1\frac{1}{8}$ ______	$\frac{7}{2}$ ______	$3\frac{1}{4}$ ______	$\frac{9}{12}$ ______	$\frac{2}{5}$ ______
2.	$\frac{7}{8}$ ______	$3\frac{1}{3}$ ______	$1\frac{3}{5}$ ______	12 ______	$\frac{3}{7}$ ______	$\frac{1}{2}$ ______
3.	$\frac{1}{10}$ ______	$\frac{3}{5}$ ______	$2\frac{1}{7}$ ______	$\frac{3}{11}$ ______	$2\frac{3}{8}$ ______	4 ______
4.	$\frac{3}{8}$ ______	$\frac{2}{7}$ ______	$\frac{4}{9}$ ______	$1\frac{3}{4}$ ______	$\frac{7}{12}$ ______	$\frac{3}{14}$ ______
5.	$\frac{2}{17}$ ______	$\frac{1}{15}$ ______	$\frac{13}{20}$ ______	$2\frac{2}{9}$ ______	3 ______	$3\frac{4}{7}$ ______
6.	5 ______	$2\frac{1}{2}$ ______	$\frac{3}{5}$ ______	$1\frac{1}{12}$ ______	$1\frac{3}{11}$ ______	$\frac{3}{16}$ ______
7.	$2\frac{3}{7}$ ______	20 ______	$\frac{8}{9}$ ______	$3\frac{5}{16}$ ______	$2\frac{1}{8}$ ______	$\frac{1}{16}$ ______

NAME ______________________

Lesson 2.11 Dividing Fractions and Mixed Numerals

To divide by a fraction, multiply by its reciprocal.

$\frac{2}{3} \div \frac{5}{8} = \frac{2}{3} \times \frac{8}{5} = \frac{16}{15} = 1\frac{1}{15}$

$1\frac{2}{3} \div 2\frac{5}{9} = \frac{5}{\cancel{3}_1} \times \frac{\cancel{9}^3}{23} = \frac{15}{23}$

Write each answer in simplest form.

	a	b	c	d
1.	$3\frac{1}{2} \div \frac{2}{3}$	$4\frac{3}{4} \div 1\frac{7}{8}$	$\frac{3}{4} \div \frac{1}{2}$	$2\frac{2}{3} \div \frac{1}{8}$
2.	$7 \div \frac{3}{5}$	$2\frac{1}{12} \div 1\frac{1}{3}$	$2\frac{1}{7} \div \frac{3}{4}$	$3 \div 5$
3.	$1\frac{1}{8} \div \frac{1}{10}$	$1\frac{2}{5} \div 2\frac{1}{3}$	$5 \div 1\frac{1}{2}$	$3\frac{1}{4} \div 1\frac{1}{2}$
4.	$6\frac{2}{3} \div \frac{2}{3}$	$3\frac{1}{8} \div \frac{2}{7}$	$4\frac{1}{4} \div \frac{1}{12}$	$14 \div \frac{1}{7}$
5.	$2\frac{3}{5} \div 1\frac{2}{7}$	$1\frac{1}{9} \div \frac{7}{11}$	$12 \div 15$	$2\frac{4}{5} \div 3$

NAME ____________________

Lesson 2.11 Dividing Fractions and Mixed Numerals

Write each answer in simplest form.

	a	b	c	d
1.	$5\frac{5}{8} \div 2\frac{1}{4}$	$3\frac{4}{7} \div 2\frac{1}{8}$	$3\frac{5}{12} \div 2\frac{1}{6}$	$5\frac{1}{4} \div 3$
2.	$8 \div 17$	$3\frac{9}{10} \div \frac{6}{15}$	$2\frac{1}{4} \div \frac{3}{8}$	$\frac{2}{3} \div \frac{5}{7}$
3.	$\frac{9}{11} \div \frac{3}{8}$	$2\frac{5}{9} \div 1\frac{1}{3}$	$3\frac{5}{12} \div 1\frac{5}{6}$	$1\frac{7}{8} \div \frac{1}{16}$
4.	$4\frac{5}{12} \div 2\frac{3}{4}$	$8 \div \frac{2}{7}$	$4\frac{1}{2} \div 5$	$3\frac{4}{7} \div \frac{5}{8}$
5.	$4\frac{1}{4} \div \frac{7}{10}$	$\frac{2}{11} \div \frac{4}{17}$	$3\frac{3}{8} \div 2$	$5\frac{1}{2} \div 2\frac{1}{3}$
6.	$\frac{7}{8} \div 3$	$6 \div \frac{1}{5}$	$2\frac{4}{9} \div \frac{5}{6}$	$7\frac{1}{4} \div 1\frac{7}{8}$

NAME ____________________

Lesson 2.12 Multiplication and Division Practice

Write each answer in simplest form.

	a	b	c	d
1.	$\frac{1}{3} \times \frac{3}{8}$	$\frac{7}{6} \times \frac{4}{13}$	$\frac{3}{7} \times \frac{4}{5}$	$\frac{2}{3} \times \frac{1}{2} \times \frac{3}{8}$
2.	$\frac{1}{2} \times \frac{5}{12}$	$\frac{2}{3} \times \frac{5}{9}$	$\frac{1}{8} \times \frac{2}{7} \times \frac{5}{6}$	$\frac{3}{5} \times \frac{2}{3} \times \frac{1}{2}$
3.	$\frac{1}{2} \times 1\frac{2}{5}$	$\frac{5}{7} \times 2\frac{1}{8}$	$1\frac{1}{2} \times 2\frac{1}{4} \times \frac{1}{3}$	$3\frac{1}{8} \times 4\frac{1}{4} \times \frac{1}{3}$
4.	$3\frac{1}{3} \times \frac{1}{4}$	$1\frac{5}{8} \times 2\frac{1}{3}$	$3\frac{4}{7} \times 1\frac{4}{5} \times 2$	$3\frac{1}{4} \times 2\frac{1}{8} \times 1\frac{5}{7}$
5.	$\frac{3}{5} \div \frac{2}{7}$	$\frac{3}{4} \div \frac{1}{2}$	$\frac{5}{8} \div \frac{3}{5}$	$\frac{5}{6} \div \frac{1}{10}$
6.	$5 \div 1\frac{1}{4}$	$3\frac{1}{2} \div \frac{2}{3}$	$1\frac{6}{7} \div 2\frac{1}{8}$	$3\frac{1}{4} \div 2$
7.	$3\frac{7}{10} \div 2\frac{1}{4}$	$5\frac{1}{2} \div 3\frac{6}{11}$	$2\frac{3}{5} \div 13$	$7\frac{1}{4} \div 3\frac{3}{8}$

NAME ______________________

Lesson 2.13 Problem Solving

SHOW YOUR WORK

Solve each problem. Write each answer in simplest form.

1. David worked $7\frac{1}{3}$ hours today and planted 11 trees. It takes him about the same amount of time to plant each tree. How long did it take him to plant each tree?

It took him __________ hour to plant each tree.

2. A car uses $3\frac{1}{8}$ gallons of gasoline per hour when driving on the highway. How many gallons will it use after $4\frac{2}{3}$ hours?

It will use __________ gallons.

3. A board was $24\frac{3}{8}$ inches long. A worker cut it into pieces that were $4\frac{7}{8}$ inches long. The worker cut the board into how many pieces?

The worker cut the board into __________ pieces.

4. Susan must pour $6\frac{1}{2}$ bottles of juice into 26 drink glasses for her party. If each glass gets the same amount of juice, what fraction of a bottle will each glass hold?

Each glass will hold __________ bottle.

5. The standard size of a certain bin holds $2\frac{2}{3}$ gallons. The large size of that bin is $1\frac{1}{4}$ times larger. How many gallons does the large bin hold?

The large bin holds __________ gallons.

6. Diana has $3\frac{1}{4}$ bags of nuts. Each bag holds $4\frac{1}{2}$ pounds. How many pounds of nuts does Diana have?

Diana has __________ pounds of nuts.

7. There is a stack of 7 crates. Each crate is $10\frac{2}{3}$ inches high. How many inches high is the stack of crates?

The stack of crates is __________ inches high.

1.
2.
3.
4.
5.
6.
7.

NAME ______________________

Check What You Learned

Fractions

Add, subtract, multiply, or divide. Write each answer in simplest form.

	a	b	c	d
1.	$\frac{3}{8} + 1\frac{5}{7}$	$2\frac{1}{4} + 3\frac{1}{3}$	$1\frac{5}{6} + 2\frac{7}{8}$	$4\frac{3}{4} + 2\frac{3}{8}$
2.	$4\frac{2}{3} - 1\frac{1}{4}$	$\frac{7}{8} - \frac{1}{2}$	$4\frac{3}{10} - 1\frac{6}{7}$	$5\frac{1}{4} - 2\frac{5}{6}$
3.	$\frac{3}{8} \times \frac{4}{5}$	$\frac{1}{2} \times \frac{3}{7}$	$\frac{5}{9} \times \frac{1}{3}$	$\frac{2}{3} \times \frac{1}{4} \times \frac{1}{8}$
4.	$3\frac{2}{7} \times \frac{5}{8}$	$2\frac{3}{4} \times 1\frac{2}{7}$	$3\frac{2}{3} \times 1\frac{5}{6}$	$2\frac{1}{3} \times 1\frac{1}{2} \times 3$
5.	$6\frac{1}{8} \div 2\frac{4}{7}$	$3\frac{2}{3} \div 8$	$5\frac{1}{2} \div 1\frac{2}{5}$	$\frac{3}{4} \div \frac{1}{8}$

NAME ____________________

Check What You Learned

SHOW YOUR WORK

Fractions

Solve each problem. Write each answer in simplest form.

6. A large patio brick weighs $4\frac{3}{8}$ pounds. A small patio brick weighs $2\frac{1}{3}$ pounds. How much more does the large brick weigh? The large brick weighs __________ pounds more.	**6.**
7. A ribbon that is $22\frac{3}{4}$ inches long must be cut into 7 equal pieces. How long will each piece be? Each piece will be __________ inches long.	**7.**
8. Fifteen cups of flour are to be stored in containers. Each container holds $2\frac{1}{3}$ cups. How many containers will the flour fill? What fraction of another container will it fill? The flour will fill __________ full containers and __________ of another container.	**8.**
9. A small bottle holds $\frac{1}{3}$ of a liter. A large bottle holds $4\frac{1}{2}$ times as much. How many liters does the large bottle hold? The large bottle holds __________ liters.	**9.**
10. The basketball team practiced $3\frac{1}{4}$ hours on Monday and $2\frac{1}{3}$ hours on Tuesday. How many hours has the team practiced so far this week? The team has practiced __________ hours this week.	**10.**
11. There are $7\frac{1}{2}$ bottles of lemonade. Each bottle holds $1\frac{5}{6}$ quarts. How many quarts of lemonade are there? There are __________ quarts of lemonade.	**11.**

CHAPTER 2 POSTTEST

NAME ____________________

Check What You Know

Decimals

Add, subtract, multiply, or divide.

	a	b	c	d
1.	$3.24 + 5.7$	$27.038 + 0.725$	$3.21 + 6.034$	$7.2043 + 0.5817 + 1.35$
2.	$3.5 - 0.7$	$21.703 - 8.6$	$17.015 - 4.251$	$6.43 - 2.5167$
3.	1.3×4.8	2.07×3.4	5.741×0.44	3.0162×2.9
4.	$3\overline{)1.56}$	$7\overline{)2.135}$	$5\overline{)4.17}$	$2\overline{)6.8374}$
5.	$1.5\overline{)6}$	$.03\overline{)72}$	$1.75\overline{)67.55}$	$0.025\overline{)300}$
6.	$3.8\overline{)15.96}$	$0.14\overline{)0.4354}$	$5.25\overline{)45.15}$	$2.003\overline{)28.8432}$

NAME ____________________

Check What You Know

Decimals

SHOW YOUR WORK

Solve each problem.

7. A recipe calls for 1.75 cups of water, 0.5 cups of oil, and 0.2 cups of vinegar. What is the total amount of liquid in the recipe?

The recipe contains ____________ cups of liquid.

7.

8. If a car averages 23.2 miles per gallon of gasoline, how far can it go on 15.25 gallons?

The car can go ____________ miles.

8.

9. Todd's bill came to $37.68. He paid with $40.70. How much change should he get?

Todd should get ____________ in change.

9.

10. Maria bought gifts for 7 of her friends. She spent $86.66. If she spent the same amount on each of her friends, how much did she spend on each?

Maria spent ____________ on each friend.

10.

11. A small tree was measured at 3.67 feet tall. It can grow to 25 times that height. What is the tallest height the tree can be expected to reach?

The tree can reach ____________ feet.

11.

12. It is 238.875 kilometers from Pikesville to Century Village. It is 422.75 kilometers from Pikesville to Fort Cedar. How much farther is it from Pikesville to Fort Cedar than from Pikesville to Century Village?

It is ____________ kilometers farther to Fort Cedar.

12.

NAME ____________________

Lesson 3.1 Converting Decimals and Fractions

Convert $\frac{2}{5}$ to tenths.

$\frac{2}{5} = \frac{2 \times 2}{5 \times 2} = \frac{4}{10} = 0.4$

Convert $\frac{3}{20}$ to hundredths.

$\frac{3}{20} = \frac{3 \times 5}{20 \times 5} = \frac{15}{100} = 0.15$

Convert $\frac{12}{25}$ to thousandths.

$\frac{12}{25} = \frac{12 \times 40}{25 \times 40} = \frac{480}{1000} = 0.480$

Convert decimals to fractions or mixed numbers.

$0.6 = \frac{6}{10}$
$= \frac{3}{5}$

$2.25 = 2\frac{25}{100}$
$= 2\frac{1}{4}$

$1.875 = 1\frac{875}{1000}$
$= 1\frac{7}{8}$

Convert each fraction to a decimal.

	a	b	c
	Convert to tenths.	Convert to hundredths.	Convert to thousandths.
1.	$1\frac{3}{5}$ ______	$2\frac{1}{4}$ ______	$\frac{48}{200}$ ______
2.	$2\frac{1}{2}$ ______	$5\frac{6}{25}$ ______	$2\frac{23}{500}$ ______
3.	$5\frac{4}{5}$ ______	$1\frac{7}{20}$ ______	$6\frac{157}{250}$ ______
4.	$6\frac{1}{5}$ ______	$2\frac{9}{10}$ ______	$3\frac{72}{100}$ ______
	Convert to ten thousandths.		
5.	$3\frac{742}{1000}$ ______	$4\frac{56}{500}$ ______	$1\frac{1287}{2500}$ ______

Convert each decimal to a fraction or mixed numeral in simplest form.

6.	0.3 ______	1.6 ______	3.7 ______
7.	0.75 ______	5.86 ______	1.13 ______
8.	0.387 ______	2.588 ______	3.090 ______
9.	0.5329 ______	6.4273 ______	5.5825 ______

NAME ______________________

Lesson 3.2 Adding Decimals

When adding decimals, keep the decimal points aligned. Add as you would add whole numbers. It may be helpful to write in 0s as placeholders.

```
 27.3824              27.3824
  1.437       OR       1.4370  <-- The zero was added
+ 3.2169             + 3.2169      to mark place value.
--------             --------
 32.0363              32.0363
```

Add.

	a	b	c	d	e
1.	0.7 + 0.4	3.2 + .8	2.6 + 1.7	5.1 + 2.6	4.2 + 9.1
2.	0.78 + 0.13	1.07 + 2.38	2.27 + 1.3	6.58 + 1.04	1.73 + 0.21
3.	0.182 + 0.317	1.077 + 3.25	1.386 + 4.851	2.01 + 3.503	3.217 + 6.5
4.	2.506 + 1.739	0.38 + 1.934	17.387 + 5.04	1.3426 + 2.5174	6.2379 + 1.586
5.	0.2837 + 5.421	12.343 + 1.6842	38.256 + 27.181	2.3 + 0.981	5.632 + 1.7563
6.	3.247 0.18 + 1.511	1.307 2.1589 + 0.3707	2.4168 2.357 + 1.5623	0.687 1.03 + 5.7	3.427 1.0324 + 0.21

NAME ______________________

Lesson 3.3 Subtracting Decimals

When subtracting decimals, keep the decimal points aligned. Subtract decimals as you would whole numbers. It may be helpful to write in 0s as placeholders.

$$\begin{array}{r} \overset{2}{\cancel{3}}\overset{15}{\cancel{6}}.\overset{10}{\cancel{1}}\overset{11}{2} \\ -\ \ 7.386 \\ \hline 28.734 \end{array} \quad \text{OR} \quad \begin{array}{r} \overset{2}{\cancel{3}}\overset{15}{\cancel{6}}.\overset{10}{\cancel{1}}\overset{11}{2}\overset{10}{\cancel{0}} \\ -\ \ 7.386 \\ \hline 28.734 \end{array}$$

Subtract.

	a	b	c	d	e
1.	0.7 − 0.2	1.38 − 0.5	2.07 − 1.13	3.821 − 1.64	5.317 − 2.436
2.	0.41 − 0.25	0.247 − 0.18	3.77 − 2.09	4.396 − 3.7	1.001 − 0.2
3.	1.3 − 1.186	2.791 − 0.918	24.22 − 3.653	3.028 − 0.959	51.347 − 12.018
4.	9.036 − 0.741	24.03 − 6.517	32 − 5.56	8.9 − 2.037	0.581 − 0.3
5.	0.6 − 0.427	3.413 − 0.6	35.5 − 6.28	2.7 − 0.56	3.893 − 1.2
6.	47 − 0.593	6.824 − 5.951	12.2 − 9.58	21.03 − 20.001	5.628 − 0.07

NAME ______________________

Lesson 3.4 Problem Solving

SHOW YOUR WORK

Solve each problem.

1. Workers are using a piece of iron that is 0.324 millimeters thick and a piece of copper that is 0.671 millimeters thick. How much thicker is the copper?

   The copper is __________ millimeters thicker.

2. Lenora bought a book for $12.36 and some school supplies for $7.29 and $5.47. How much did she spend?

   She spent __________.

3. Joe's bill at the grocery store came to $6.08. He paid with a ten dollar bill and a dime. How much change did he get?

   He received __________ in change.

4. One bottle holds 67.34 ounces and another bottle holds 48.5 ounces. Combined, how much do they hold?

   The bottles hold __________ ounces combined.

5. A basic stereo system costs $189.67. An upgraded model costs $212.09. How much more does the upgraded model cost?

   The upgraded model costs __________ more.

6. Lin ran 0.683 kilometers on Wednesday and 0.75 kilometers on Thursday. How far did he run on the two days combined?

   He ran __________ kilometers over the two days.

7. A certain cabinet door is actually made of three thin boards that are pressed together. The boards are 0.371 inches, 0.13 inches, and 0.204 inches thick. How thick is the cabinet door?

   The door is __________ inches thick.

1.
2.
3.
4.
5.
6.
7.

NAME ______________________

Lesson 3.5 Multiplying Decimals

When multiplying decimals, count the number of decimal places in each factor to figure out the placement of the decimal point in the product.

$\begin{array}{r} 3 \\ \times\ 5 \\ \hline 15 \end{array}$	$\begin{array}{r} 0.3 \\ \times\ 5 \\ \hline 1.5 \end{array}$	$\begin{array}{r} 0.3 \\ \times 0.5 \\ \hline 0.15 \end{array}$	$\begin{array}{r} 0.3 \\ \times 0.05 \\ \hline 0.015 \end{array}$
0 + 0 = 0 decimal places	1 + 0 = 1 decimal place	1 + 1 = 2 decimal places	1 + 2 = 3 decimal places

Multiply.

	a	b	c	d	e
1.	$\begin{array}{r} 1.2 \\ \times\ 3 \\ \hline \end{array}$	$\begin{array}{r} 0.61 \\ \times\ 4 \\ \hline \end{array}$	$\begin{array}{r} 0.58 \\ \times\ 12 \\ \hline \end{array}$	$\begin{array}{r} 1.212 \\ \times\ 3 \\ \hline \end{array}$	$\begin{array}{r} 32.7 \\ \times\ 2 \\ \hline \end{array}$
2.	$\begin{array}{r} 3.7 \\ \times 1.5 \\ \hline \end{array}$	$\begin{array}{r} 6.24 \\ \times\ 2.8 \\ \hline \end{array}$	$\begin{array}{r} 3.73 \\ \times 0.77 \\ \hline \end{array}$	$\begin{array}{r} 4.389 \\ \times\ 0.6 \\ \hline \end{array}$	$\begin{array}{r} 1.7924 \\ \times\ 2.5 \\ \hline \end{array}$
3.	$\begin{array}{r} 5.06 \\ \times\ 1.1 \\ \hline \end{array}$	$\begin{array}{r} 7.301 \\ \times\ 0.2 \\ \hline \end{array}$	$\begin{array}{r} 3.46 \\ \times\ 8.7 \\ \hline \end{array}$	$\begin{array}{r} 0.571 \\ \times\ 9 \\ \hline \end{array}$	$\begin{array}{r} 1.6342 \\ \times\ 2.7 \\ \hline \end{array}$
4.	$\begin{array}{r} 6.07 \\ \times\ 3 \\ \hline \end{array}$	$\begin{array}{r} 5.826 \\ \times\ 0.4 \\ \hline \end{array}$	$\begin{array}{r} 2.103 \\ \times\ 1.01 \\ \hline \end{array}$	$\begin{array}{r} 4.35 \\ \times\ 0.8 \\ \hline \end{array}$	$\begin{array}{r} 7.4213 \\ \times\ 6 \\ \hline \end{array}$

NAME ____________________

Lesson 3.6 Dividing Decimals by Whole Numbers

When dividing a decimal by any whole number, place the decimal point in the quotient directly above the decimal point in the dividend.

$$\begin{array}{r} 5.4 \\ 6\overline{)32.4} \\ -30 \\ \hline 24 \\ -24 \\ \hline 0 \end{array} \qquad \begin{array}{r} 0.54 \\ 6\overline{)3.24} \\ -30 \\ \hline 24 \\ -24 \\ \hline 0 \end{array} \qquad \begin{array}{r} .054 \\ 6\overline{)0.324} \\ -30 \\ \hline 24 \\ -24 \\ \hline 0 \end{array} \qquad \begin{array}{r} .0054 \\ 6\overline{)0.0324} \\ -30 \\ \hline 24 \\ -24 \\ \hline 0 \end{array}$$

Divide.

	a	b	c	d
1.	$4\overline{)0.48}$	$2\overline{)7.6}$	$5\overline{)1.75}$	$3\overline{)9.03}$
2.	$9\overline{)8.181}$	$7\overline{)2.877}$	$3\overline{)15.024}$	$2\overline{)1.3548}$
3.	$3\overline{)0.0096}$	$2\overline{)1.54}$	$4\overline{)3.228}$	$5\overline{)2.570}$
4.	$6\overline{)0.696}$	$8\overline{)7.216}$	$9\overline{)0.1899}$	$7\overline{)7.6349}$

NAME ______________________

Lesson 3.7 Dividing Whole Numbers by Decimals

Multiply the divisor and dividend by 10, 100, or 1000 so the new divisor is a whole number.

$0.7\overline{)49} = 7\overline{)490}$, $490 - 490 = 0$, quotient 70

$.06\overline{)24} = 6\overline{)2400}$, $2400 - 2400 = 0$, quotient 400

$.005\overline{)3} = 5\overline{)300}$, $30 - 30 = 0$ (as printed), quotient 60

Divide.

	a	b	c	d
1.	$0.3\overline{)42}$	$0.5\overline{)25}$	$0.04\overline{)24}$	$0.06\overline{)6}$
2.	$3.3\overline{)99}$	$2.5\overline{)10}$	$0.18\overline{)72}$	$0.009\overline{)63}$
3.	$1.2\overline{)6}$	$0.21\overline{)42}$	$0.05\overline{)75}$	$0.025\overline{)50}$
4.	$0.7\overline{)84}$	$0.08\overline{)128}$	$0.003\overline{)132}$	$0.002\overline{)344}$

NAME ______________________

Lesson 3.8 Dividing Decimals by Decimals

Multiply the divisor and the dividend by the same power of 10 to change the divisor to a whole number.

$$1.5\overline{)40.5} = 15\overline{)405} \quad \begin{array}{r} 27 \\ 15\overline{)405} \\ -30 \\ \hline 105 \\ -105 \\ \hline 0 \end{array}$$

$$1.05\overline{)2.415} = 105\overline{)241.5} \quad \begin{array}{r} 2.3 \\ 105\overline{)241.5} \\ -210 \\ \hline 315 \\ -315 \\ \hline 0 \end{array}$$

Divide.

	a	b	c	d
1.	$0.03\overline{)45.6}$	$1.7\overline{)20.4}$	$3.8\overline{)16.72}$	$0.5\overline{)1.875}$
2.	$7.4\overline{)28.86}$	$1.07\overline{)67.41}$	$0.22\overline{)8.03}$	$0.15\overline{)0.9423}$
3.	$0.08\overline{)2.524}$	$0.027\overline{)6.561}$	$1.5\overline{)9.5025}$	$6.4\overline{)27.04}$
4.	$0.95\overline{)0.6175}$	$0.008\overline{)0.1736}$	$0.175\overline{)3.0625}$	$2.388\overline{)3.3432}$

NAME ____________________

Lesson 3.9 Multiplication and Division Practice

Multiply or divide.

	a	b	c	d
1.	0.2×1.3	4.37×2.6	3.771×0.5	1.3794×4.6
2.	8.7×6.2	0.301×1.02	5.007×2.8	0.2109×3.4
3.	3)0.36	5)4.55	7)0.63	8)0.048
4.	7)14.42	9)36.081	2)5.422	6)3.6090
5.	0.5)45	1.3)39	3.6)324	0.04)12
6.	0.15)5.4	8.01)10.413	2.9)98.02	0.08)1.896
7.	0.0009)54	2.01)7.638	4.17)10.6335	1.003)37.111

NAME ______________________

Lesson 3.10 Problem Solving

SHOW YOUR WORK

Solve each problem.

1. Fred bought 7 games on clearance for $104.65. Each game was on sale for the same price. How much did each game cost?

Each game cost ___________.

1.

2. Gas costs $1.64 a gallon. Elaine spent $23.78 at the gas station. How many gallons of gas did she buy?

Elaine bought ___________ gallons of gas.

2.

3. There are 2.5 servings in a can of tuna fish. How many servings are there in 7 cans?

There are ___________ servings in 7 cans.

3.

4. A grain distributor can process 14.6 tons of grain an hour. How much can the distributor process in 8.75 hours?

The distributor can process ___________ tons of grain.

4.

5. Rhonda earned $324.65 delivering newspapers. She promised her sister 0.2 of her earnings for helping her. How much does Rhonda owe her sister?

Rhonda owes her sister ___________.

5.

6. A car traveled 48.36 miles in one hour. What was its average speed per minute?

Its average speed was ___________ miles per minute.

6.

7. There are 5.28 cups of pudding to be put into 6 dishes. How much pudding should be put into each dish to make them equal?

Each dish should get ___________ cups of pudding.

7.

NAME ________________________

Check What You Learned

Decimals

Add, subtract, multiply, or divide.

	a	b	c	d
1.	0.23 + 0.9	78.07 + 1.34	9.065 + 2.78	48.761 + 9.0374
2.	1.379 + 6.04 + 3.4173	28.46 + 3.7748 + 0.011	5.8 − 2.9	33.04 − 6.75
3.	29.083 − 2.1	13.732 − 8.64	3.89 − 1.476	8.201 − 3.9376
4.	6.2 × 0.4	3.05 × 2.83	5.736 × 8.2	4.0327 × 1.1
5.	7)9.52	2)3.586	0.25)65	0.04)19
6.	0.7)13.237	3.8)22.8	7.3)2.847	3.107)43.1873

NAME ____________________

Check What You Learned

Decimals

SHOW YOUR WORK

Solve each problem.

7. Sheila bought three books for $12.63, $9.05, and $14.97. How much did she spend?

Sheila spent ____________ on the three books.

7.

8. Roberto bought a 12-pack of bottled water. Each bottle held 0.75 liters. How many liters of water did he buy?

Roberto bought ____________ liters.

8.

9. The highest batting average on the Owls baseball team is 0.427. The lowest batting average is 0.189. What is the difference?

The difference is ____________.

9.

10. Lou spent $17.65 to buy 5 items of equal value. How much did he spend on each?

Lou spent ____________ on each item.

10.

11. A hike is 26.4 miles. Alicia wants to divide it equally over 3 days. How far does she need to hike each day?

She needs to hike ____________ miles each day.

11.

12. There are 6.75 buckets of sand in a sandbox. If each full bucket holds 4.32 pounds of sand, how many pounds of sand are there in the sandbox?

There are ____________ pounds of sand in the sandbox.

12.

NAME ____________________

Check What You Know

Finding Percents

CHAPTER 4 PRETEST

Change each of the following to percents.

	a	b	c
1.	$\frac{41}{50}$ = ______%	$\frac{7}{20}$ = ______%	$\frac{3}{5}$ = ______%
2.	3.5 = ______%	7.25 = ______%	0.3 = ______%

Change each of the following to decimals.

3.	20% = ______	38% = ______	127% = ______
4.	$12\frac{1}{2}$% = ______	$7\frac{3}{5}$% = ______	$22\frac{1}{4}$% = ______

Change each of the following to fractions in simplest form.

5.	25% = ______	40% = ______	320% = ______

Complete the following.

6.	______ is 8% of 20.	______ is 25% of 56.	______ is 40% of 6.
7.	______ is 110% of 90.	______ is 2% of 2.	______ is 75% of 80.
8.	8 is 25% of ______.	25 is 12.5% of ______.	70 is 200% of ______.
9.	3.5 is 20% of ______.	0.2 is 5% of ______.	1.65 is $5\frac{1}{2}$% of ______.
10.	100 is ______% of 400.	0.4 is ______% of 0.5.	74 is ______% of 37.
11.	9 is ______% of 60.	12 is ______% of 600.	23 is ______% of 115.

NAME ____________________

Check What You Know

Finding Percents

SHOW YOUR WORK

Solve each problem.

12. A grocery store is offering a 2% savings if customers bag their own groceries. How much will Akira save on a purchase of $215.50? He will save ___________.	**13.**
13. A home improvement company gives a 30% discount for all projects over $1,000. If the original cost of Praveen's project is $2,545, how much will he save with the discount? He will save ___________.	**13.**
14. A restaurant charges an automatic 20% tip for groups of 6 or more. A group of 8 people had a bill of $187. How much was their tip? Their tip was ___________.	**14.**
15. A department store has a policy of charging a 15% service charge on all returned checks. If a check for $725 is returned, how much will the service charge be? The service charge will be ___________.	**15.**
16. A mail order company charges $4\frac{1}{2}$% for shipping and handling on all orders. How much is the shipping and handling charge on an order of $52? The shipping charge is ___________.	**16.**
17. The phone company charges a 1.5% service fee on all long distance calls. If a long distance bill is $32, how much is the service fee? The service fee is ___________.	**17.**

NAME ____________________

Lesson 4.1 Understanding Percents

Percent means how many out of 100 and is expressed with the symbol **%**. Percents can also be expressed as fractions with a denominator of 100 and as decimals.

$25\% = \frac{25}{100} = \frac{1}{4}$ or 0.25 $9\% = \frac{9}{100}$ or 0.09

Complete the following. Write fractions in simplest form.

	Percent	Fraction	Decimal
1.	7%	______	______
2.	13%	______	______
3.	48%	______	______
4.	71%	______	______
5.	27%	______	______
6.	2%	______	______
7.	15%	______	______
8.	39%	______	______
9.	10%	______	______
10.	62%	______	______
11.	75%	______	______
12.	97%	______	______
13.	53%	______	______
14.	82%	______	______

NAME ______________________

Lesson 4.2 Comparing Percents, Fractions, and Decimals

Use inequality symbols to compare percents, fractions, and decimals.

Express the numbers in the same format so they are easier to compare.

Symbol	Meaning
$>$	greater than
$<$	less than
$=$	equal to

$\frac{1}{5}$ ______ 30%			0.45 ______ 38%
20% ______ 30%	Convert 1 of the numbers.		45% ______ 38%
20% __$<$__ 30%	Compare the numbers		45% __$>$__ 38%

Write $>$, $<$, or $=$ on the line to compare the given quantities.

	a	b	c
1.	13% ______ $\frac{2}{5}$	0.35 ______ $\frac{1}{8}$	$\frac{1}{4}$ ______ 0.25
2.	87% ______ 0.79	18 ______ 18%	$\frac{1}{2}$ ______ 0.42
3.	$\frac{9}{10}$ ______ 9%	40% ______ $\frac{4}{5}$	0.72 ______ $\frac{2}{3}$
4.	0.82 ______ $\frac{41}{50}$	63% ______ $\frac{1}{2}$	14% ______ 0.014
5.	$\frac{1}{3}$ ______ 50%	$\frac{4}{5}$ ______ 80%	0.07 ______ $\frac{1}{10}$
6.	$\frac{250}{100}$ ______ 2.5	0.25 ______ $\frac{1}{3}$	318 ______ 3.18%
7.	50% ______ $\frac{2}{3}$	93% ______ 0.93	22% ______ $\frac{1}{4}$
8.	0.67 ______ $\frac{3}{5}$	$\frac{1}{2}$ ______ 20%	642% ______ 6.42
9.	0.08 ______ 80%	50% ______ $\frac{3}{4}$	$\frac{1}{2}$ ______ 0.050
10.	$\frac{2}{5}$ ______ 2.5	70% ______ $\frac{7}{10}$	$\frac{147}{100}$ ______ 14%
11.	$\frac{45}{100}$ ______ 55%	1238% ______ 12.38	$16\frac{2}{5}$ ______ 16.25
12.	3.75 ______ 375%	0.15 ______ $\frac{1}{5}$	7.5 ______ $\frac{3}{4}$
13.	$\frac{13}{25}$ ______ 49%	0.45 ______ $\frac{7}{20}$	3% ______ 0.03
14.	25% ______ $\frac{11}{50}$	$12\frac{1}{5}$ ______ 12.2	18% ______ $\frac{1}{4}$

NAME ____________________

Lesson 4.3 Ordering Percents, Fractions, and Decimals

To put percents, fractions, and decimals in a certain order, first write the numbers in the same format so they are easier to compare. Compare and order the numbers. Then, rewrite the numbers in their original forms.

Order 25%, $\frac{2}{3}$, $\frac{4}{5}$, and 0.37 from greatest to least.

Rewrite: 0.25, 0.67, 0.8, 0.37

Order: 0.8, 0.67, 0.37, 0.25

Rewrite: $\frac{4}{5}$, $\frac{2}{3}$, 0.37, 25%

Order from least to greatest.

	a	b
1.	13%, $\frac{1}{3}$, 0.35, $\frac{1}{4}$ ____________	$\frac{3}{4}$, 72%, 0.02, 0.34 ____________
2.	$\frac{2}{5}$, 45%, 0.25, $\frac{1}{3}$ ____________	$\frac{1}{10}$, 1%, $\frac{11}{100}$, 0.15 ____________
3.	143%, 14.5, $\frac{14}{25}$, $\frac{14}{100}$ ____________	68%, 0.55, $\frac{3}{5}$, 0.63 ____________

Order from greatest to least.

	a	b
4.	$3\frac{1}{2}$, 35%, 320%, $\frac{3}{100}$ ____________	$\frac{1}{4}$, $\frac{1}{5}$, 0.4, 0.5, 30% ____________
5.	0.625, $\frac{7}{8}$, 60%, $\frac{3}{4}$ ____________	17%, $\frac{1}{7}$, 1.7, 0.017 ____________
6.	406%, 4.1, $\frac{40}{100}$, $\frac{4}{5}$ ____________	$\frac{16}{5}$, $5\frac{2}{5}$, 32%, 16% ____________

NAME ________________

Lesson 4.4 Percent to Fraction and Fraction to Percent

Multiply by $\frac{1}{100}$ to change a percent to a fraction or mixed numeral in simplest form.

$$120\% = 120 \times \frac{1}{100} = \frac{120}{100} = \frac{6}{5} = 1\frac{1}{5}$$

Multiply by a factor of 100 to change a fraction or mixed numeral to a percent.

$$2\frac{3}{5} = \frac{13}{5} \times \frac{20}{20} = \frac{260}{100} = 260 \times \frac{1}{100} = 260\%$$

Change fractions and mixed numerals to percents. Change percents to fractions or mixed numerals in simplest form.

	a	b	c	d
1.	75% = ______	$\frac{7}{25}$ = ______%	$\frac{16}{50}$ = ______%	98% = ______
2.	56% = ______	48% = ______	$2\frac{2}{5}$ = ______%	$9\frac{3}{10}$ = ______%
3.	$\frac{31}{50}$ = ______%	$\frac{9}{20}$ = ______%	12% = ______	425% = ______
4.	$7\frac{3}{5}$ = ______%	15% = ______	$2\frac{1}{4}$ = ______%	31% = ______
5.	60% = ______	$\frac{1}{5}$ = ______%	$\frac{1}{2}$ = ______%	72% = ______
6.	$3\frac{3}{4}$ = ______%	135% = ______	40% = ______	$\frac{14}{25}$ = ______%
7.	$\frac{17}{20}$ = ______%	$\frac{5}{8}$ = ______%	65% = ______	10% = ______
8.	5% = ______	$10\frac{4}{25}$ = ______%	50% = ______	$3\frac{7}{20}$ = ______%

NAME ______________________

Lesson 4.5 Percent to Decimal and Decimal to Percent

Study how a percent is changed to a decimal and a decimal is changed to a percent.

$$6.75\% = 6.75 \times 0.01 = 0.0675 \qquad 1.35 = \frac{135}{100} = 135\%$$

Change each of the following percents to decimals and decimals to percents.

	a	b	c
1.	85% = ________	1.47 = ________%	17% = ________
2.	0.38 = ________%	8.32% = ________	0.69 = ________%
3.	27% = ________	0.05 = ________%	2.1% = ________
4.	1.50 = ________%	15% = ________	0.426 = ________%
5.	33.5% = ________	0.65 = ________%	9.25% = ________
6.	0.039 = ________%	52.6% = ________	4.85 = ________%
7.	5.5% = ________	0.225 = ________%	6.25% = ________
8.	0.005 = ________%	525% = ________	0.7 = ________%
9.	0.1% = ________	0.1 = ________%	63.2% = ________

NAME ____________________

Lesson 4.5 Percent to Decimal and Decimal to Percent

If a percent is expressed as a fraction, first change that fraction to a decimal. Then, change the percent to a decimal.

$$2\frac{1}{2}\% = 2.5\% = 2.5 \times 0.01 = 0.025$$

Change each of the following to decimals.

	a	b	c
1.	$25\frac{1}{4}\%$ = ______	$3\frac{1}{2}\%$ = ______	$2\frac{7}{10}\%$ = ______
2.	$15\frac{1}{20}\%$ = ______	$63\frac{1}{5}\%$ = ______	$12\frac{17}{25}\%$ = ______
3.	$5\frac{3}{4}\%$ = ______	$11\frac{3}{10}\%$ = ______	$42\frac{3}{4}\%$ = ______
4.	$17\frac{1}{2}\%$ = ______	$22\frac{2}{5}\%$ = ______	$75\frac{9}{20}\%$ = ______
5.	$9\frac{3}{5}\%$ = ______	$18\frac{2}{25}\%$ = ______	$52\frac{1}{4}\%$ = ______
6.	$3\frac{19}{50}\%$ = ______	$39\frac{1}{10}\%$ = ______	$83\frac{12}{25}\%$ = ______
7.	$15\frac{1}{5}\%$ = ______	$79\frac{4}{25}\%$ = ______	$27\frac{3}{4}\%$ = ______
8.	$38\frac{19}{20}\%$ = ______	$8\frac{9}{10}\%$ = ______	$93\frac{18}{25}\%$ = ______
9.	$48\frac{33}{50}\%$ = ______	$3\frac{2}{5}\%$ = ______	$81\frac{7}{10}\%$ = ______
10.	$50\frac{1}{2}\%$ = ______	$14\frac{1}{2}\%$ = ______	$45\frac{3}{4}\%$ = ______

NAME ____________________

Lesson 4.6 Finding the Percent of a Number

To find a percent of a number, express the percent as a fraction or a decimal and multiply.

______ $= 20\%$ of 65	______ $= 20\%$ of 65
______ $= \frac{1}{5} \times 65$	______ $= 0.2 \times 65$
______ $= \frac{65}{5} = 13$	______ $= 13$
13 is 20% of 65.	13 is 20% of 65.

Complete the following.

	a	b	c
1.	______ is 25% of 50.	______ is 30% of 65.	______ is 50% of 38.5.
2.	______ is 20% of 73.	______ is 5% of 32.	______ is 12% of 47.
3.	______ is 25% of 14.	______ is 45% of 93.	______ is $6\frac{1}{4}\%$ of 30.
4.	______ is 52% of 6.	______ is $5\frac{1}{2}\%$ of 16.	______ is 20% of 412.
5.	______ is $7\frac{3}{4}\%$ of 16.	______ is 10% of 3.6.	______ is 49% of 7.8.
6.	______ is 3% of 98.	______ is 15% of 23.2.	______ is 75% of 45.
7.	______ is 5% of 3.	______ is 30% of 11.	______ is 40% of 126.
8.	______ is $2\frac{1}{2}\%$ of 320.	______ is 95% of 125.	______ is 80% of 60.
9.	______ is 4% of 20.	______ is $9\frac{1}{2}\%$ of 109.	______ is 55% of 95.
10.	______ is 45% of 105.	______ is 70% of 565.	______ is 35% of 7.

NAME ____________________

Lesson 4.6 Finding the Percent of a Number

11.7 is what percent of 65?

$11.7 = n\% \times 65$		Write the expression as a sentence.
$11.7 = \frac{n}{100} \times \frac{65}{1}$		Express the percent as a fraction
$\frac{11.7}{1} = \frac{n \times 65}{100}$		Rewrite both sides as fractions.
$1170 = n \times 65$		Multiply both sides by 100.
$\frac{1170}{65} = n$		Divide both sides by 65.
$18 = n$		11.7 is <u>18%</u> of 65.

Complete the following.

	a	b	c
1.	12 is ______% of 48.	75 is ______% of 300.	37 is ______% of 74.
2.	7.2 is ______% of 30.	160 is ______% of 80.	60 is ______% of 40.
3.	3 is ______% of 20.	7 is ______% of 5.	27.9 is ______% of 93.
4.	28.8 is ______% of 72.	11.25 is ______% of 15.	29.6 is ______% of 37.
5.	17.25 is ______% of 100.	16 is ______% of 80.	6.25 is ______% of 125.
6.	5 is ______% of 25.	5 is ______% of 50.	5 is ______% of 100.
7.	4 is ______% of 400.	4.5 is ______% of 60.	11 is ______% of 20.
8.	11.25 is ______% of 90.	10 is ______% of 40.	50 is ______% of 80.
9.	76.5 is ______% of 90.	25 is ______% of 500.	72 is ______% of 60.
10.	250 is ______% of 50.	100 is ______% of 800.	16.5 is ______% of 16.5.

NAME ____________

Lesson 4.6 Finding the Percent of a Number

17 is 25% of what number?

$17 = 25\% \times n$			Write the question as a number sentence.
$\frac{17}{1} = \frac{25}{100} \times \frac{n}{1}$	OR	$17 = 0.25 \times n$	Express as fraction or decimal.
$1700 = 25 \times n$			Multiply.
$\frac{1700}{25} = n$		$\frac{17}{0.25} = \frac{0.25 \times n}{0.25}$	Divide.
$68 = n$		$68 = n$	17 is 25% of <u>68</u>.

Complete the following.

	a	b	c
1.	32 is 50% of ______.	7 is 20% of ______.	15 is 12% of ______.
2.	5 is 200% of ______.	83 is 25% of ______.	10 is 25% of ______.
3.	75 is 25% of ______.	12 is 80% of ______.	4.5 is 9% of ______.
4.	7.25 is 2.5% of ______.	80 is 40% of ______.	35 is 70% of ______.
5.	3.86 is 20% of ______.	0.3 is 60% of ______.	8 is 8% of ______.
6.	33 is 66% of ______.	5.25 is 35% of ______.	6.25 is 25% of ______.
7.	15.75 is 35% of ______.	17.16 is 22% of ______.	78.85 is 83% of ______.
8.	55.2 is 120% of ______.	1.12 is 2% of ______.	71 is 71% of ______.
9.	100 is 20% of ______.	146 is 200% of ______.	0.8 is 40% of ______.
10.	75.24 is 22% of ______.	1.5 is 10% of ______.	11 is 55% of ______.

NAME ____________________

Lesson 4.7 Problem Solving

SHOW YOUR WORK

Solve each problem.

1. Mika's lunch came to $12.50. She wants to leave an 18% tip. How much should she leave?

She should leave a __________ tip.

1.

2. A store is having a 25%-off sale. If an item originally cost $19.36, how much should be taken off the price?

__________ should be taken off the original price.

2.

3. Dario bought a new bike for $90.00. Sales tax is $5\frac{1}{2}$%. How much tax does he have to pay? How much is his total bill?

Dario's tax is __________.

Dario's total bill is __________.

3.

4. Tai used a coupon and bought a sweater for $32. The full retail price of the sweater was $40. What percent did Tai save with her coupon?

Tai saved __________% with her coupon.

4.

5. Owen made a down payment of $1,600 on a car. That was 20% of the total price. What was the total price of the car?

The total price of the car was __________.

5.

6. A store allows customers to buy 3 items of the same price and get 2 more of the same items free. What percent savings does this represent?

This represents a __________% savings.

6.

NAME ____________________

Check What You Learned

Finding Percents

Change each of the following to percents.

	a	b	c
1.	$\frac{2}{5}$ = ______ %	$\frac{9}{10}$ = ______ %	$\frac{3}{20}$ = ______ %
2.	0.42 = ______ %	1.3 = ______ %	0.01 = ______ %

Change each of the following to decimals.

3.	53% = ______	250% = ______	8% = ______
4.	$7\frac{3}{4}$% = ______	$29\frac{1}{5}$% = ______	$5\frac{1}{10}$% = ______

Change each of the following to fractions in simplest form.

5.	475% = ______	60% = ______	155% = ______

Complete the following.

6.	______ is 20% of 10.	______ is 5% of 76.	______ is 60% of 120.
7.	______ is 140% of 80.	______ is 75% of 0.4.	______ is 10% of 0.08.
8.	95 is ______ % of 23.75.	60 is ______ % of 80.	45 is ______ % of 300.
9.	0.15 is ______ % of 30.	33 is ______ % of 110.	63 is ______ % of 126.
10.	11 is 80% of ______.	0.5 is 10% of ______.	24 is 300% of ______.
11.	8 is 40% of ______.	45 is 4.5% of ______.	123.75 is 75% of ______.

CHAPTER 4 POSTTEST

NAME ______________________________

Check What You Learned

SHOW YOUR WORK

Finding Percents

Solve each problem.

12. A store is offering a special on CDs. If a customer buys four CDs at the regular price, the fifth one is 25% off. If the regular price is $16.76, how much will the customer save on the fifth CD? The customer will save __________.	**12.**
13. Vito bought a book that retails for $23.80. He used a coupon for 15% off. How much money did he save? Vito saved __________.	**13.**
14. Diana bought some art supplies. The total came to $38.00, plus tax. There is a $6\frac{1}{2}$% sales tax. How much tax did she pay? Diana paid __________ in tax.	**14.**
15. Pete wants to buy a car for $8,200. Pete has to make a down payment of $1,640. What percent of the car's total price is that? The down payment is __________% of the car's total price.	**15.**
16. Danielle bought a gift for a friend that originally cost $32. She used a coupon to get $5 off. What percent did she save? Danielle saved __________%.	**16.**
17. Ines is saving to buy some computer equipment that costs $690. Her parents have offered to pay for 45% of the equipment. How much money does Ines need to save? Ines needs to save __________.	**17.**

CHAPTER 4 POSTTEST

NAME ______________________

Check What You Know

Calculating Interest

CHAPTER 5 PRETEST

Complete the following.

	Principal	Rate	Time	Interest	Total Amount
1.	$525	6%	1 year	______	______
2.	$380	8%	1 year	______	______
3.	$714	12%	1 year	______	______
4.	$1,250	7%	1 year	______	______
5.	$500	9%	3 years	______	______
6.	$650	$3\frac{1}{4}$%	4 years	______	______
7.	$820	$5\frac{1}{2}$%	2 years	______	______
8.	$300	$7\frac{3}{4}$%	6 years	______	______
9.	$1,000	$2\frac{1}{4}$%	$1\frac{1}{2}$ years	______	______
10.	$520	$3\frac{1}{2}$%	$2\frac{3}{4}$ years	______	______
11.	$4,200	6%	$5\frac{1}{4}$ years	______	______
12.	$1,700	$4\frac{1}{2}$%	$3\frac{1}{2}$ years	______	______
13.	$50	8%	$\frac{1}{2}$ year	______	______
14.	$1,400	$12\frac{1}{2}$%	$\frac{3}{4}$ year	______	______
15.	$280	$6\frac{1}{2}$%	$\frac{1}{4}$ year	______	______

NAME ____________________

Check What You Know

Calculating Interest

SHOW YOUR WORK

Solve each problem.

16. Sarah has \$480 in her savings account earning $4\frac{1}{4}$% interest. How much interest will she earn in $2\frac{1}{2}$ years? How much money will be in the account after $2\frac{1}{2}$ years?

Sara will earn ________ in interest in $2\frac{1}{2}$ years.

After $2\frac{1}{2}$ years, ________ will be in Sarah's account.

16.

17. The Turners borrowed \$20,000 to invest in a new business. The loan is for 15 years at $5\frac{1}{4}$% interest. How much interest will they pay? How much will their total payments be?

The Turners will pay ________ in interest.

Their total payments will be ________.

17.

18. Bianca borrowed \$120 for 9 months ($\frac{3}{4}$ year) at $3\frac{1}{2}$% interest. How much interest will she pay? What is the total amount she will pay back?

Bianca will pay ________ in interest.

The total amount she will pay back is ________.

18.

19. Ed bought a \$50 bond that pays $8\frac{1}{4}$% interest. It comes due in 2 years. How much interest will he get? How much will the bond be worth?

Ed will get ________ in interest.

The bond will be worth ________.

19.

20. A store allows customers 1 year to pay for their purchases, but it charges 14% interest. How much interest would be charged on a purchase of \$620? What is the total amount the customer would pay?

The interest would be ________.

The customer would pay a total amount of ________.

20.

NAME ______________________

Lesson 5.1 Simple Interest for One Year

Simple interest is determined by multiplying the amount of money (principal, or *p*) by the rate of interest (*r*) by the number of years (time, or *t*). This can be written as $I = prt$.

What is the simple interest on $400 deposited in a savings account paying 3% for 1 year?

$I = prt$

$I = 400 \times 0.03 \times 1$

$I = \$12.00$

Complete the following.

	Principal	Rate	Time	Interest
1.	$650	3%	1 year	______
2.	$700	2%	1 year	______
3.	$400	4%	1 year	______
4.	$175	5%	1 year	______
5.	$250	7%	1 year	______
6.	$325	6%	1 year	______
7.	$415	4%	1 year	______
8.	$318.80	5%	1 year	______
9.	$725	3%	1 year	______
10.	$850	7%	1 year	______
11.	$575	8%	1 year	______
12.	$925	5%	1 year	______
13.	$545.50	4%	1 year	______
14.	$1,380	7%	1 year	______

NAME ___________________________

Lesson 5.1 Problem Solving

SHOW YOUR WORK

Solve each problem.

1. Mr. Johnson borrowed $750 for 1 year. He has to pay 6% simple interest. How much interest will he pay?

   Mr. Johnson will pay __________ in interest.

2. Mrs. Soto invested in a certificate of deposit that pays 8% interest. Her investment was $325. How much interest will she receive in 1 year?

   Mrs. Soto will receive __________ in interest.

3. Andrea put $52 in a savings account that pays 4% interest. How much interest will she earn in 1 year?

   Andrea will earn __________ in interest.

4. Ms. Wilson took out a $1,500 loan. The interest rate is 7%. How much interest will she pay in 1 year?

   Ms. Wilson will pay __________ in interest.

5. Mr. Perez loaned $450 to his son for 1 year at 2% interest. How much interest will he collect?

   Mr. Perez will collect __________ in interest.

6. Jackson's savings account contains $827.50. If the interest rate is 4%, how much interest will the money earn in 1 year?

   The money will earn __________.

7. A special bond is being issued. It pays 13% for investments of $2,500. How much interest will it pay in 1 year?

   The bond will pay __________ in interest.

1.
2.
3.
4.
5.
6.
7.

NAME ______________________

Lesson 5.2 Simple Interest for More Than One Year

What is the simple interest on \$700 deposited in a savings account for 4 years paying $5\frac{1}{4}\%$ interest? How much money will be in the account at the end of 4 years?

$$I = p \times r \times t = 700 \times 0.0525 \times 4$$
$$= 147$$
$$\text{Total} = I + p = 147 + 700 = \$847 \text{ in the account.}$$

Complete the following.

	Principal	Rate	Time	Interest	Total Amount
1.	\$500	$10\frac{1}{2}\%$	2 years	________	________
2.	\$750	8%	3 years	________	________
3.	\$425	$9\frac{1}{2}\%$	4 years	________	________
4.	\$600	$4\frac{1}{4}\%$	6 years	________	________
5.	\$350	12%	4 years	________	________
6.	\$700	$3\frac{1}{2}\%$	3 years	________	________
7.	\$850	7%	7 years	________	________
8.	\$1,025	$5\frac{1}{2}\%$	4 years	________	________
9.	\$800	$4\frac{3}{4}\%$	5 years	________	________
10.	\$1,500	$6\frac{1}{2}\%$	2 years	________	________
11.	\$2,250	5%	3 years	________	________
12.	\$1,385	$2\frac{1}{2}\%$	6 years	________	________

NAME ____________________

Lesson 5.2 Simple Interest for More Than One Year

What is the simple interest on $800 deposited in a savings account for $3\frac{1}{2}$ years paying 4% interest? How much money will be in the account at the end of $3\frac{1}{2}$ years?

$$I = p \times r \times t = 800 \times 0.04 \times 3.5$$
$$= 112$$
$$I + p = 112 + 800 = \$912 \text{ in the account.}$$

Complete the following.

	Principal	Rate	Time	Interest	Total Amount
1.	$500	$5\frac{1}{2}$%	$3\frac{1}{2}$ years	______	______
2.	$180	10%	$1\frac{3}{4}$ years	______	______
3.	$720	$6\frac{1}{2}$%	$2\frac{1}{4}$ years	______	______
4.	$650	$4\frac{1}{4}$%	4 years	______	______
5.	$585	8%	$5\frac{1}{2}$ years	______	______
6.	$1,600	$9\frac{1}{4}$%	$2\frac{1}{2}$ years	______	______
7.	$60	$2\frac{1}{2}$%	$3\frac{1}{2}$ years	______	______
8.	$700	6%	$3\frac{1}{4}$ years	______	______
9.	$2,200	$5\frac{1}{4}$%	$4\frac{1}{2}$ years	______	______
10.	$1,350	7%	$6\frac{1}{2}$ years	______	______
11.	$400	12%	$5\frac{3}{4}$ years	______	______
12.	$5,000	18%	$6\frac{3}{4}$ years	______	______

NAME ____________________

Lesson 5.3 Simple Interest for Less Than One Year

What is the simple interest on a \$500 loan at $6\frac{1}{2}\%$ interest for $\frac{1}{2}$ year? How much total will be paid back?

$$I = p \times r \times t = 500 \times 0.065 \times 0.5$$
$$= 16.25$$
$$I + p = 16.25 + 500 = \$516.25 \text{ to be paid.}$$

Complete the following.

	Principal	Rate	Time	Interest	Total Amount
1.	\$700	6%	$\frac{3}{4}$ year	________	________
2.	\$500	$4\frac{1}{2}\%$	$\frac{1}{2}$ year	________	________
3.	\$850	8%	$\frac{1}{4}$ year	________	________
4.	\$1,200	$6\frac{1}{2}\%$	$\frac{1}{4}$ year	________	________
5.	\$425	4%	$\frac{3}{4}$ year	________	________
6.	\$200	18%	$\frac{1}{2}$ year	________	________
7.	\$2,500	7%	$\frac{3}{4}$ year	________	________
8.	\$3,000	$5\frac{1}{2}\%$	$\frac{1}{4}$ year	________	________
9.	\$50	3%	$\frac{1}{2}$ year	________	________
10.	\$720	11%	$\frac{3}{4}$ year	________	________

NAME ____________

Lesson 5.3 Problem Solving

SHOW YOUR WORK

Solve each problem.

1. Crystal borrowed \$500 for $\frac{1}{4}$ year at 8% interest. How much interest did the bank charge? How much total did she pay at the end of the term?

   The bank charged ____________ in interest.

   Crystal paid ____________ total.

2. Drew invested \$360 for $2\frac{1}{2}$ years at $7\frac{1}{4}$% interest. How much interest did he earn? How much money did he have after $2\frac{1}{2}$ years?

   Drew earned ____________ in interest.

   Drew had a total of ____________ after $2\frac{1}{2}$ years.

3. Jonas purchased a 42-month ($3\frac{1}{2}$ year) certificate of deposit. It cost \$600 and pays 7% interest. How much interest will he get? How much will the certificate be worth when he cashes it in?

   Jonas will get ____________ in interest.

   The certificate will be worth ____________.

4. Rick borrowed \$50 from his sister for 3 months ($\frac{1}{4}$ year). She charged him 14% interest. How much does Rick have to pay to his sister?

   Rick must pay his sister a total of ____________.

5. The grocery store borrowed \$15,000 to remodel. The term is 7 years and the interest rate is $4\frac{1}{4}$%. How much interest will the store pay? What is the total amount to be repaid?

   The store will pay ____________ in interest.

   The total amount to be repaid is ____________.

1.

2.

3.

4.

5.

NAME ______________________

Check What You Learned

Calculating Interest

Complete the following.

	Principal	Rate	Time	Interest	Total Amount
1.	$450	8%	1 year	________	________
2.	$630	5%	1 year	________	________
3.	$275	4%	1 year	________	________
4.	$595.50	6%	1 year	________	________
5.	$360	$5\frac{1}{2}$%	2 years	________	________
6.	$420	$8\frac{1}{4}$%	4 years	________	________
7.	$750	7%	5 years	________	________
8.	$580	$3\frac{1}{4}$%	3 years	________	________
9.	$1,300	4%	$3\frac{1}{2}$ years	________	________
10.	$1,060	5%	$4\frac{1}{4}$ years	________	________
11.	$600	$3\frac{1}{2}$%	$2\frac{3}{4}$ years	________	________
12.	$520	$6\frac{1}{2}$%	$5\frac{1}{4}$ years	________	________
13.	$880	$4\frac{1}{4}$%	$\frac{3}{4}$ year	________	________
14.	$1,500	8%	$\frac{1}{4}$ year	________	________
15.	$700	$1\frac{1}{2}$%	$\frac{1}{2}$ year	________	________

CHAPTER 5 POSTTEST

NAME ____________________

Check What You Learned

SHOW YOUR WORK

Calculating Interest

Solve each problem.

16. Luis has \$660 in his savings account earning $4\frac{1}{2}$% interest. How much interest will he earn in 2 years? How much money will be in the account?

Luis will earn __________ in interest.

He will have a total of __________ in his account.

16.

17. Mrs. Cole borrowed \$1,200 for 6 months ($\frac{1}{2}$ year) at $3\frac{1}{4}$% interest. How much interest will she pay? What is the total amount she has to pay?

Mrs. Cole will pay __________ in interest.

She will pay a total of __________.

17.

18. Flo invested in a 6-year certificate. If she invested \$750 and it pays $5\frac{3}{4}$% interest, how much interest will she get? What will the certificate be worth after 6 years?

Flo will get __________ in interest.

The certificate will be worth a total of __________.

18.

19. Interest on a $2\frac{1}{2}$ year loan of \$920 was charged at the rate of $8\frac{1}{4}$% a year. How much interest was charged? What is the total amount to be paid back on the loan?

The interest charged was __________.

A total of __________ must be paid back.

19.

20. Juan bought a new computer on credit. He has $\frac{3}{4}$ of a year to repay \$890 at 4% interest. How much interest will he pay? What is the total he will be paying for the computer?

Juan will pay __________ in interest.

He will pay a total of __________.

20.

CHAPTER 5 POSTTEST

NAME ______________________

Check What You Know

Ratio and Proportion

Solve each of the following.

	a	b	c
1.	$\frac{8}{15} = \frac{24}{n}$ ______	$\frac{3}{6} = \frac{n}{2}$ ______	$\frac{7}{n} = \frac{14}{16}$ ______
2.	$\frac{8}{n} = \frac{1}{3}$ ______	$\frac{n}{10} = \frac{4}{8}$ ______	$\frac{6}{n} = \frac{16}{24}$ ______
3.	$\frac{n}{25} = \frac{2}{5}$ ______	$\frac{4}{25} = \frac{n}{100}$ ______	$\frac{32}{16} = \frac{2}{n}$ ______
4.	$\frac{9}{5} = \frac{n}{20}$ ______	$\frac{18}{54} = \frac{1}{n}$ ______	$\frac{50}{75} = \frac{n}{6}$ ______
5.	$\frac{n}{3} = \frac{16}{6}$ ______	$\frac{20}{60} = \frac{n}{33}$ ______	$\frac{42}{n} = \frac{12}{2}$ ______

NAME ______________________

Check What You Know

Ratio and Proportion

SHOW YOUR WORK

Solve each problem.

6. Three baskets of oranges weigh 120 pounds. How many pounds are in 4 baskets?

There are __________ pounds in 4 baskets.

7. A scale drawing of a car is 3 inches to 12 inches. If the car is 48 inches high, how high is the drawing?

The drawing is __________ inches high.

8. There are 60 pencils in 4 pencil boxes. How many pencils are in 7 boxes?

There are __________ pencils in 7 boxes.

9. The supply store sells 4 pencils for every 5 pens. The store sold 28 pencils yesterday. How many pens did it sell?

The store sold __________ pens.

10. The ratio of chaperones to students on a field trip is 2 to 9. If 252 students went on the trip, how many chaperones were there?

There were __________ chaperones on the field trip.

11. On a map, each inch represents 25 miles. What is the length of a highway if it is 6 inches long on a map?

The highway is __________ miles long.

12. A survey found that 3 out of 8 students have pets. If 27 students have pets, how many students were surveyed?

__________ students were surveyed.

6.
7.
8.
9.
10.
11.
12.

NAME ______________________

Lesson 6.1 Ratio and Proportion

A **ratio** is a comparison of two numbers. A **proportion** expresses the equality of two ratios.

A ratio can be expressed as 1 to 2, 1:2, or $\frac{1}{2}$, and it means that for every 1 of the first item, there are 2 of the other item.

Cross-multiply to determine if two ratios are equal.

$$\frac{2}{4}, \frac{3}{6} \qquad 2 \times 6 = 12 \qquad 3 \times 4 = 12 \qquad \frac{2}{4} = \frac{3}{6}$$

Circle the ratios that are equal. Show your work.

	a	b	c
1.	$\frac{1}{3}, \frac{2}{6}$	$\frac{3}{8}, \frac{1}{4}$	$\frac{3}{5}, \frac{9}{15}$
2.	$\frac{3}{4}, \frac{9}{12}$	$\frac{1}{2}, \frac{4}{8}$	$\frac{5}{6}, \frac{15}{18}$
3.	$\frac{5}{8}, \frac{4}{7}$	$\frac{1}{2}, \frac{1}{4}$	$\frac{4}{3}, \frac{16}{12}$
4.	$\frac{6}{18}, \frac{2}{6}$	$\frac{3}{25}, \frac{6}{50}$	$\frac{1}{8}, \frac{2}{10}$
5.	$\frac{1}{4}, \frac{2}{4}$	$\frac{5}{10}, \frac{3}{6}$	$\frac{4}{24}, \frac{7}{42}$
6.	$\frac{3}{5}, \frac{5}{3}$	$\frac{7}{8}, \frac{21}{24}$	$\frac{8}{23}, \frac{9}{46}$
7.	$\frac{7}{4}, \frac{28}{16}$	$\frac{3}{9}, \frac{1}{3}$	$\frac{16}{20}, \frac{9}{10}$
8.	$\frac{8}{100}, \frac{80}{50}$	$\frac{8}{12}, \frac{10}{14}$	$\frac{15}{20}, \frac{3}{4}$
9.	$\frac{9}{2}, \frac{12}{3}$	$\frac{6}{3}, \frac{8}{4}$	$\frac{1}{3}, \frac{11}{33}$
10.	$\frac{12}{7}, \frac{36}{21}$	$\frac{10}{12}, \frac{15}{20}$	$\frac{3}{4}, \frac{9}{16}$

NAME ______________________

Lesson 6.2 Solving Proportion Problems

A proportion can be used in problem solving.

The ratio of apples to oranges is 4 to 5. There are 20 oranges in the basket. How many apples are there?

$\frac{4}{5} = \frac{n}{20}$	Set up a proportion, using *n* for the missing number.
$4 \times 20 = 5 \times n$	Cross-multiply.
$\frac{80}{5} = n$	Solve for *n*.
$16 = n$	There are 16 apples.

Solve each of the following.

	a	b	c
1.	$\frac{1}{3} = \frac{n}{24}$ ________	$\frac{4}{9} = \frac{n}{36}$ ________	$\frac{5}{45} = \frac{n}{9}$ ________
2.	$\frac{3}{5} = \frac{n}{15}$ ________	$\frac{10}{70} = \frac{n}{7}$ ________	$\frac{25}{40} = \frac{n}{16}$ ________
3.	$\frac{7}{12} = \frac{n}{36}$ ________	$\frac{13}{26} = \frac{n}{4}$ ________	$\frac{7}{1} = \frac{n}{3}$ ________
4.	$\frac{8}{5} = \frac{n}{40}$ ________	$\frac{2}{6} = \frac{n}{33}$ ________	$\frac{5}{13} = \frac{n}{39}$ ________
5.	$\frac{5}{6} = \frac{n}{18}$ ________	$\frac{9}{8} = \frac{n}{32}$ ________	$\frac{2}{3} = \frac{n}{15}$ ________

NAME ____________________

Lesson 6.3 Solving Proportion Problems

The missing number can appear any place in a proportion.
Solve the same way.

$\frac{2}{3} = \frac{6}{n}$	$\frac{3}{5} = \frac{n}{10}$	$\frac{3}{n} = \frac{6}{8}$	$\frac{n}{4} = \frac{3}{6}$
$3 \times 6 = 2 \times n$	$3 \times 10 = 5 \times n$	$3 \times 8 = 6 \times n$	$4 \times 3 = 6 \times n$
$\frac{18}{2} = n$	$\frac{30}{5} = n$	$\frac{24}{6} = n$	$\frac{12}{6} = n$
$9 = n$	$6 = n$	$4 = n$	$2 = n$

Solve each of the following.

	a	b	c
1.	$\frac{n}{3} = \frac{3}{9}$ ______	$\frac{5}{3} = \frac{15}{n}$ ______	$\frac{2}{n} = \frac{1}{4}$ ______
2.	$\frac{15}{30} = \frac{2}{n}$ ______	$\frac{4}{6} = \frac{n}{24}$ ______	$\frac{n}{7} = \frac{15}{21}$ ______
3.	$\frac{6}{n} = \frac{15}{20}$ ______	$\frac{n}{12} = \frac{9}{18}$ ______	$\frac{9}{2} = \frac{27}{n}$ ______
4.	$\frac{7}{9} = \frac{n}{63}$ ______	$\frac{15}{n} = \frac{12}{4}$ ______	$\frac{40}{100} = \frac{n}{25}$ ______
5.	$\frac{35}{n} = \frac{4}{8}$ ______	$\frac{16}{4} = \frac{36}{n}$ ______	$\frac{n}{12} = \frac{25}{30}$ ______

NAME ______________________

Lesson 6.4 Problem Solving

SHOW YOUR WORK

Solve each problem.

1. The ratio of cars to minivans in the parking lot is 2 to 3. There are 96 minivans. How many cars are in the lot?

There are __________ cars in the lot.

1.

2. The ratio of skateboards to bicycles at the park is 5 to 2. If there are 12 bicycles, how many skateboards are there?

There are __________ skateboards.

2.

3. An ice cream shop sells 4 vanilla cones for every 3 chocolate cones. The store sold 48 vanilla cones today. How many chocolate cones did it sell?

The store sold __________ chocolate cones.

3.

4. A flower arrangement has 8 carnations for every 4 roses. There are 14 carnations. How many roses are in the arrangement?

There are __________ roses in the arrangement.

4.

5. There are 18 girls in the school choir. The ratio of girls to boys is 1 to 2. How many boys are in the choir?

There are __________ boys in the choir.

5.

6. A baseball player strikes out 3 times for every 2 hits he gets. If the player strikes out 15 times, how many hits does he get? If the player gets 46 hits, how many times does he strike out?

The player gets __________ hits for every 15 times he strikes out.

If the player gets 46 hits, he strikes out __________ times.

6.

NAME ____________________

Lesson 6.5 Proportions and Scale Drawings

A **scale drawing** is a drawing of a real object in which all of the dimensions are proportional to the real object. A scale drawing can be larger or smaller than the object it represents. The **scale** is the ratio of the drawing size to the actual size of the object.

A drawing of a person has a scale of 2 inches = 1 foot. If the drawing is 11 inches high, how tall is the person?

$\frac{2}{1} = \frac{11}{n}$	Write a proportion.
$\frac{1 \times 11}{2} = n$	Solve for n.
$5\frac{1}{2} = n$	The person is $5\frac{1}{2}$ feet tall.

SHOW YOUR WORK

Solve each problem. Write a proportion in the space to the right.

1. A bridge is 440 yards long. A scale drawing has a ratio of 1 inch = 1 yard. How long is the drawing?

The drawing is ____________ inches long.

2. A map of the county uses a scale of 2 inches = 19 miles. If the county is 76 miles wide, how wide is the map?

The map is ____________ inches wide.

3. A picture of a goldfish has a scale of 8 centimeters to 3 centimeters. If the actual goldfish is 12 centimeters long, how long is the drawing?

The drawing is ____________ centimeters long.

4. An architect made a scale drawing of a house to be built. The scale is 2 inches to 3 feet. The house in the drawing is 24 inches tall. How tall is the actual house?

The actual house is ____________ feet tall.

1.

2.

3.

4.

NAME ___________________________

Lesson 6.6 Problem Solving

SHOW YOUR WORK

Solve each problem.

1. The proportion of nickels to dimes in a coin jar is 2 to 5. If there are 35 dimes, how many nickels are there?

There are __________ nickels in the jar.

2. On a map, each centimeter represents 45 kilometers. Two towns are 135 kilometers apart. What is the distance between the towns on the map?

The towns are __________ centimeters apart on the map.

3. A certain recipe calls for 2 cups of flour and 3 ounces of oil. If the recipe is increased to use 8 cups of flour, how much oil should be used?

__________ ounces of oil should be used.

4. An 8-inch by 12-inch portrait is reduced to be "pocket size." If the shorter side is now 2 inches, how long is the longer side?

The longer side is __________ inches.

5. Tim practices guitar 3 hours for every 1 hour he plays basketball. He practiced guitar 24 hours last month. How many hours did he play basketball?

Tim played basketball __________ hours last month.

6. The shipping charge on a 30-pound package is $6. How much would the shipping cost be on a 50-pound package?

The shipping cost would be __________.

7. A new school has a teacher-to-student ratio of 2:15. The school has 42 teachers. How many students are there in the school?

There are __________ students in the school.

1.
2.
3.
4.
5.
6.
7.

NAME ______________________

Check What You Learned

Ratio and Proportion

Solve each of the following.

	a	b	c
1.	$\frac{3}{2} = \frac{n}{6}$ ______	$\frac{17}{34} = \frac{1}{n}$ ______	$\frac{n}{16} = \frac{6}{4}$ ______
2.	$\frac{7}{n} = \frac{21}{12}$ ______	$\frac{5}{8} = \frac{n}{40}$ ______	$\frac{1}{2} = \frac{56}{n}$ ______
3.	$\frac{n}{12} = \frac{2}{3}$ ______	$\frac{9}{n} = \frac{12}{8}$ ______	$\frac{36}{50} = \frac{n}{100}$ ______
4.	$\frac{24}{3} = \frac{8}{n}$ ______	$\frac{n}{9} = \frac{4}{12}$ ______	$\frac{6}{n} = \frac{18}{75}$ ______
5.	$\frac{5}{2} = \frac{n}{12}$ ______	$\frac{4}{2} = \frac{32}{n}$ ______	$\frac{3}{n} = \frac{15}{20}$ ______

CHAPTER 6 POSTTEST

NAME ____________________

Check What You Learned

SHOW YOUR WORK

Ratio and Proportion

CHAPTER 6 POSTTEST

Solve each problem.

6. Three out of every 7 houses in the neighborhood are painted white. There are 224 houses in the neighborhood. How many houses are white? There are ________ white houses in the neighborhood.	**6.**
7. A plan for a new development is created as a scale drawing. On the plan, 8 centimeters equal 75 meters. The width of the development is 675 meters. How wide is the plan drawing? The drawing is ________ centimeters wide.	**7.**
8. A 6-inch by 4-inch photograph is enlarged so that the shorter side is 26 inches. How long is the longer side? The longer side is ________ inches.	**8.**
9. There are 9 chairs for every 2 tables in the lunchroom. There are 81 chairs. How many tables are there? There are ________ tables in the lunchroom.	**9.**
10. Lois spends 3 hours doing French homework for every 2 hours she spends on history. Last month, she had 24 hours of history homework. How many hours of French homework did she have? She had ________ hours of French homework.	**10.**
11. Six buckets of gravel weigh 48 pounds. How much would 4 buckets weigh? Four buckets of gravel would weigh ________ pounds.	**11.**
12. On a map, a road is 7 inches long. If the scale is 1 inch = 14 miles, how long is the actual road? The actual road is ________ miles long.	**12.**

NAME ______________________

Mid-Test Chapters 1–6

Add, subtract, multiply, or divide. Write each answer in simplest form.

	a	b	c	d
1.	$127 + 46 + 352$	$2079 + 114 + 17$	$5\frac{1}{2} + 7\frac{2}{3}$	$3\frac{7}{8} + 2\frac{2}{5}$
2.	$346 - 72$	$480 - 119$	$6\frac{2}{9} - 3\frac{1}{4}$	$5\frac{1}{2} - 2\frac{3}{7}$
3.	275×56	312×9	1717×34	5806×42
4.	$\frac{1}{4} \times \frac{5}{6}$	$\frac{3}{8} \times \frac{2}{3}$	$2\frac{5}{7} \times \frac{4}{9}$	$\frac{1}{2} \times \frac{3}{5} \times \frac{2}{3}$
5.	$8\overline{)72}$	$19\overline{)384}$	$52\overline{)6147}$	$8\overline{)1352}$
6.	$\frac{2}{3} \div \frac{4}{7}$	$3\frac{1}{2} \div \frac{5}{6}$	$\frac{4}{9} \div \frac{1}{12}$	$2\frac{2}{3} \div 1\frac{1}{8}$

CHAPTERS 1–4 MID-TEST

NAME ____________________

Mid-Test Chapters 1–6

Add, subtract, multiply, or divide.

	a	b	c	d
7.	14 5138 + 203	72024 315642 + 1357	5.73 0.212 + 1.6	28.3052 1.071 + 5.58
8.	586423 − 7982	43248 − 19156	42.5 − 16.304	7.28 − 0.959
9.	586 × 3.7	2.1 × 0.8	3.507 × 2.6	38.2 × 7.58
10.	98 × 0.4	370 × 6.4	7.0215 × 9	42.36 × 13
11.	2.5)10	0.03)36	9)7.2	8)5.664
12.	4.8)24.96	0.37)2.2755	9.06)66.138	1.205)4.2175

NAME ____________________

Mid-Test Chapters 1–6

Change to percents.

	a	b	c
13.	$\frac{3}{20}$ = ________ %	$\frac{4}{5}$ = ________ %	$\frac{14}{50}$ = ________ %

Change to decimals.

14.	30% = ________	$72\frac{1}{4}$% = ________	346% = ________

Change to fractions.

15.	75% = ________	20% = ________	140% = ________

Complete.

16.	________ is 9% of 30.	________ is 8% of 15.	________ is 22% of 90.
17.	36.9 is 45% of ________.	0.36 is 12% of ________.	120 is 150% of ________.
18.	13 is ________% of 52.	5 is ________% of 125.	38 is ________% of 40.

Complete the following.

	Principal	Rate	Time	Interest	Total Amount
19.	$720	$3\frac{1}{4}$%	4 years	________	________
20.	$500	$5\frac{1}{2}$%	$3\frac{1}{2}$ years	________	________
21.	$60	4%	$\frac{3}{4}$ year	________	________
22.	$480	$12\frac{1}{2}$%	$5\frac{1}{4}$ years	________	________

NAME ______________________

Mid-Test Chapters 1–6

SHOW YOUR WORK

Solve each problem.

23. A can of mixed nuts has 5 peanuts for every 2 cashews. There are 175 peanuts in the can. How many cashews are there?

There are __________ cashews in the can.

23.

24. A savings account pays $4\frac{1}{2}$% interest. How much interest will be earned on $450 in 3 years? How much money will be in the account in 3 years?

The account will earn ________ in interest in 3 years.

There will be ________ in the account in 3 years.

24.

25. A drawing of an office building has a scale of 2 inches = 30 feet. The building is 105 feet tall. How tall is the drawing?

The drawing is __________ inches tall.

25.

26. A company charges $2\frac{1}{4}$% for shipping and handling on all purchases. How much is shipping and handling on a purchase of $180? What is the total cost to the customer?

The shipping and handling charge is ________.

The total cost to the customer is ________.

26.

27. The Kendalls make monthly deposits into their savings plan. In 7 months, they have deposited $224. If they continue at this rate, how much will they have deposited in 12 months?

They will have deposited ________.

27.

28. During the first half of his shift, a server made $63 in tips on bills totaling $350. At this rate, what will be his total tips if the bills for the evening total $775? What percent was the server tipped?

His total tips will be ________.

The server was tipped __________%.

28.

CHAPTERS 1–4 MID-TEST

Check What You Know

Customary Measurement

Convert the following.

	a	b	c
1.	14 yd. = ______ ft.	$4\frac{1}{4}$ mi. = ______ yd.	$2\frac{1}{2}$ mi. = ______ ft.
2.	2.5 ft. = ______ in.	81 ft. = ______ yd.	5940 ft. = ______ mi.
3.	16 yd. 2 ft. = ______ ft.	7 ft. 3 in. = ______ in.	1 mi., 320 ft. = ______ ft.
4.	8052 yd. = ______ mi.	69 in. = ____ ft. ____ in.	42 yd. = ______ in.
5.	22 c. = ______ qt.	6.5 pt. = ______ c.	82 c. = ______ gal.
6.	9 qt. = ______ gal.	$13\frac{1}{4}$ gal. = ______ qt.	27 pt. = ____ qt. ____ pt.
7.	43 pt. = ______ c.	6 qt. = ______ pt.	$2\frac{3}{4}$ gal. = ______ pt.
8.	19 c. = ____ pt. ____ c.	13 qt. = ____ gal. ____ qt.	5 gal. 2 qt. = ______ qt.
9.	24 oz. = ______ lb.	2400 lb. = ______ T.	5.5 lb. = ______ oz.
10.	6.25 T. = ______ lb.	13 lb. = ______ oz.	1500 lb. = ______ T.
11.	6200 lb. = ______ T.	12 oz. = ______ lb.	2.6 T. = ______ lb.
12.	18 oz. = ____ lb. ____ oz.	40 oz. = ____ lb. ____ oz.	0.25 lb. = ______ oz.
13.	$5\frac{1}{2}$ hr. = ______ min.	380 sec. = ______ min.	0.25 hr. = ______ sec.
14.	108 hr. = ______ days	72 min. = ______ hr.	204 hr. = ____ days ____ hr.
15.	560 sec. = ____ min. ____ sec.	3.25 days = ______ hr.	23 min. = ______ sec.
16.	2.5 days = ______ min.	18 hr. = ______ days	15 hr. = ______ min.

NAME ____________________

Check What You Know

Customary Measurement

SHOW YOUR WORK

Solve each problem.

17. Betsy kept track of her homework minutes by subject for one month. Her results were: English: 443 minutes; history: 474 minutes; math: 382 minutes; science: 527 minutes; Spanish: 438 minutes. How long did she study each subject, in hours and minutes? How many total days, hours, and minutes did she study?

English: __________ hours __________ minutes

History: __________ hours __________ minutes

Math: __________ hours __________ minutes

Science: __________ hours __________ minutes

Spanish: __________ hours __________ minutes

Total: _____ day _____ hours _____ minutes

17.

18. The Linders invited 38 people to a cookout. They need 6 ounces of meat per person. How many total ounces do they need? How many pounds is that?

The Linders need _____ ounces. That is _____ pounds.

18.

19. The Linders in **problem 18** also want to have 3 cups of lemonade for each person. How many quarts do they need? How many gallons is that?

The Linders need _____ quarts. That is _____ gallons.

19.

20. The Linders in **problem 18** want to use 10.5 feet of their patio for the food serving area. Express that in yards, feet, and inches.

The serving area will be _____ yards _____ foot _____ inches.

20.

21. The walking path at the park is 1,254 feet. If Paul walks the path 8 times, how many miles will he walk?

Paul will walk __________ miles.

21.

NAME ______________________________

Lesson 7.1 Units of Length (inches, feet, yards, and mile)

1 foot (ft.) = 12 inches (in.)
1 yard (yd.) = 3 ft. = 36 in.
1 mile (mi.) = 1760 yd. = 5280 ft.

Use the table and multiply or divide to convert units of measure.

3.2 ft. = ________ in.
3.2 ft. = (3.2 × 12) = 38.4 in.

4224 yd. = ________ mi.
4224 yd. ÷ 1760 = 2.4 mi.

Convert the following.

	a	b	c
1.	17 yd. = ________ ft.	8 mi. = ________ ft.	5280 yd. = ________ mi.
2.	280.8 in. = ________ yd.	8.5 mi. = ________ yd.	708 in. = ________ ft.
3.	3 yd. 1 ft. = ________ in.	111 ft. = ________ yd.	12 mi. = ________ yd.
4.	4 mi. 182 yd. = ________ yd.	13 ft. 5 in. = ________ in.	2.4 mi. = ________ ft.
5.	328 in. = ____ yd. ____ in.	41.6 mi. = ________ yd.	22000 yd. = ________ mi.
6.	64.4 ft. = ________ in.	37.8 mi. = ________ ft.	2 mi. 311 ft. = ________ ft.

SHOW YOUR WORK

Solve each problem.

7. The race track at the high school is 0.25 miles long. How many yards is it?

   The track is ________ yards long.

8. Lisa swam in the 600-foot race at the swim meet. How many yards is this race?

   The race is ________ yards.

9. Rich measured 1.6 miles from his house to the library. How many yards is this? How many feet?

   The distance is ________ yards or ________ feet.

7.

8.

9.

NAME ___________________________

Lesson 7.2 Liquid Volume (cups, pints, quarts, gallons)

1 pint (pt.) = 2 cups (c.)
1 quart (qt.) = 2 pt. = 4 c.
1 gallon (gal.) = 4 qt. = 8 pt. = 16 c.

Use the table and multiply or divide to convert units of measure.

11 pt. = ________ c.
11 pt. = (11 × 2) c.
11 pt. = 22 c.

12 pt. = ________ gal.
12 pt. = (12 ÷ 8) gal.
12 pt. = 1.5 gal.

Convert the following.

	a	b	c
1.	13 c. = ________ pt.	2.5 gal. = ________ qt.	7 qt. = ________ pt.
2.	72 c. = ________ gal.	4 qt. 1 pt. = ________ pt.	5.4 gal. = ________ qt.
3.	3 gal. = ________ pt.	8.5 qt. = ________ c.	11 qt. = ____ gal. ____ qt.
4.	32 c. = ________ qt.	5.25 gal. = ________ c.	27 c. = ____ pt. ____ c.
5.	9.5 pt. = ________ qt.	9.5 qt. = ________ pt.	33 pt. = ____ gal. ____ pt.

SHOW YOUR WORK

Solve each problem.

6. A serving size is 1 cup of orange juice. How many servings are in a $\frac{1}{2}$ gallon bottle?

There are ________ servings in the bottle.

7. If a teakettle holds 1.75 quarts of water, how many cups of tea can be made?

________ cups of tea can be made.

8. Rey's bathtub holds 42 gallons of water. How many quarts is this? How many pints?

The bathtub holds _____ quarts. It holds _____ pints.

6.

7.

8.

NAME ____________________

Lesson 7.3 Problem Solving

SHOW YOUR WORK

Solve each problem.

1. The instructions on a package of garden fertilizer say to mix a spoonful of the powder with 9 pints of water. How many cups would this make? How many quarts? How many gallons?

This would make __________ cups.

This would make __________ quarts.

This would make __________ gallons.

2. In an 880 relay race, 4 runners on a team each run 880 yards. How many total yards is this race? How many feet is this? How many miles is this?

This is __________ yards.

This is __________ feet.

This is __________ miles.

3. Bill is 58 inches tall. Nikki is 4.75 feet tall. Elias is 1.5 yards tall. How tall are Bill, Nikki, and Elias in feet and inches? Who is the tallest?

Bill is __________ feet __________ inches.

Nikki is __________ feet __________ inches.

Elias is __________ feet __________ inches.

__________ is the tallest.

4. June needs to buy gas for her lawn mower. Her gas can holds 5.75 quarts. How many gallons is that?

The gas can holds __________ gallons.

5. A water pitcher holds 0.75 gallons of water. How many pints is this? How many cups?

The pitcher holds __________ pints.

The pitcher holds __________ cups.

1.
2.
3.
4.
5.

NAME ______________________

Lesson 7.4 Weight (ounces, pounds, tons)

1 pound (lb.) = 16 ounces (oz.)
1 ton (T.) = 2000 lb. = 32000 oz.

Multiply or divide to convert units of measure.

3.6 lb. = ________ oz.
3.6 lb. = (3.6 × 16) oz.
3.6 lb. = 57.6 oz.

11000 lb. = ________ T.
11000 lb. = (11000 ÷ 2000) lb.
11000 lb. = 5.5 T.

Convert the following.

	a	b	c
1.	3.5 T. = ________ lb.	72 oz. = ________ lb.	$\frac{3}{4}$ lb. = ________ oz.
2.	9000 lb. = ________ T.	64000 oz. = ________ T.	430 oz. = ________ lb.
3.	10689 lb. = ____ T. ____ lb.	$3\frac{1}{4}$ lb. = ________ oz.	3800 lb. = ________ T.
4.	9 lb. 14 oz. = ________ oz.	24700 lb. = ________ T.	6.8 T. = ________ lb.
5.	519 oz. = ____ lb. ____ oz.	6.5 lb. = ________ oz.	13 T. = ________ lb.

SHOW YOUR WORK

Solve each problem.

6. A dump truck can carry 3,200 pounds of dirt. How many tons is that?

The truck can carry ________ tons.

6.

7. At his last veterinary visit, Jerry's cat weighed 12.8 pounds. How many ounces is that?

Jerry's cat weighed ________ ounces.

7.

8. For the class picnic, the class needs one 4-ounce beef patty for each student. There are 27 students in the class. How many total ounces are needed? How many pounds is that?

A total of _____ ounces or _____ pounds are needed.

8.

NAME ______________________

Lesson 7.5 Time

1 minute (min.) = 60 seconds (sec.)
1 hour (hr.) = 60 min. = 3600 sec.
1 day = 24 hr. = 1440 min.

Multiply or divide to convert units of measure.

75 min. = ________ hr.
75 min. = (75 ÷ 60) hr.
75 min. = 1.25 hr.

16 min. = ________ sec.
16 min. = (16 × 60) sec.
16 min. = 960 sec.

Convert the following.

	a	b	c
1.	12 min. = ________ hr.	900 sec. = ________ min.	3.5 hr. = ________ min.
2.	8 days = ________ hr.	7 min. = ________ sec.	84 hr. = ________ days
3.	320 min. = ___ hr. ___ min.	$5\frac{1}{4}$ hr. = ________ min.	396 sec. = ________ min.
4.	150 hr. = ___ days ___ hr.	1800 sec. = ________ hr.	6.5 hr. = ________ min.
5.	42 days = ________ hr.	3 hr. 15 min. = ______ min.	3.75 min. = ________ sec.

SHOW YOUR WORK

Solve each problem.

6. Jenna swam two laps in 96 seconds. How many minutes did it take her?

It took Jenna ________ minutes to swim two laps.

7. According to the recipe, an apple spice cake has to bake for 90 minutes. How many hours is that?

The cake has to bake ________ hours.

8. Mickey is counting the hours until his trip to the ocean. It is now 228 hours away. How many days and hours are there until the trip?

The trip is in _____ days and _____ hours.

6.

7.

8.

NAME ______________________

Lesson 7.6 Problem Solving

SHOW YOUR WORK

Solve each problem.

1. Daniel, Trent, and Will competed in a race. Daniel's time was 0.09 hours, Trent's time was 5.8 minutes, and Will's time was 322 seconds. Express each runner's time in minutes and seconds. Who had the fastest time?

Daniel's time was ________ minutes ________ seconds.

Trent's time was ________ minutes ________ seconds.

Will's time was ________ minutes ________ seconds.

____________ had the fastest time.

1.

2. Bobbie bought 5 bags of trail mix. Each bag weighs 36 ounces. How many pounds of trail mix did she buy?

Bobbie bought ____________ pounds of trail mix.

2.

3. Helen has a washtub that holds 16.5 quarts of water. How many gallons does it hold? How many pints? How many cups?

The washtub holds ____________ gallons.

It holds ____________ pints.

It holds ____________ cups.

3.

4. An engineer determined that it would take $14\frac{1}{2}$ tons of steel to build the structure she designed. How many pounds of steel is that?

That is ____________ pounds of steel.

4.

5. Allen kept track of his time working on his science project. When he added it all up, he found that he spent 138 hours on his science project. How many days is that?

Allen spent ____________ days on his science project.

5.

6. A stationery store sells paper by the pound. Patty bought 4.2 pounds of paper. How many ounces is that?

Patty bought ____________ ounces of paper.

6.

NAME ______________________

Check What You Learned

Customary Measurement

Convert the following.

	a	b	c
1.	72 ft. = ________ yd.	18 in. = ________ ft.	1.2 mi. = ________ yd.
2.	12.5 yd. = ________ ft.	6600 yd. = ________ mi.	62 ft. = ____ yd. ____ ft.
3.	2 yd. 8 in. = ________ in.	38 yd. = ________ ft.	11880 ft. = ________ mi.
4.	3 mi. 540 yd. = ______ yd.	32.5 ft. = ________ in.	83 ft. = ____ yd. ____ ft.
5.	17 pt. = ________ qt.	6 c. = ________ pt.	41 qt. = ________ gal.
6.	$3\frac{1}{2}$ qt. = ________ c.	2.75 gal. = ________ qt.	3 gal. 5 c. = ________ c.
7.	13 c. = ____ pt. ____ c.	7 qt. = ________ gal.	32 pt. = ________ gal.
8.	8.5 pt. = ________ qt.	3.25 gal. = ________ pt.	4 gal. 3 qt. = ________ qt.
9.	28 oz. = ________ lb.	3.5 T. = ________ lb.	2.5 lb. = ________ oz.
10.	8200 lb. = ________ T.	11 lb. 3 oz. = ________ oz.	54 oz. = ________ lb.
11.	56 oz. = ____ lb. ____ oz.	7.25 T. = ________ lb.	32 oz. = ________ lb.
12.	4.6 lb. = ________ oz.	2.75 T. = ________ lb.	5.25 lb. = ________ oz.
13.	3.5 days = ________ hr.	4 hr. 23 min. = ______ min.	6.25 min. = ________ sec.
14.	210 sec. = ________ min.	88 hr. = ____ days ____ hr.	315 min. = ________ hr.
15.	45 min. = ________ hr.	3.2 min. = ________ sec.	12 hr. = ________ days
16.	6 min. 42 sec. = ______ sec.	8.75 days = ___ days ___ hr.	6.5 hr. = ________ min.

NAME ____________________

Check What You Learned

SHOW YOUR WORK

Customary Measurement

CHAPTER 7 POSTTEST

Solve each problem.

17. A construction crew removed 6,820 pounds of fill dirt. How much is that in tons and pounds?

The crew removed ______ tons ______ pounds of dirt.

17.

18. It is exactly 1.5 miles from the post office to the bank. How many yards is that? How many feet?

The distance is ____________ yards.

The distance is ____________ feet.

18.

19. The Jeffersons bought a 45-gallon hot water heater. How many quarts is that? How many cups?

The water heater holds ____________ quarts.

It holds ____________ cups.

19.

20. There are 18 children in the preschool class, and they each get 1 pint of juice a day. How many total cups is that? How many quarts? How many gallons?

That is ____________ cups.

It is ____________ quarts.

It is ____________ gallons.

20.

21. Shari spent 93 minutes working in her flower garden. She spent 42 minutes trimming the hedges. How many total hours and minutes did she spend working in her yard?

Shari worked ________ hours ________ minutes.

21.

22. Sofia used 18.5 yards of ribbon for a craft project. How many inches is that? How many feet and inches?

Sofia used ____________ inches.

That is ________ feet ________ inches.

22.

Check What You Know

Metric Measurement

Convert the following.

	a		b	
1.	4.8 km = ______________ m		1.2 m = ______________ cm	
2.	0.7 m = ______________ mm		2475 m = ______________ km	
3.	3 cm = ______________ mm		682 mm = ______________ m	
4.	804 mm = ______________ cm		13.1 km = ______________ m	
5.	520 cm = ______________ m		480 m = ______________ km	
6.	2.4 g = ______________ mg		6800 kg = ______________ MT	
7.	12 kg = ______________ g		460 mg = ______________ g	
8.	4.86 MT = ______________ kg		2.7 kg = ______________ g	
9.	743 g = ______________ kg		0.8 g = ______________ mg	
10.	375 kg = ______________ MT		2162 mg = ______________ g	
11.	0.71 kL = ______________ L		560 mL = ______________ L	
12.	87 L = ______________ kL		8.94 L = ______________ mL	
13.	1720 L = ______________ kL		346 mL = ______________ L	
14.	2635 mL = ______________ L		500 kL = ______________ L	
15.	0.63 L = ______________ mL		500 L = ______________ kL	

NAME ____________________

Check What You Know

SHOW YOUR WORK

Metric Measurement

Solve each problem.

16. A small can of juice is 355 milliliters. A bottle of juice is 1.4 liters. Which holds more, 4 cans or 1 bottle?

__________ hold(s) more.

16.

17. A jar of peanut butter weighs 1.13 kilograms. How many grams is that?

The jar weighs __________ grams.

17.

18. Lucita's house is 743 meters from her cousin's house. Lucita walks to her cousin's house and back home 3 times a week. How many kilometers does she walk in a week?

Lucita walks __________ kilometers.

18.

19. A pen is 147 millimeters long. How many centimeters is that?

The pen is __________ centimeters long.

19.

20. The tanks at a processing plant each hold 651 liters of fluid. There are 7 tanks. In total, how many kiloliters do they hold?

The tanks hold __________ kiloliters.

20.

21. A can of soda contains 40 milligrams of sodium. How many cans would it take to consume a gram of sodium?

It would take __________ cans.

21.

22. A book weighs 723 grams. How much does it weigh in kilograms? in milligrams?

The book weighs _____ kilograms or _____ milligrams.

22.

NAME ______________________

Lesson 8.1 Units of Length (millimeters, centimeters, meters, and kilometers)

1 centimeter (cm) = 10 millimeters (mm)	1 mm = 0.1 cm = 0.001 m
1 meter (m) = 100 cm = 1000 mm	1 cm = 0.01 m
1 kilometer (km) = 1000 m	1 m = 0.001 km

Multiply to convert units of measure.

23.8 m = ________ cm	23.8 m = ________ mm	23.8 m = ________ km
23.8 m = (23.8 × 100) cm	23.8 m = (23.8 × 1000) mm	23.8 m = (23.8 × 0.001) km
23.8 m = 2380 cm	23.8 m = 23800 mm	23.8 m = 0.0238 km

Convert the following.

	a	b	c
1.	3.5 km = ____________ m	4 m = ____________ cm	1.1 m = ____________ mm
2.	2500 m = ____________ km	5200 mm = ____________ m	13 cm = ____________ mm
3.	0.04 km = ____________ m	500 m = ____________ mm	230 cm = ____________ m
4.	3.27 m = ____________ cm	1.6 m = ____________ km	18 m = ____________ cm
5.	720 cm = ____________ m	860 mm = ____________ cm	0.75 km = ____________ m

SHOW YOUR WORK

Solve each problem.

6. A pencil is 13.6 centimeters long. How many millimeters is that?

The pencil is ____________ millimeters.

7. The bike path is 2,830 meters long. Cindy rode it 4 times. How many kilometers did she ride?

Cindy rode ____________ kilometers.

6.

7.

NAME ____________________

Lesson 8.2 Liquid Volume (milliliters, liters, and kiloliters)

1 liter (L) = 1000 milliliters (mL)	1 mL = 0.001 liter
1 kiloliter (kL) = 1000 liters	1 liter = 0.001 kL

Multiply to convert units of measure.

8 kL = ______ liters	750 mL = ______ liters
8 kL = (8 × 1000) liters	750 mL = (750 × 0.001) liters
8 kL = 8000 liters	750 mL = 0.75 liters

Convert the following.

	a	b
1.	2.5 kL = ______________ L	17 L = ______________ mL
2.	560 L = ______________ kL	0.82 L = ______________ mL
3.	427 mL = ______________ L	1.34 kL = ______________ L
4.	1826 L = ______________ kL	38 mL = ______________ L
5.	7.48 L = ______________ mL	75 L = ______________ kL

SHOW YOUR WORK

Solve each problem.

6. Nick has a scoop that holds 20 milliliters of water. How many scoops will it take to fill a 1 liter container?

It will take __________ scoops.

6.

7. A supplier had 4.3 kiloliters of milk. Customers bought a total of 620 liters this morning. How many kiloliters of milk are left?

There are __________ kiloliters of milk left.

7.

NAME ____________________

Lesson 8.3 Weight (milligrams, grams, kilograms, and metric tons)

1 gram (g) = 1000 milligrams (mg)	1 mg = 0.001 g
1 kilogram (kg) = 1000 g	1 g = 0.001 kg
1 metric ton (MT) = 1000 kg	1 kg = 0.001 MT

Multiply to convert units of measure.

3.5 kg = ______ g	180 mg = ______ g
3.5 kg = (3.5 × 1000) g	180 mg = (180 × 0.001) g
3.5 kg = 3500 g	180 mg = 0.18 g

Convert the following.

	a	b
1.	0.75 kg = ______________ g	3410 kg = ______________ MT
2.	827 g = ______________ kg	8.45 MT = ______________ kg
3.	6.2 g = ______________ mg	1.3 kg = ______________ g
4.	250 kg = ______________ MT	630 mg = ______________ g
5.	9 kg = ______________ g	0.8 g = ______________ mg

SHOW YOUR WORK

Solve each problem.

6. One liter of water weighs 1 kilogram. What is the weight in kilograms of 2.75 liters? What is the weight in grams?

The water weighs ______ kilograms or ______ grams.

7. The combined weight of the people on a bus is 1,316 kilograms. How much is that in metric tons?

The people weigh __________ metric tons.

6.

7.

NAME ___________________________

Lesson 8.4 Problem Solving

SHOW YOUR WORK

Solve each problem.

1. Marta is training for the 75-meter dash. She ran the dash 43 times last week. How many meters did she run? How many kilometers?

   Marta ran __________ meters.

   She ran __________ kilometers.

2. Booker is using a 3-liter bucket to fill a 0.81 kiloliter tub. How many buckets will it take to fill the tub?

   It will take __________ buckets.

3. There are 3.6 metric tons of cargo on a cargo ship. How many kilograms is that?

   The ship is carrying __________ kilograms.

4. A table is 193 centimeters long. How many meters is that?

   The table is __________ meters long.

5. A glass holds 450 milliliters of water. A bottle holds 1.5 liters. Which holds more, 3 glasses or 1 bottle?

   __________ hold(s) more.

6. A certain insect weighs about 340 milligrams. How much would a colony of 168 insects weigh, in grams?

   A colony would weigh __________ grams.

7. Pablo is 1.554 meters tall. Ruby is 150 centimeters 48 millimeters tall. Express their height in meters, centimeters, and millimeters. Who is taller?

   Pablo is _____ meter(s), _____ centimeters, and _____ millimeters tall.

   Ruby is _____ meter(s), _____ centimeters, and _____ millimeters tall.

   __________ is taller.

1.

2.

3.

4.

5.

6.

7.

NAME ______________________

Check What You Learned

Metric Measurement

Convert the following.

	a	b
1.	623 cm = __________ m	346 m = __________ km
2.	211 mm = __________ cm	8.7 km = __________ m
3.	1.3 cm = __________ mm	512 mm = __________ m
4.	0.2 m = __________ mm	3864 m = __________ km
5.	3.6 km = __________ m	8.82 m = __________ cm
6.	422 kg = __________ MT	5847 mg = __________ g
7.	394 g = __________ kg	0.24 g = __________ mg
8.	2.91 MT = __________ kg	3.12 kg = __________ g
9.	8.2 kg = __________ g	643 mg = __________ g
10.	9.6 g = __________ mg	3425 kg = __________ MT
11.	0.51 L = __________ mL	832 L = __________ kL
12.	6235 mL = __________ L	26 kL = __________ L
13.	4807 L = __________ kL	918 mL = __________ L
14.	36 L = __________ kL	6.47 liters = __________ mL
15.	0.68 kL = __________ L	390 mL = __________ L

CHAPTER 8 POSTTEST

NAME ____________________

Check What You Learned

Metric Measurement

SHOW YOUR WORK

Solve each problem.

16. A serving of cereal has 70 milligrams of potassium. The recommended daily allowance of potassium is 3.5 grams. How many servings of cereal would it take to consume that much potassium?

It would take __________ servings of cereal.

16.

17. A small box of clips weighs 215 grams. The giant size box weighs 1.2 kilograms. Which weighs more, 5 small boxes or 1 giant box?

__________ weighs more.

17.

18. The diameter of a nickel is about 2 centimeters. How many nickels would have to be lined up side by side to be 1 meter in length?

It would take __________ nickels to equal 1 meter.

18.

19. A glass holds 420 milliliters and a jar holds 1.47 liters. How many glasses would it take to fill 1 jar?

It would take __________ glasses to fill 1 jar.

19.

20. A spring water company bottled 4,800 bottles of water yesterday. Each bottle holds 0.25 liters. How many kiloliters did they bottle?

The company bottled __________ kiloliters.

20.

21. Alvin's paper route includes 7 streets. Five of the streets are 334 meters long. The other 2 streets are 587 meters long. How many kilometers is Alvin's route?

Alvin's route is __________ kilometers.

21.

22. There were 221 runners in a race. Each runner drank 45 milliliters of water before the race. How many liters did they drink?

The runners drank __________ liters.

22.

NAME ______________________________

Check What You Know

Probability and Statistics

Use the following data set to complete the problems.

Daily High Temperature (°F)

66, 68, 72, 79, 67, 82, 73, 85, 68, 81, 73, 82, 69, 73, 74

1. Make a stem-and-leaf plot for the data.

2. Complete the frequency table to represent the data.

Temperature	Cumulative Frequency	Relative Frequency	Frequency
66°–70°			%
71°–75°			%
76°–80°			%
81°–85°			%

3. Make a line plot to display this data.

4. Make a box-and-whisker plot for this data.

5. Find the mean, median, mode, range, upper extreme, and lower extreme of the data.

a	b
mean: ____________	range: ____________
median: ____________	upper extreme: ____________
mode: ____________	lower extreme: ____________

NAME ______________________

Check What You Know

Probability and Statistics

6. Pepi's Pizza has a choice of thin crust or thick crust. The available toppings are mushrooms, onions, pepperoni, and sausage. Make a tree diagram showing the possible outcomes for a 1-topping pizza.

Use your tree diagram to answer the following questions.

7. How many possible outcomes are there? ______________

8. What is the probability that a pizza will be thin crust? ______________

9. What is the probability that a pizza will have onions? ______________

10. What is the probability that a pizza will be thick crust and have mushrooms? ______________

Use the circle graph at the right to answer the following questions.

11. Which two days combined account for exactly half of the people? ______________________

12. Which day did the fewest people pick? ______________

13. How many people chose Friday? ______________

14. What is the angle measure for Saturday? ______________

15. Use the data in the circle graph to make a histogram.

What Day Do You Go Grocery Shopping?

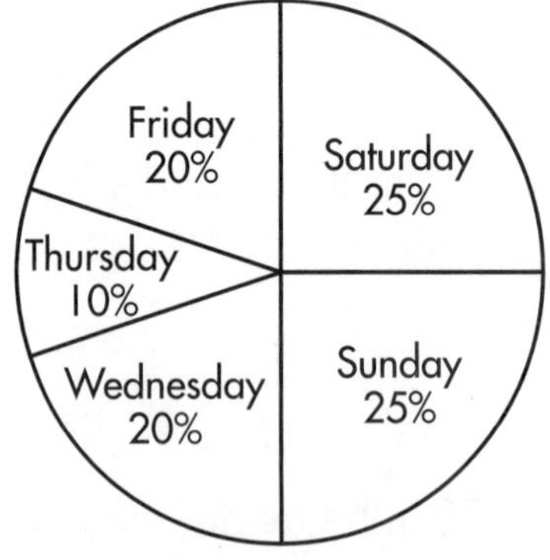

20 people responded.

NAME ____________________

Lesson 9.1 Bar Graphs

Bar graphs are used to compare data that has been collected from two or more data sets. Different colors or patterns are used for the bars to identify each category of a **multiple bar graph**.

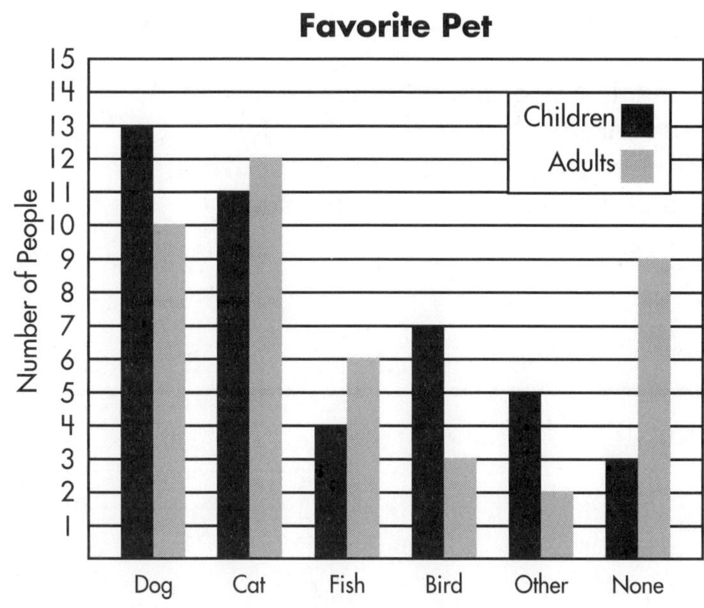

This graph shows the favorite pets of adults and children who were surveyed.

Use the bar graph above to answer each question.

1. How many people responded to the survey? ____________

2. How many adults responded? How many children? adults: ________ children: ________

3. How many adults chose fish? ____________

4. How many children chose cat? ____________

5. How many more adults than children preferred cats? ____________

6. How many more children chose dog than bird? ____________

7. Which pet was chosen by the most adults? ____________

8. Which pet (other than none) was chosen by the fewest children? ____________

9. How many total people chose bird? ____________

NAME ______________________

Lesson 9.2 Histograms

A **histogram** is a type of bar chart in which the categories are consecutive and the intervals are equal.

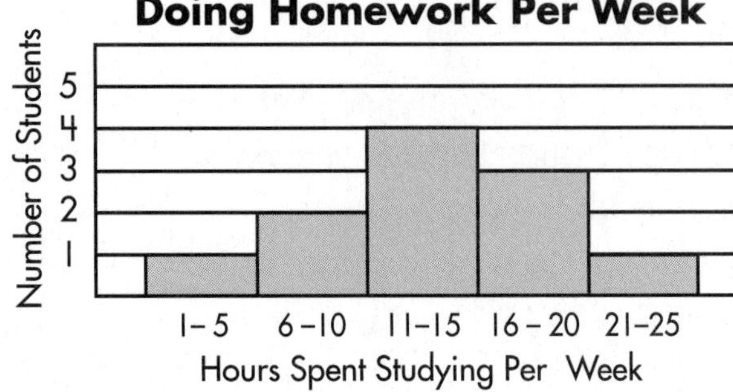

In this histogram, each bar represents an **interval** of 5 hours. The intervals are equal. The bars are **consecutive**, or in sequence one after the other.

Use the histogram above to answer each question.

1. How many students were surveyed? ______________

2. Which two intervals (bars) were selected by an equal number of students? ______________ and ______________

How many students chose each of those intervals? ______________

3. Which interval was selected by the most students? ______________

4. How many more students do 16–20 hours of homework than 1–5 hours? ______________

Use the histogram at the right to answer the following questions.

Snowfall per Month

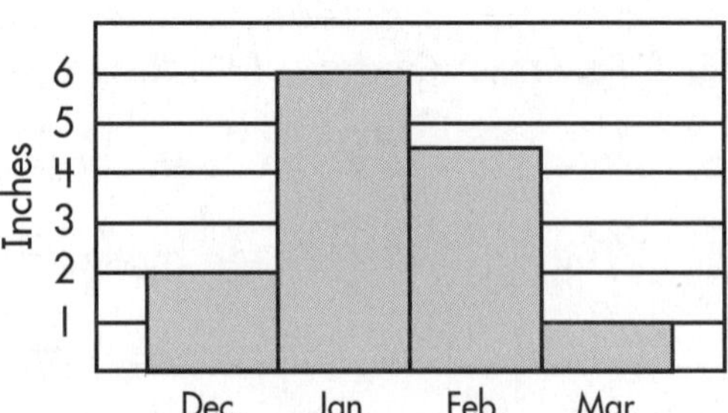

5. Which month had the most snowfall? ______________

6. How many inches of snow fell in January through March? ______________

7. How many more inches of snow fell in February than in March? ______________

8. How many inches of snow fell in December? ______________

NAME ____________________

Lesson 9.3 Line Graphs

Line graphs are used to show how a variable changes over time. Multiple lines can be used on the same graph to compare 2 or more variables.

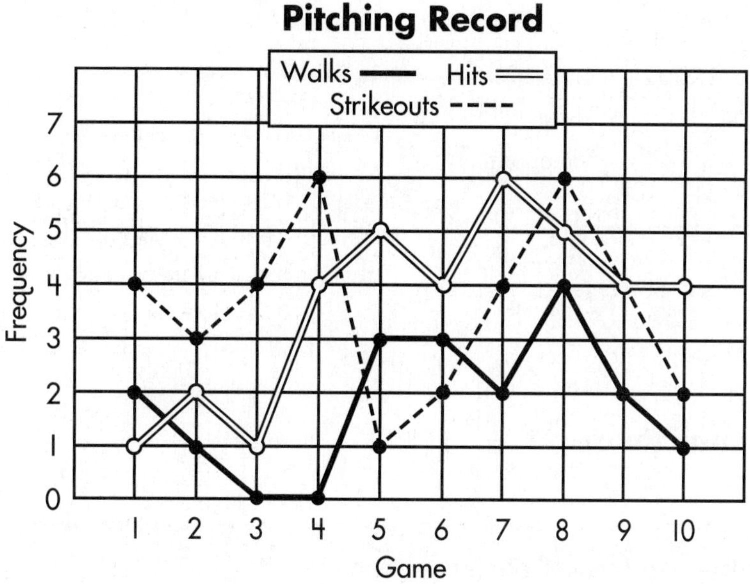

This graph shows the pitching record for the first 10 baseball games. As shown in the key, a different kind of line is used for each event being recorded.

Use the line graph above to answer the following questions.

1. How many total hits were given up? ____________
2. What was the total number of walks? ____________
3. Which game had the same number of strikeouts and hits? ____________
4. How many games had no walks? ____________
5. Which game(s) had 6 strikeouts? ____________
6. In which game(s) did the pitcher give up the fewest hits? ____________
7. Over the course of 10 games, were there more walks or more strikeouts? ____________
8. How many more hits were there in game 5 than in game 4? ____________

NAME ____________________

Lesson 9.4 Circle Graphs

A **circle graph** shows the relationship of parts to a whole. The circle is divided into sectors which add up to 100%. The sectors are determined by the central angles, and the sum of all those angles is 360°.

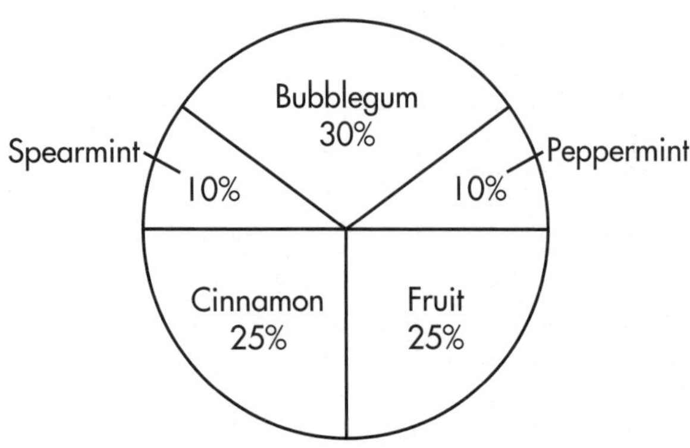

Favorite Gum Flavor

This circle graph shows the favorite gum flavor of 400 people. The sectors show the percent who prefer each flavor.

Use the circle graph above to answer each question.

1. Which flavor is preferred by the most people? ____________

2. How many people prefer spearmint? ____________

3. How many people prefer cinnamon? ____________

4. Which flavor is preferred by the same number of people who prefer cinnamon? ____________

5. Which two flavors combined account for exactly half of the people? ____________

6. How many people prefer bubblegum? ____________

7. What is the measure of the angle for the peppermint sector of the graph? ____________

8. What is the measure of the angle for the fruit sector of the graph? ____________

9. What is the measure of the angle for the bubblegum sector of the graph? ____________

Lesson 9.5 Scattergrams

A **scattergram** shows the relationship between two sets of data. It is made up of points. The points are plotted by using the values from the two sets of data as coordinates.

Note: Before working Lesson 9.5 activities, you may find it helpful to work Lesson 10.11, *Plotting Ordered Pairs.*

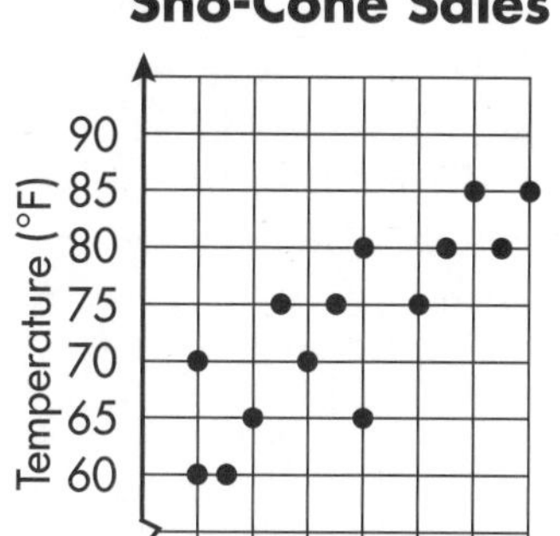

This scattergram shows the relationship between the temperature and the number of sno-cones sold. As one value increases, the other appears to increase as well. This indicates a *positive* relationship.

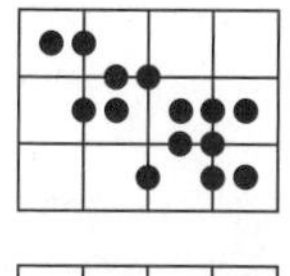

A *negative* relationship would show that more sno-cones are sold as the temperature decreases.

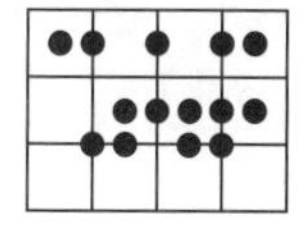

No relationship would show no clear trend in the data.

Use the scattergram above to complete the data table. Include the coordinates for all 14 points.

1.

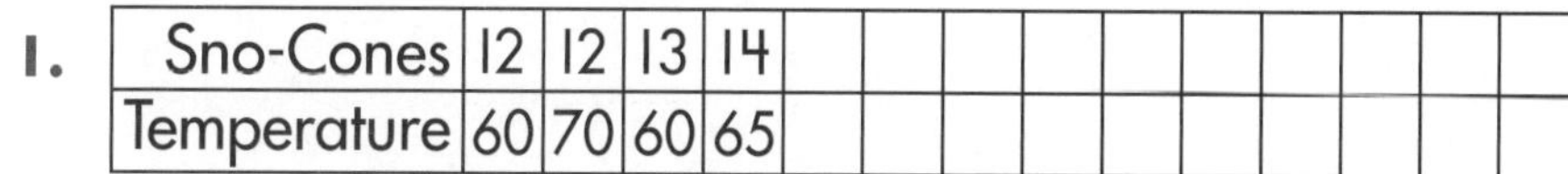

Sno-Cones	12	12	13	14										
Temperature	60	70	60	65										

Does each scattergram below indicate a positive relationship, a negative relationship, or no relationship?

2.

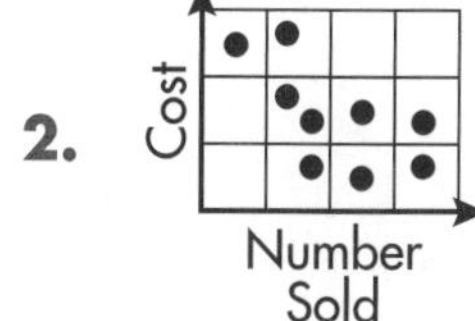

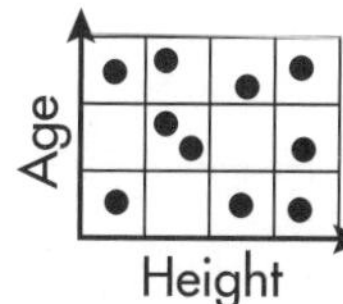

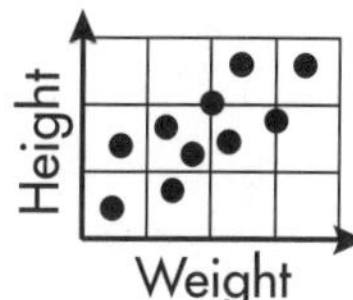

____________ ____________ ____________

Use the data below to create a scattergram on the grid. Be sure to include all labels.

3.

Hours Studying	0.5	0.5	0.75	0.75	1	1	1.25	1.25	1.5	2
Test Grade	71	72	70	76	74	80	82	83	80	85

NAME ____________________

Lesson 9.6 Measures of Central Tendency

The **mean** is the average of a set of numbers. It is found by adding the set of numbers and then dividing by the number of addends.

The **median** is the middle number of a set of numbers that is ordered from least to greatest. When there is an even amount of numbers, it is the mean of the two middle numbers.

The **mode** is the number that appears most often in a set of numbers. There is no mode if all numbers appear the same number of times.

The **range** is the difference between the greatest and least numbers in the set.

Find the mean, median, mode, and range of the following set of numbers.

34, 32, 39, 33, 37, 36, 39, 38

mean: $34 + 32 + 39 + 33 + 37 + 36 + 39 + 38 = \frac{288}{8} = 36$

Arrange the numbers from least to greatest to find median, mode, and range.

32, 33, 34, 36, 37, 38, 39, 39

median: $\frac{36+37}{2} = 36.5$ mode: 39 range: $39 - 32 = 7$

Find the mean, median, mode, and range of the following sets of numbers.

	a	b
1.	8, 6, 9, 11, 12, 4, 9, 10, 9, 2	40.7, 23.1, 18.5, 43.6, 52.1, 50.9, 44.8, 23.1
	mean: ______	mean: ______
	median: ______	median: ______
	mode: ______	mode: ______
	range: ______	range: ______
2.	152, 136, 171, 208, 193, 163, 124, 212, 216, 171	349, 562.5, 612, 349, 187, 612, 530, 716.5, 349, 902
	mean: ______	mean: ______
	median: ______	median: ______
	mode: ______	mode: ______
	range: ______	range: ______

NAME ____________________

Lesson 9.7 Stem-and-Leaf Plots

A **stem-and-leaf** plot is used to arrange data in order from least to greatest. It is displayed in two columns. The right column shows the **leaves**—the ones digit of each number. The other digits form the **stems** and are shown in the left column. The **key** explains how to read the plot.

Use the following data to create a stem-and-leaf plot.

71, 73, 87, 106, 95, 73, 86,

99, 104, 82, 93, 74, 101, 90

Stem	Leaves
7	1 3 3 4
8	2 6 7
9	0 3 5 9
10	1 4 6

Key: 7 | 1 = 71

Create a stem-and-leaf plot for each set of data.

	a	b
1.	18, 17, 12, 24, 17, 33, 21, 22, 14, 31, 30, 20, 16, 35	122, 120, 135, 130, 148, 131, 142, 122, 133, 143, 135, 132
2.	32, 46, 21, 33, 51, 65, 22, 45	78, 109, 73, 82, 95, 112, 93, 86, 109
3.	135, 146, 128, 164, 137, 152, 167, 150	346, 327, 368, 342, 339, 351, 346, 329

Lesson 9.8 Frequency Tables

A **frequency table** shows how often an item, a number, or a range of numbers occurs. The **cumulative frequency** is the sum of all frequencies up to and including the current one. The **relative frequency** is the percent of a specific frequency.

Make a frequency table for these test scores:

71, 85, 73, 92, 86, 79, 87,
98, 82, 93, 81, 89, 88, 96

Test Scores

Score	Frequency	Cumulative Frequency	Relative Frequency
71–75	2	2	14.3%
76–80	1	3	7.1%
81–85	3	6	21.4%
86–90	4	10	28.6%
91–95	2	12	14.3%
96–100	2	14	14.3%

Use the following data to complete the frequency table.

1. Cats' weights:

9.4375 lb., 11.375 lb., 12.1875 lb., 11.625 lb., 8.625 lb., 9.6875 lb., 8.875 lb., 12.5 lb., 9.375 lb., 10.25 lb., 10.625 lb., 12.0625 lb., 11.875 lb., 8.9375 lb., 9.75 lb., 10.1875 lb., 10.125 lb., 10.1875 lb., 12.0 lb., 9.125 lb.

Cats' Weights

Weight in pounds	Frequency	Cumulative Frequency	Relative Frequency
8.6–8.99			%
9–9.5			%
9.6–9.99			%
10–10.5			%
10.6–10.99			%
11–11.5			%
11.6–11.99			%
12–12.5			%

Answer the following questions about the frequency table above.

2. How many cats weigh 12–12.5 pounds? ____________

3. How many cats weigh 10.6–10.99 pounds? ____________

4. How many cats weigh less than 10 pounds? ____________

5. How many cats weigh 11 pounds or more? ____________

6. What percent of cats is 10–10.5 pounds? ____________

7. What percent of cats is less than 9 pounds? ____________

NAME ____________________

Lesson 9.9 Line Plots

A **line plot** is a graph that shows the frequency of data on a number line. Line plots make it easy to identify the mode, range, and any outliers in a data set. **Outliers** are data points that are much larger or smaller than other values.

To make a line plot, draw a number line from the least to the greatest value in the number set. Then, make an x above each number every time it appears in the set.

Make a line plot for the following data:

8, 9, 11, 8, 10, 11, 8, 9, 12, 8, 17, 12

The mode is 8. The range is 17 − 8 = 9. 17 is an outlier.

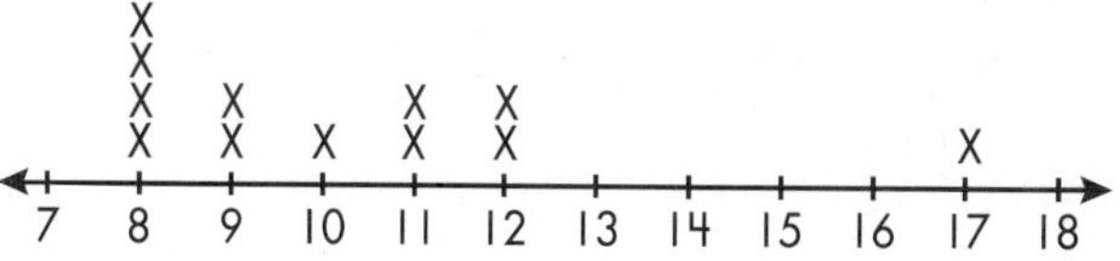

Answer the questions about the line plots below.

Number of Siblings

1. How many people responded to the sibling survey? ________
2. What is the mode of the sibling survey? What is the range?

   mode: ________ range: ________
3. How many people have 3 or more siblings? ________
4. What number is an outlier on the sibling survey? ________

Hours Studying For Test

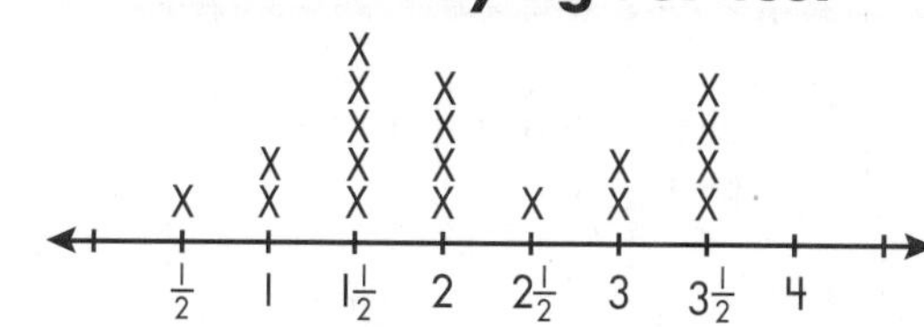

5. How many people responded to the test survey? ________
6. What is the mode of the test survey? What is the range?

   mode: ________ range: ________
7. How many people studied 2 or fewer hours? ________
8. How many people studied 4 or more hours? ________
9. Did more people study 2 or more hours or less than 2 hours?

   More people studied ________ hours.

NAME ______________________

Lesson 9.10 Box-and-Whisker Plots

A **box-and-whisker** plot displays data along a number line. Quartiles are used to divide the data into four equal parts. Each quartile is 25% of the number of items. The upper and lower quartiles, representing 50% of the data, form the box.
The upper extreme (highest value) and lower extreme (lowest value) form the whiskers.

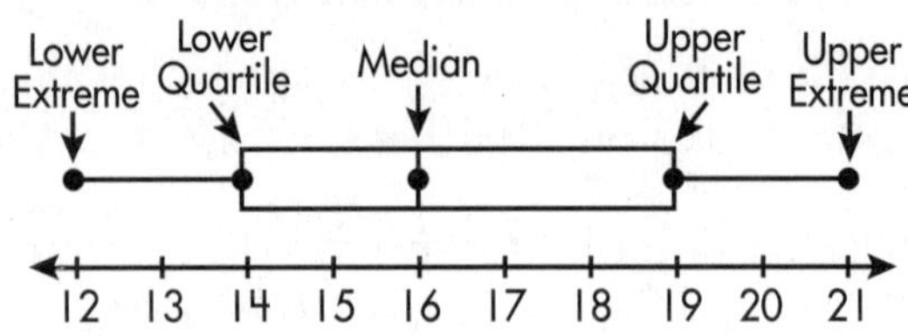

This box-and-whisker plot represents the following data:

12, 13, 14, 14, 15, 16, 17, 18, 19, 19, 21

Upper Extreme: 21
Lower Extreme: 12
Middle Quartile (median): 16
Upper Quartile (median of upper half): 19
Lower Quartile (median of lower half): 14

Use the box-and-whisker plots below to answer the following questions.

Miles Walked in Walk-a-Thon

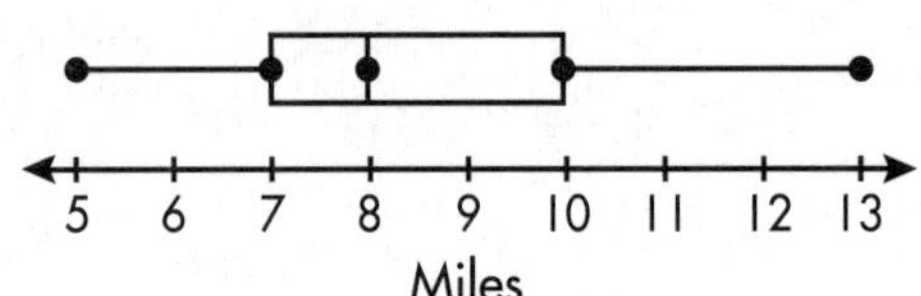

1. What is the median number of miles walked? ______________

2. What are the lowest and highest numbers of miles walked?

lowest: __________ highest: __________

3. If 126 people participated in the walkathon, how many people walked 7–10 miles? ______________

4. What percentage of the people walked more than 10 miles? ______________

Books Read Over the Summer

2 4 6 8 10 12 14 16 18 20 22

5. What is the median number of books read? ______________

6. What is the upper quartile? ______________

7. What percentage of the people who responded to the survey read 4 or fewer books? ______________

8. What is the most number of books anyone read? ______________

9. If 82 people responded to this survey, how many read from 4 to 18 books? ______________

NAME ______________________

Lesson 9.11 Tree Diagrams

A **sample space** is a set of all possible outcomes (or possible results) for an activity or experiment. To determine the sample space, it is helpful to organize the possibilities using a list, chart, picture, or tree diagram.

Show the sample space for tossing a nickel, a dime, and a quarter.

Nickel	Dime	Quarter	Possible Outcomes
Heads (H)	H	H	HHH
		T	HHT
	T	H	HTH
		T	HTT
Tails (T)	H	H	THH
		T	THT
	T	H	TTH
		T	TTT

There are 8 possible outcomes or possible results.

Make a tree diagram for each situation. Determine the number of possible outcomes.

1. The concession stand offers the drink choices shown in the table.

Drinks	Sizes
Lemonade	Small
Fruit Punch	Medium
Apple Cider	Large
	Jumbo

There are __________ possible outcomes.

2. The Kellys are planning their vacation activities. The first day they can go to the zoo or the museum. The second day they can go to the pier or the dunes. The third day they have to choose sailing, swimming, or horseback riding.

There are __________ possible outcomes.

NAME ______________________

Lesson 9.12 Calculating Probability

An **outcome** is any of the possible results of an activity or experiment. **Probability** is the likelihood that a specific outcome or set of outcomes will occur. Probability is the ratio of desired outcome(s) to the sample space. It can be expressed as a ratio, fraction, decimal, or percent.

When tossing a coin, what is the probability that it will land on heads?

desired outcome: heads sample space: heads, tails probability: 1:2, $\frac{1}{2}$, 50%, 0.5

Find the probability. Express your answer as a fraction in simplest form.

A box contains 3 red pencils, 4 blue pencils, 2 green pencils, and 1 regular pencil. If you take 1 pencil without looking, what is the probability of picking each of the following?

1. a red pencil ______________

2. a blue pencil ______________

3. a green pencil ______________

4. a regular pencil ______________

If you spin the spinner shown at the right, what is the probability of the spinner stopping on each of the following?

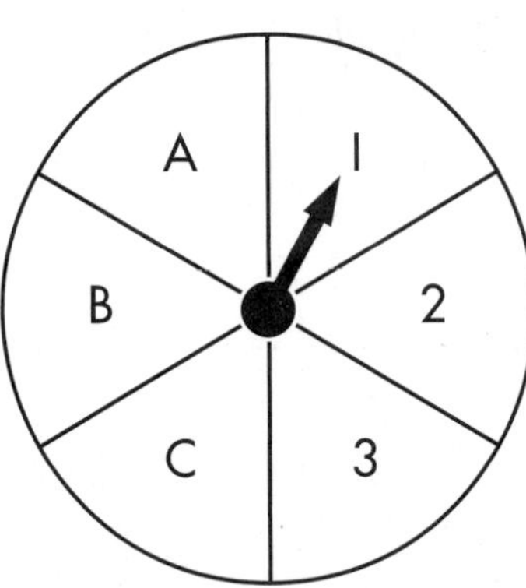

5. a letter ______________

6. an odd number ______________

7. an even number ______________

8. a vowel ______________

9. the number 3 ______________

10. a consonant ______________

NAME ______________________

Check What You Learned

Probability and Statistics

Use the following data set to complete the problems.

Number of Cars Across the Bridge

93, 105, 92, 111, 98, 97, 108, 101, 112, 115, 96, 104, 103, 91, 97

1. Make a stem-and-leaf plot to represent the data.

2. Make a frequency table for this data.

3. Make a line plot to display this data.

4. Make a box-and-whisker plot for this data.

5. Find the mean, median, mode, range, upper quartile, and lower quartile for this data.

a	b
mean: ____________	range: ____________
median: ____________	upper quartile: ____________
mode: ____________	lower quartile: ____________

CHAPTER 9 POSTTEST

NAME ___________________________

Check What You Learned

Probability and Statistics

6. Paul is getting a new bike. He can get either a racing bike or a mountain bike. His color choices are red, black, and silver. Make a tree diagram showing Paul's possible outcomes.

Use your tree diagram to answer the following questions.

7. How many possible outcomes are there? ____________

8. What is the probability that Paul will get a racing bike? ____________

9. What is the probability that the bike will be red? ____________

10. What is the probability that Paul will get a silver mountain bike? ____________

Use the circle graph at the right to answer the following questions.

11. How many people exercise 10–12 hours per week? ____________

12. What is the angle measure for 7–9 hours? ____________

13. How many hours do the most people exercise? ____________

14. Which group can be combined with the people who exercise 7–9 hours to account for exactly half of the people? ____________

15. Use the data in the circle graph to make a histogram.

Hours of Exercise Per Week

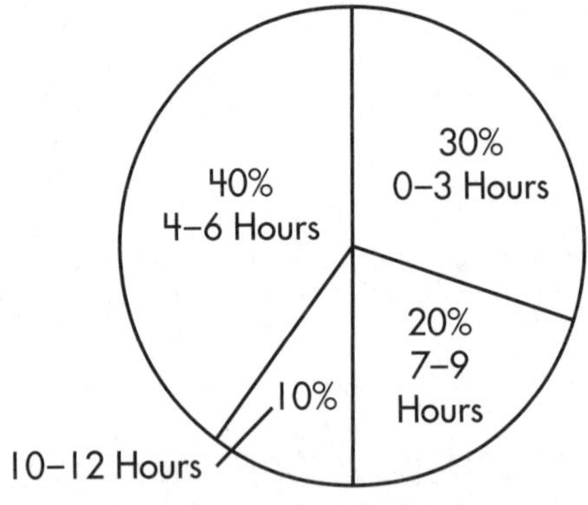

40 people responded.

Check What You Know

Geometry

Identify the following.

a b c

1. • T ____________ R S ____________ Y X ____________

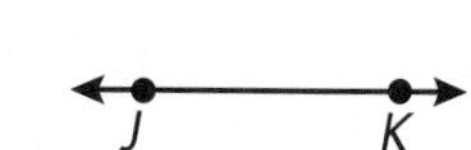

C D J K Q R

2. ____________ ____________ ____________

Name the angle, rays, and vertex.

3.

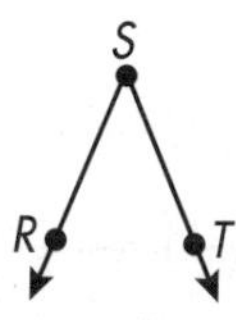

angle: ____________ rays: ____________ vertex: ____________

4.

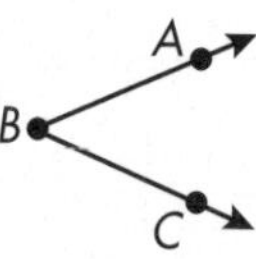

angle: ____________ rays: ____________ vertex: ____________

Use the figure at the right to complete the following.

5. Which two lines are parallel? ____________

6. If ∠4 is 120°, What is the measure of ∠3? ____________

7. Is ∠3 acute, obtuse, or right? ____________

8. What angle is vertical to ∠11? ____________

9. What angle is supplementary to ∠6? ____________

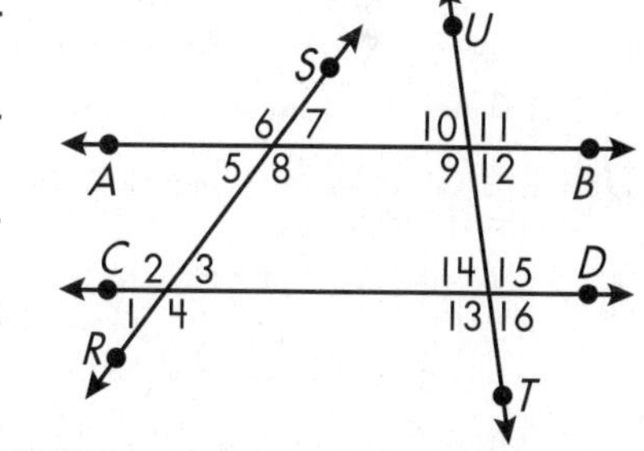

Name the transversal that forms each pair of angles. Write whether the angles are alternate interior, alternate exterior, or corresponding.

10. ∠4 and ∠6 ____________ ____________

11. ∠15 and ∠9 ____________ ____________

12. ∠11 and ∠5 ____________ ____________

13. ∠10 and ∠14 ____________ ____________

NAME ____________________

Check What You Know

Geometry

Write whether each triangle is acute, right, or obtuse and equilateral, isosceles, or scalene.

	a	b	c
14.			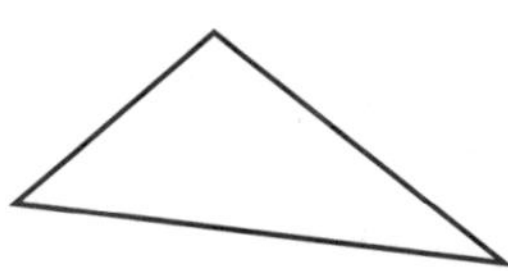
	____________	____________	____________

Identify the following shapes. If more than one name applies, use the name that is most specific.

15.	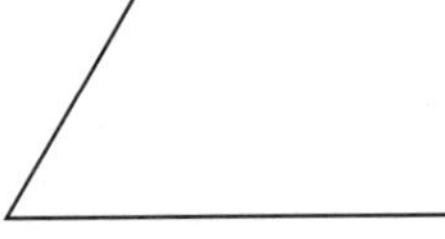		
	____________	____________	____________
16.	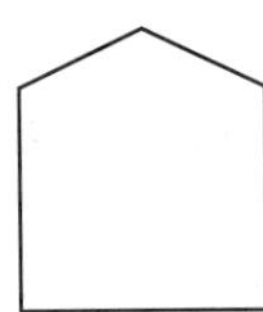	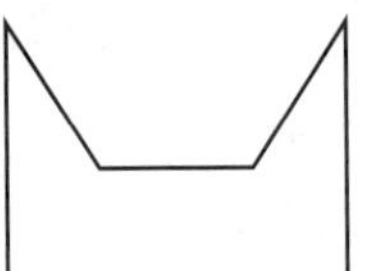	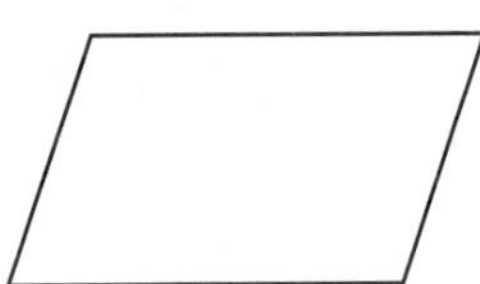
	____________	____________	____________

Use the grid at the right to answer the following.

17. What type of transformation is represented by figures *ABCDEFGH* and *IJKLMNOP*? ____________

18. What is the ordered pair of Point *S*? ____________

19. What is the ordered pair of Point *B*? ____________

20. What point is at coordinates (−3, −2)? ____________

21. What point is at coordinates (1, 2)? ____________

22. In which quadrant is Point *T*? ____________

23. Are the two figures in Quadrants I and II congruent? ____________

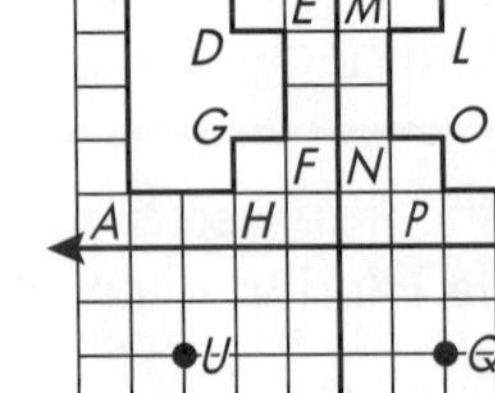

NAME ______________________

Lesson 10.1 Points and Lines

A **point** is a location. It is represented by a dot. *Point R* is shown below.

•*R*

A **line** is a straight path that extends indefinitely in opposite directions. The line below could be identified as *Line ST, Line TS*, $\overleftrightarrow{ST}$, or $\overleftrightarrow{TS}$.

A **line segment** is a straight path between two end points. The line segment below could be identified as *Line Segment UV, Line Segment VU*, $\overline{UV}$, or $\overline{VU}$.

Complete the following.

		a	b
1.	R, S (line)	line *RS* or *SR*	$\overleftrightarrow{RS}$ or $\overleftrightarrow{SR}$
2.	P, Q (line)	line ________ or ________	________ or ________
3.	M, N (line)	line ________ or ________	________ or ________

		a	b	c
4.	X, Y	line segment *XY* or ____	$\overline{XY}$ or ____	endpoints ____ and ____
5.	A, B	line segment ____ or ____	____ or ____	endpoints ____ and ____
6.	C, D	line segment ____ or ____	____ or ____	endpoints ____ and ____

Draw the following.

	a	b
7.	line *TU*	$\overleftrightarrow{OP}$
8.	$\overline{GH}$	$\overleftrightarrow{JK}$
9.	line segment *XY*	$\overline{WX}$

NAME ____________________

Lesson 10.2 Rays and Angles

A **ray** is a part of a line. It has one endpoint and extends indefinitely in one direction. The ray below could be identified as *Ray RS* or $\overrightarrow{RS}$.

An **angle** is formed by two rays that intersect at a common endpoint. The angle below could be identified as *Angle ABC, Angle CBA,* $\angle ABC$, or $\angle CBA$.

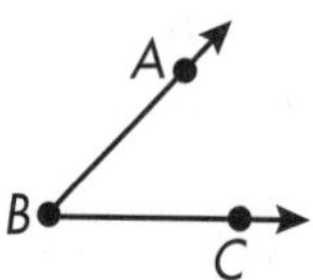

The common endpoint of two rays is also called a **vertex**. In $\angle ABC$ to the left, the vertex is *B*.

Complete the following.

		a	b
1.	A, B	ray *AB* $\overrightarrow{AB}$	endpoint *A*
2.	C, D	ray ________ ________	endpoint ________
3.	E, F	ray ________ ________	endpoint ________
4.	G, H, I	angle *GHI* or *IHG* rays: $\overrightarrow{HG}$ and $\overrightarrow{HI}$	$\angle GHI$ or $\angle IHG$ vertex *H*
5.	J, K, L	angle ________ or ________ rays: ________ and ________	________ or ________ vertex ________
6.	M, N, O	angle ________ or ________ rays: ________ and ________	________ or ________ vertex ________

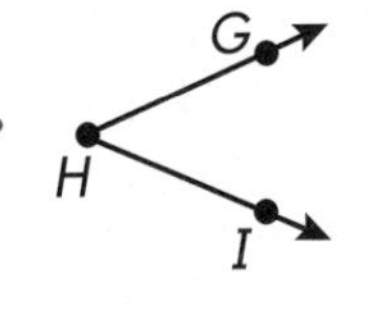

Use the points given to draw the following.

	a		b	
7.	$\overrightarrow{XY}$	Y X	$\overrightarrow{TU}$	T U
8.	$\angle RST$	R S T	$\angle PQR$	R Q P

Lesson 10.3 Measuring Angles

Use a protractor to measure an angle.

The measure of a **right angle** is 90°.

The measure of an **acute angle** is less than 90°.

The measure of an **obtuse angle** is greater than 90°.

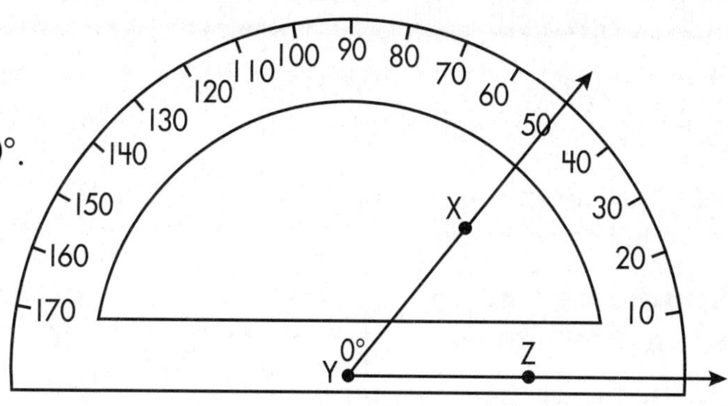

The measure of $\angle XYZ$ is 50°.

right angle

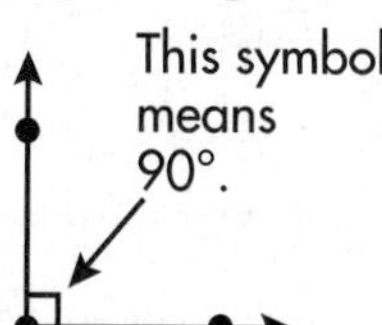

obtuse angle

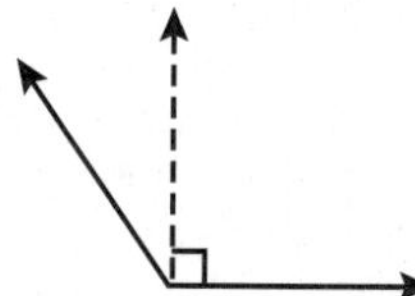

acute angle

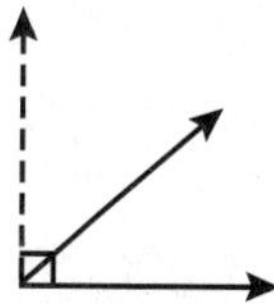

Find the measure of each angle. Write whether the angle is right, acute, or obtuse.

	a	b

1.

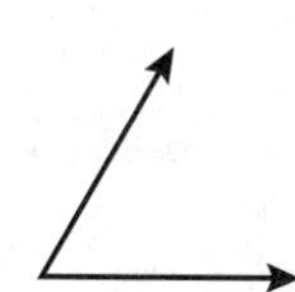

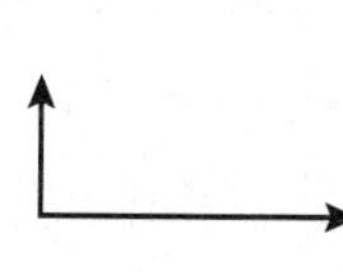

2.

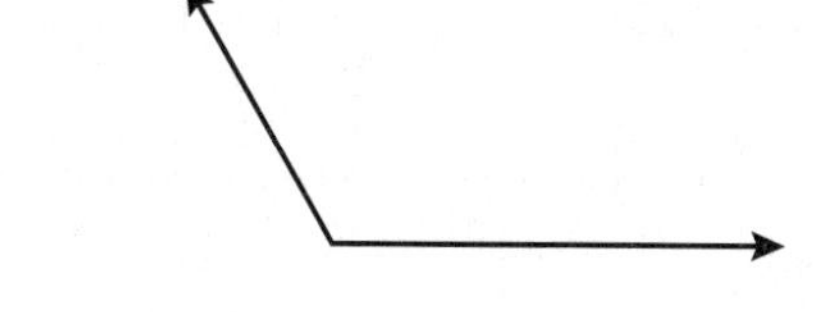

3.

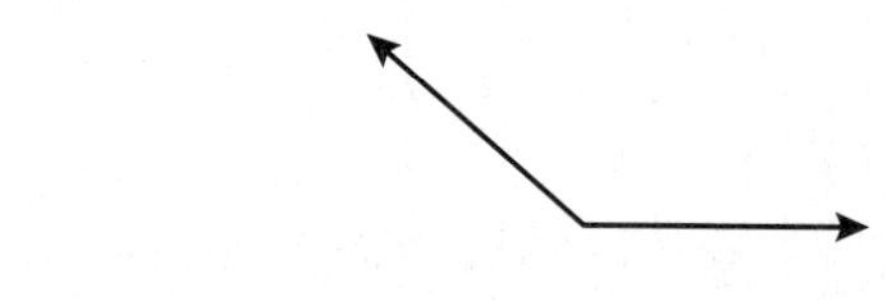

NAME ______________________________

Lesson 10.4 Vertical, Supplementary, and Complementary Angles

When two lines intersect, they form angles that have special relationships.

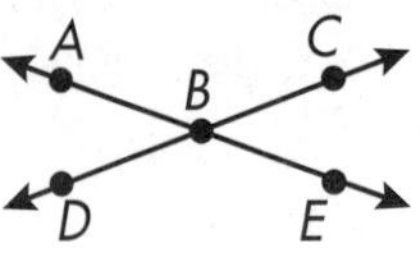

∠ABC and ∠DBE are vertical.

∠ABD and ∠DBE are supplementary.

Vertical angles are opposite angles that have the same measure.

Supplementary angles are two angles whose measures have a sum of 180°.

Complementary angles are two angles whose measures have a sum of 90°.

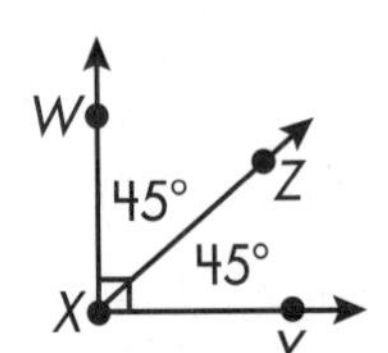

∠WXZ and ∠ZXY are complementary.

$\overrightarrow{XZ}$ is the bisector of ∠WXY.

A **bisector** divides an angle into two angles of equal measure.

Use the figure at the right to answer questions 1–4.

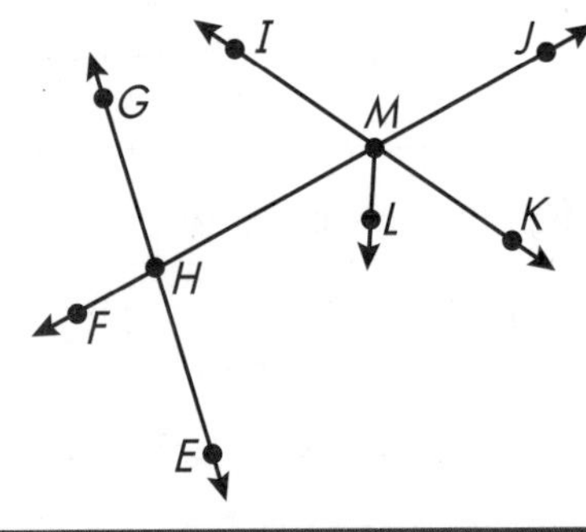

1. Name an angle that is vertical to ∠EHF. ______________

2. Name an angle that is vertical to ∠EHM. ______________

3. Name an angle that is supplementary to ∠IMJ. ______________

4. Name the bisector of ∠HMK. ______________

Use the figure at the right to answer questions 5 and 6.

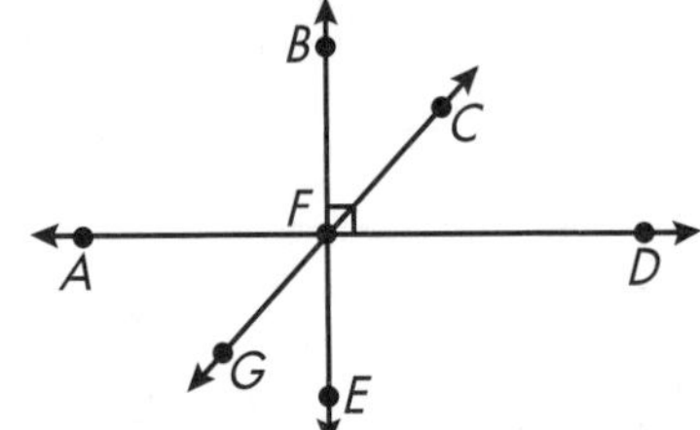

5. Name an angle complementary to ∠BFC. ______________

6. Name an angle complementary to ∠AFG. ______________

Solve.

7. ∠RST is supplementary to angle ∠PSO. The measure of ∠RST is 103°.
What is the measure of ∠PSO? ______________

8. ∠MNO and ∠NOP are complementary. The measure of ∠NOP is 22°.
What is the measure of ∠MNO? ______________

9. ∠XYZ is bisected by $\overrightarrow{YW}$. The measure of ∠XYW is 52°.
What is the measure of ∠WYZ? What is the measure of ∠XYZ?

The measure of ∠WYZ is ______________. The measure of ∠XYZ is ______________.

NAME ______________________________

Lesson 10.5 Transversals

A **transversal** is a line that intersects two or more lines at different points. The angles that are formed are called **alternate interior angles** and **alternate exterior angles**. **Parallel lines** are lines that will never intersect. When a transversal intersects parallel lines, **corresponding angles** are formed.

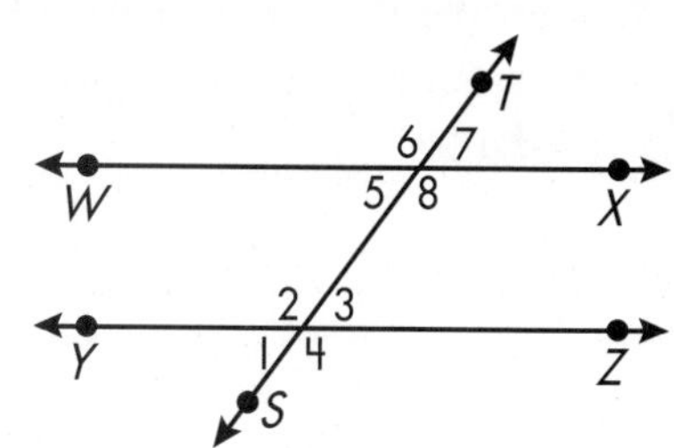

In the figure, $\overleftrightarrow{ST}$ is a transversal. $\overleftrightarrow{WX}$ and $\overleftrightarrow{YZ}$ are parallel.

The alternate interior angles are $\angle 2$ and $\angle 8$, and $\angle 3$ and $\angle 5$.

The alternate exterior angles are $\angle 4$ and $\angle 6$, and $\angle 1$ and $\angle 7$.

The corresponding angles are $\angle 1$ and $\angle 5$, $\angle 2$ and $\angle 6$, $\angle 3$ and $\angle 7$, and $\angle 4$ and $\angle 8$.

Use the figure to the right. Name the transversal that forms each pair of angles. Write whether the angles are alternate interior, alternate exterior, or corresponding.

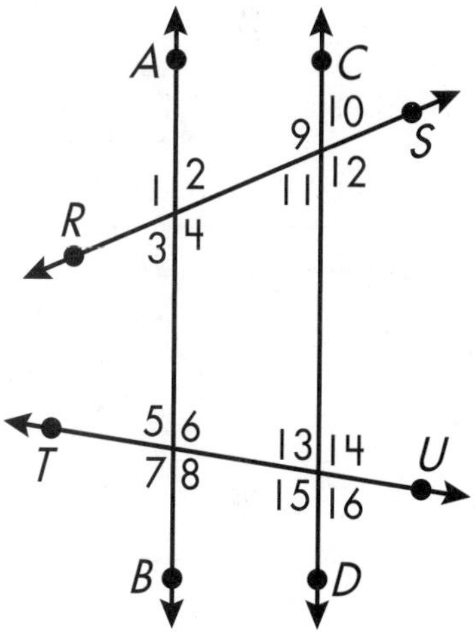

1. $\angle 1$ and $\angle 9$ ____________ ______________________

2. $\angle 5$ and $\angle 4$ ____________ ______________________

3. $\angle 11$ and $\angle 3$ ____________ ______________________

4. $\angle 5$ and $\angle 16$ ____________ ______________________

5. $\angle 13$ and $\angle 8$ ____________ ______________________

6. $\angle 15$ and $\angle 10$ ____________ ______________________

7. $\angle 7$ and $\angle 14$ ____________ ______________________

8. $\angle 8$ and $\angle 16$ ____________ ______________________

9. $\angle 6$ and $\angle 3$ ____________ ______________________

10. $\angle 12$ and $\angle 13$ ____________ ______________________

11. $\angle 10$ and $\angle 2$ ____________ ______________________

12. $\angle 5$ and $\angle 13$ ____________ ______________________

NAME ______________________

Lesson 10.6 Triangles (by angles)

The sum of the measures of the angles of a triangle is always 180°. Two of the angles are always acute. The triangle can be classified by the measure of the third angle as **right**, **acute**, or **obtuse**.

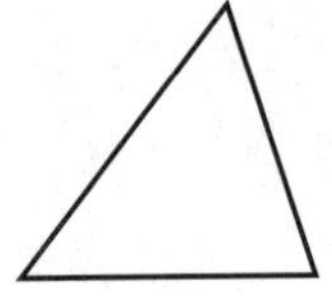

acute triangle
All angles are less than 90°.

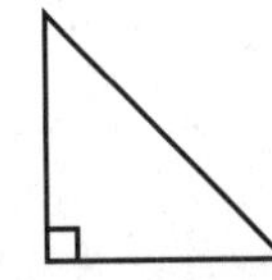

right triangle
One angle is 90°.

obtuse triangle
One angle is more than 90°.

Write whether each triangle is acute, right, or obtuse.

	a	b	c
1.	 ______	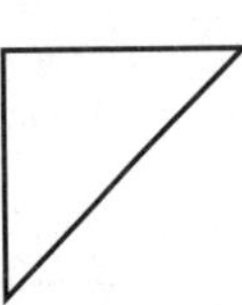 ______	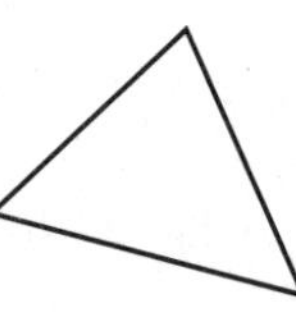 ______
2.	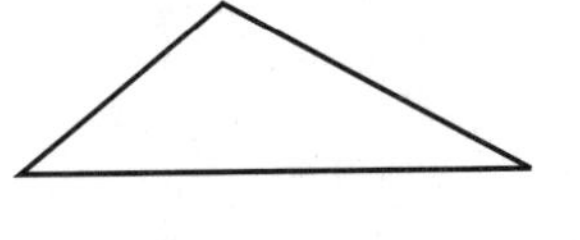 ______	 ______	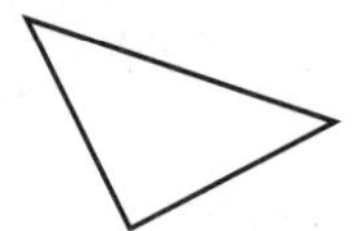 ______
3.	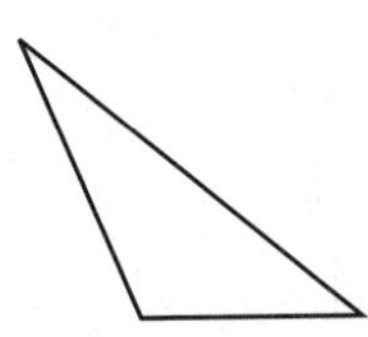 ______	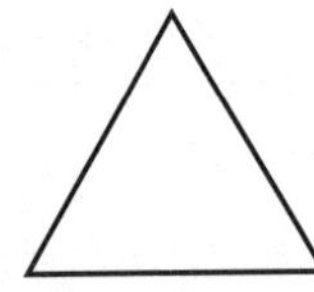 ______	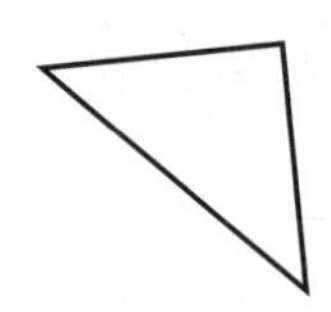 ______
4.	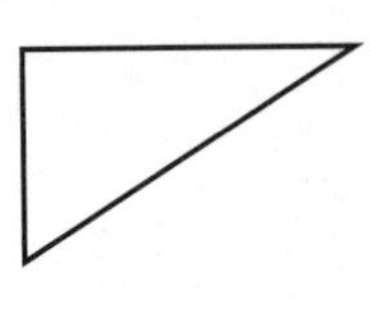 ______	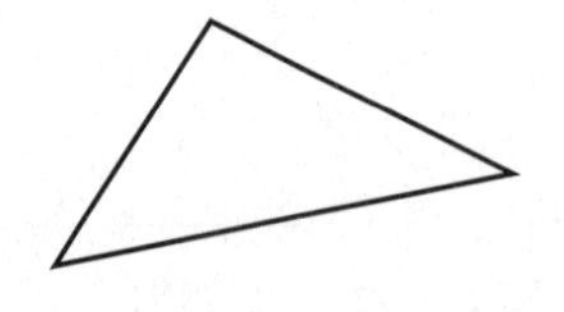 ______	 ______

NAME ______________________________

Lesson 10.7 Triangles (by side)

Triangles can be classified by the number of congruent (equal) sides that they have.

No two sides are congruent in a **scalene triangle**.

At least two sides are congruent in an **isosceles triangle**.

All three sides are congruent in an **equilateral triangle**.

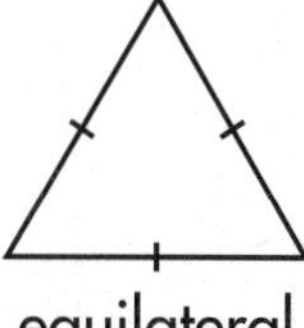
equilateral

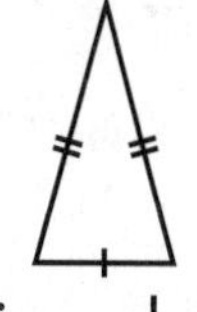
isosceles

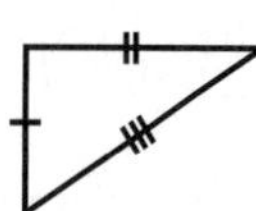
scalene

Use a ruler to measure each triangle. Write if it is equilateral, isosceles, or scalene.

	a	b	c
1.	  ______________	 ______________	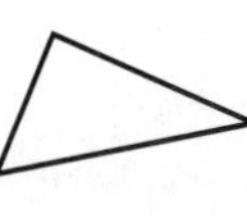 ______________
2.	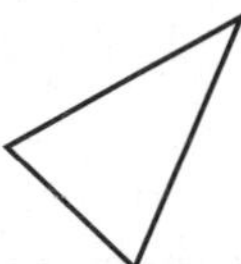 ______________	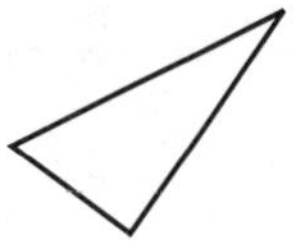 ______________	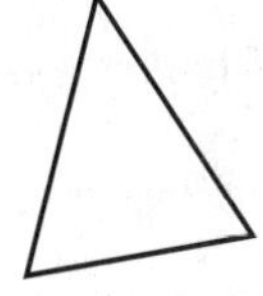 ______________
3.	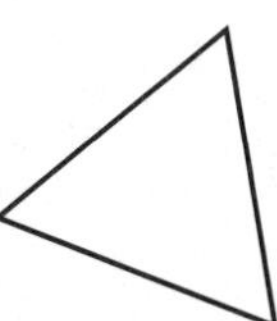 ______________	 ______________	 ______________

NAME ______________________

Lesson 10.8 Quadrilaterals

A **quadrilateral** is a closed figure with 4 sides.

A **parallelogram** is a quadrilateral whose opposite sides are parallel and congruent.

A **rectangle** is a parallelogram with four right angles.

A **rhombus** is a parallelogram with four congruent sides.

A **square** has four right angles and four congruent sides.

A **trapezoid** is a quadrilateral with only one pair of parallel sides.

parallelogram | rectangle | rhombus | square | trapezoid

Complete the following.

1. Which quadrilaterals have four right angles? ______________________

2. Which quadrilaterals have four congruent sides? ______________________

3. Are all parallelograms also rectangles? ____________

4. Are all rectangles also parallelograms? ____________

5. Are all squares also rectangles? ____________

6. Are all rectangles also squares? ____________

7. Is a square also a rhombus? ____________

Identify the following shapes. Use all terms that apply.

	a	b
8.	____________ ____________	____________ ____________
9.	 ____________ ____________	 ____________ ____________

NAME ___________________________

Lesson 10.9 Polygons

A **polygon** is a closed figure whose sides are all line segments. Polygons can be classified by the number of sides they have. The table shows some of the prefixes of polygons and the number of sides they represent.

Prefix	# of sides
penta-	5
hexa-	6
hepta-	7
octa-	8
nona-	9
deca-	10

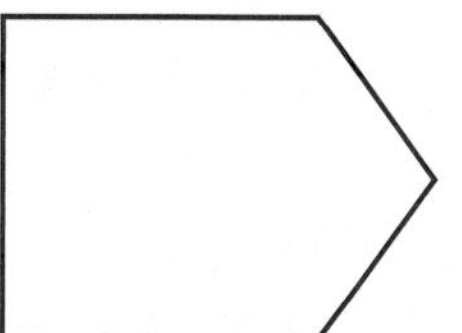
pentagon
5 sides

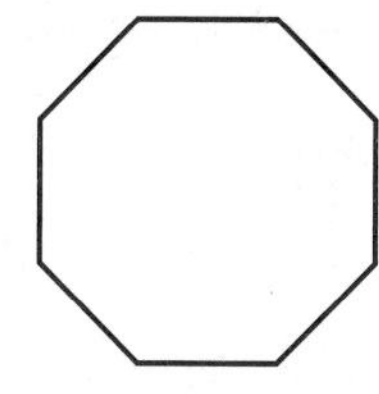
octagon
8 sides

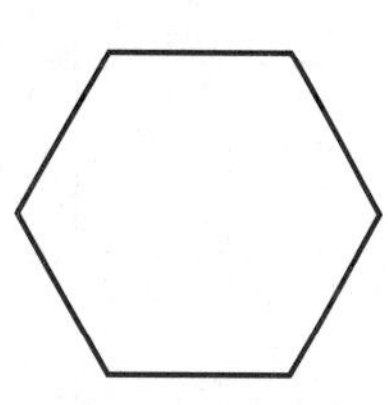
hexagon
6 sides

Write the name for each polygon.

	a	b
1.	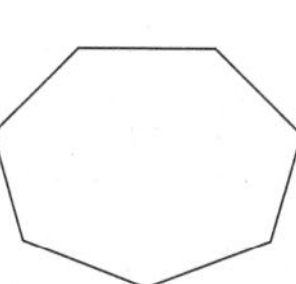 ______________	 ______________
2.	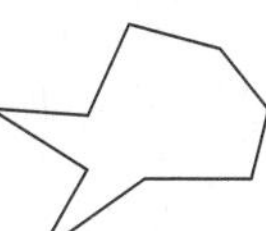 ______________	______________
3.	 ______________	 ______________
4.	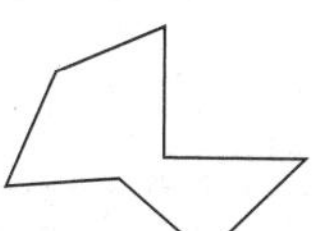 ______________	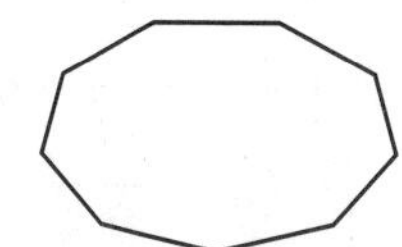 ______________

NAME ______________________

Lesson 10.10 Similar Figures

Two figures are **similar** if their corresponding angles are congruent and the lengths of their corresponding sides are proportional. Write a ratio to determine if the sides are proportional.

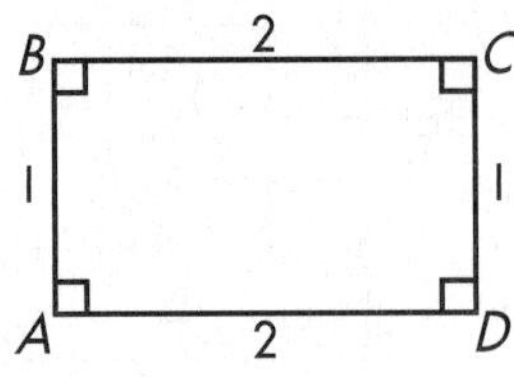

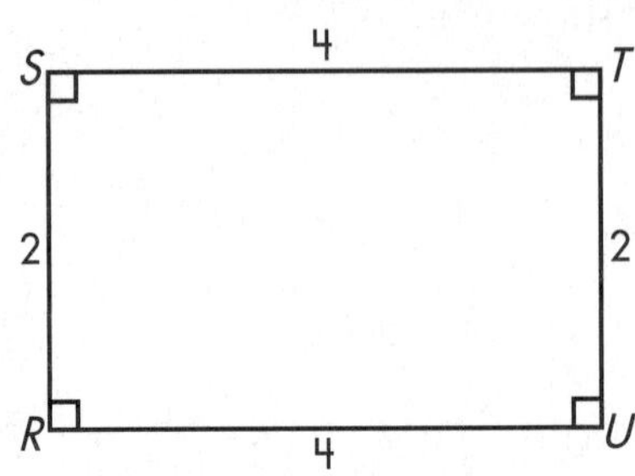

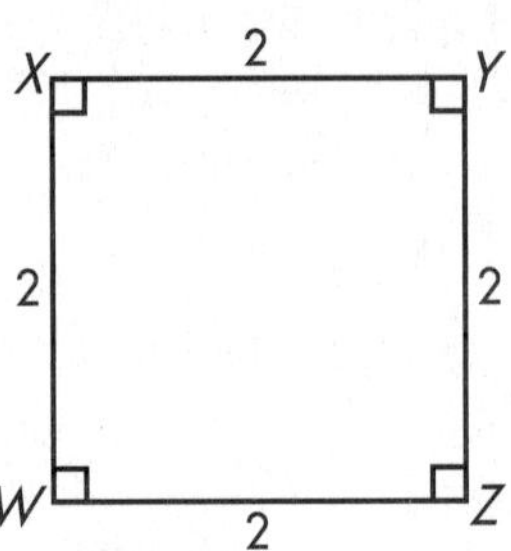

$\frac{AB}{SR} = \frac{BC}{ST}$? $\frac{1}{2} = \frac{2}{4}$ Similar

$\frac{AB}{WX} = \frac{BC}{XY}$? $\frac{1}{2} \neq \frac{2}{2}$ Not Similar

In the following figures, the angle marks indicate which angles are congruent. Use the measures given for the lengths of the sides. Write ratios to determine if the sides are proportional. Then, write *similar* or *not similar* for each pair of figures.

a **b**

1.

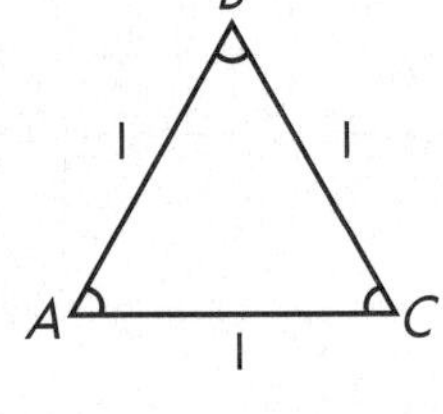

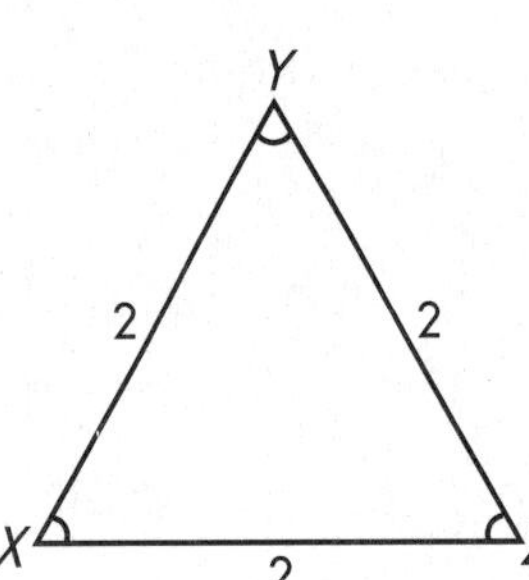

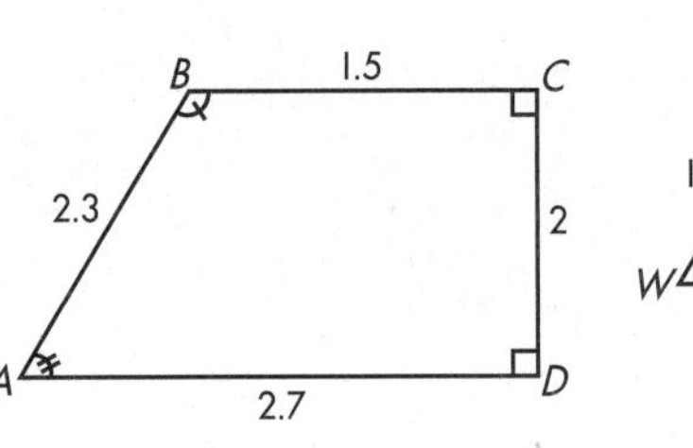

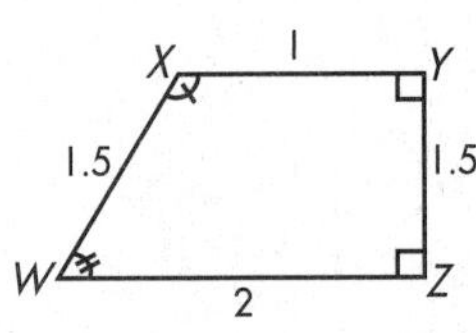

______________________ ______________________

2.

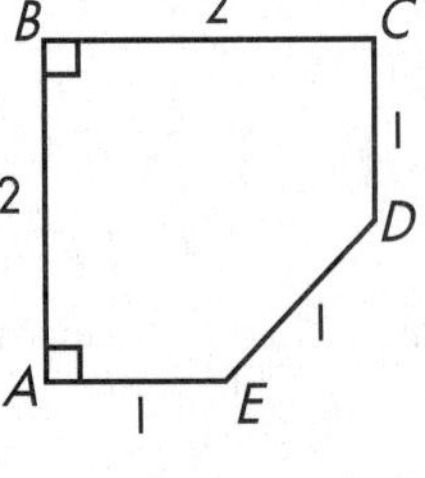

U 3 V

3 2

W

1

T 2 X

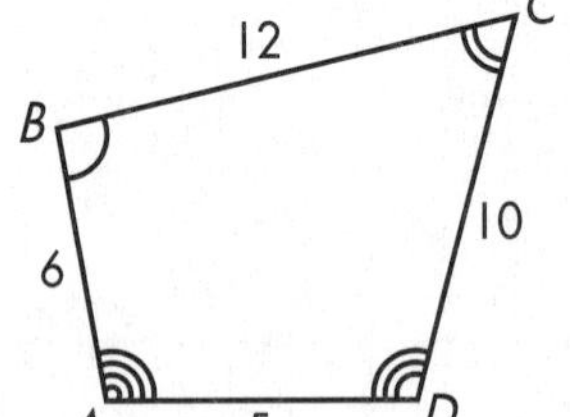

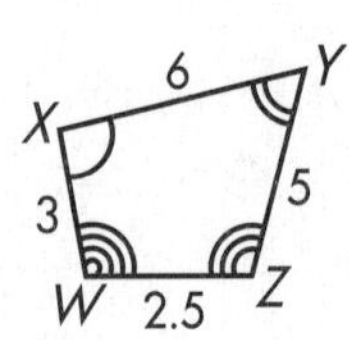

______________________ ______________________

NAME ___________________________

Lesson 10.11 Plotting Ordered Pairs

In a **coordinate plane**, the axes are labeled *x* and *y*. The coordinates of a point are represented by the ordered pair (x, y). The plane is divided into four quadrants, which are named in counterclockwise order. The signs on the ordered pairs in Quadrant I are (+, +), Quadrant II are (−, +), Quadrant III are (−, −) and Quadrant IV are (+, −).

Note: Before you complete this lesson, you may find it helpful to work through Lesson 12.7 *Adding and Subtracting Integers.*

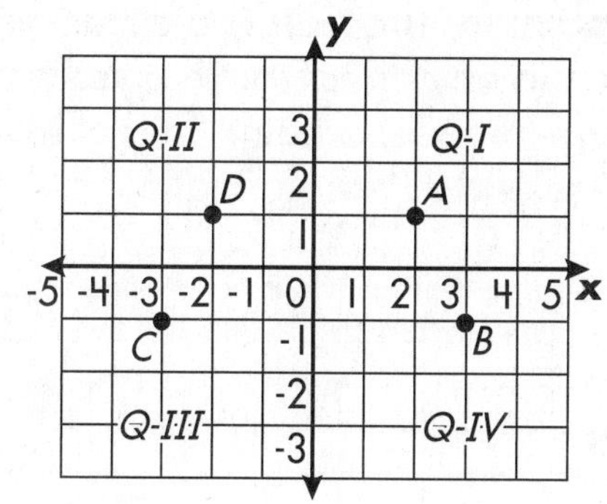

Point *A* has the coordinates (2, 1)
Point *B* has the coordinates (3, − 1)
Point *C* has the coordinates (−3, − 1)
Point *D* has the coordinates (−2, 1)

Use Grid 1 to name the point for each ordered pair.

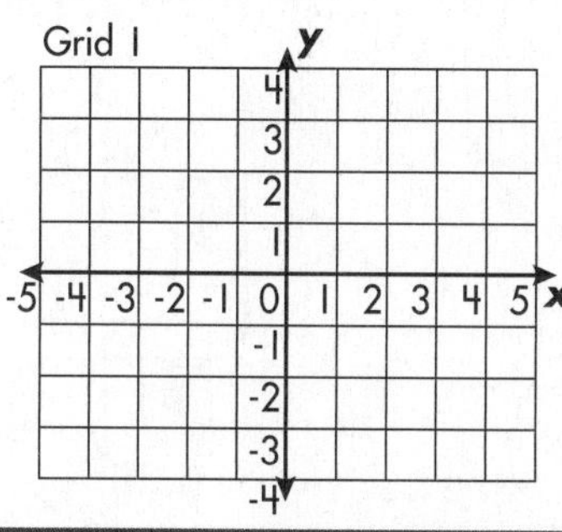

	a	b
1.	(2, 3) ____________	(3, − 1) ____________
2.	(−2, −2) ____________	(−2, 3) ____________
3.	(1, −2) ____________	(1, 1) ____________

Use Grid 2 to find the ordered pair for each point.

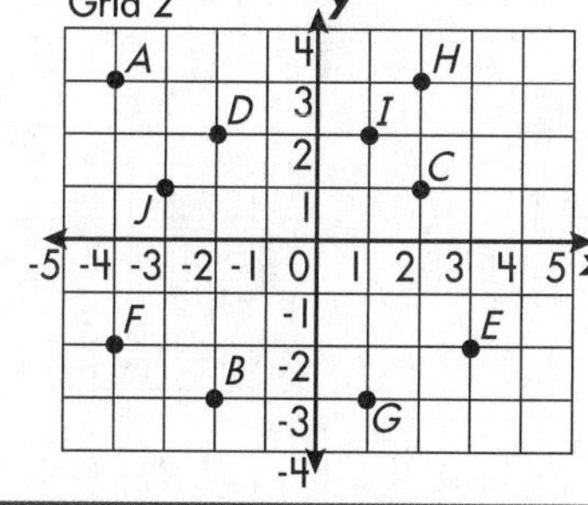

	a	b
4.	*A* ____________	*F* ____________
5.	*B* ____________	*G* ____________
6.	*C* ____________	*H* ____________

Plot the following points on Grid 3.

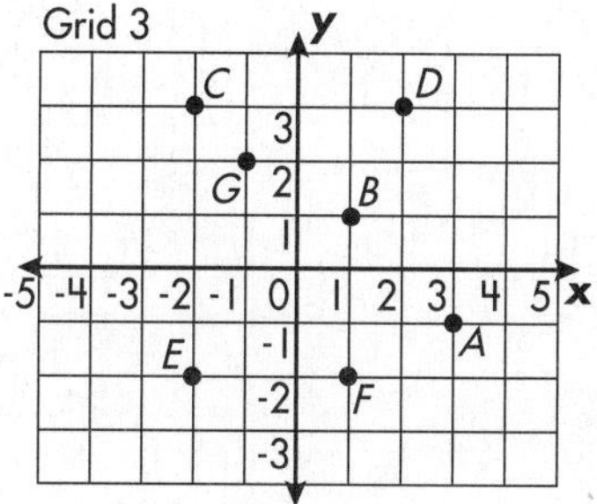

	a	b
7.	*A* (2, 3)	*D* (2, −3)
8.	*B* (−1, 4)	*E* (3, 2)
9.	*C* (−2, −3)	*F* (−4, 2)

NAME ____________________

Lesson 10.12 Transformations

A **transformation** is a change of the position or size of an image. In a **translation**, an image slides in any direction. In a **reflection**, an image is flipped over a line. In a **rotation**, an image is turned about a point. In a **dilation**, an image is enlarged or reduced. One way to view an image and its transformation is to graph it on a coordinate plane.

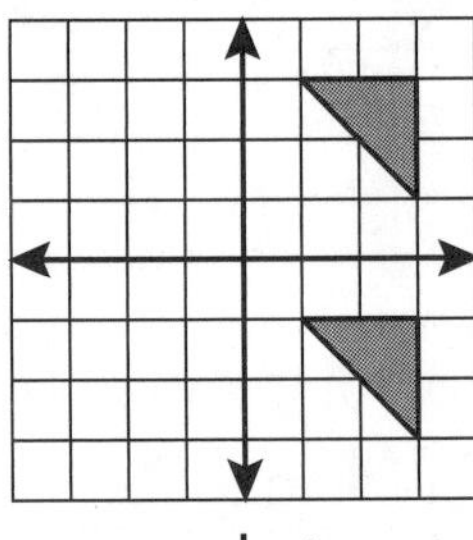
translation

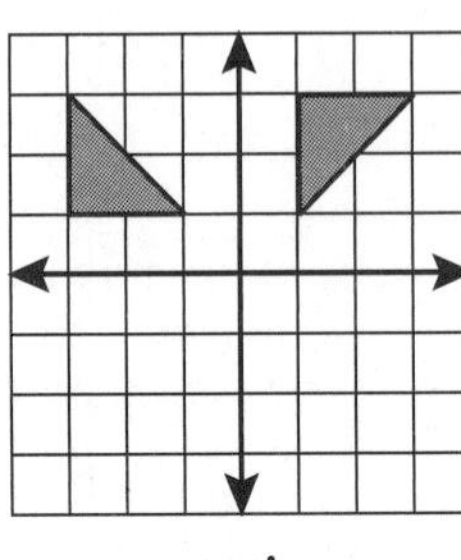
rotation

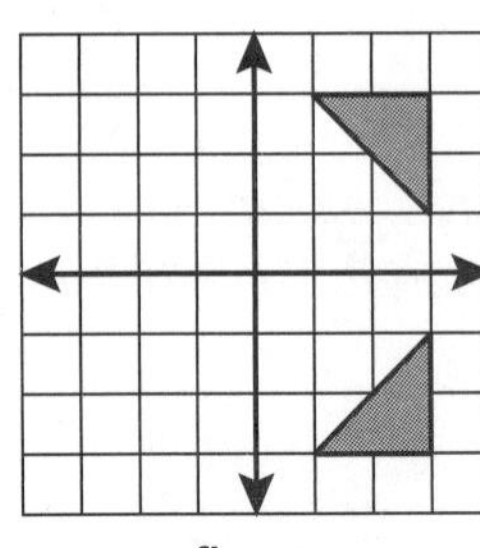
reflection

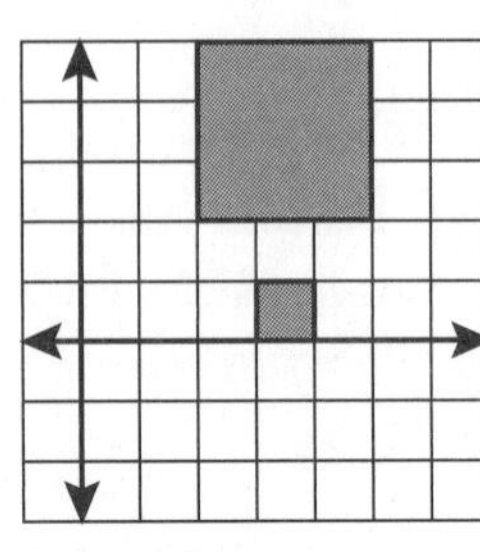
dilation

Write whether each transformation is a translation, rotation, reflection, or dilation.

	a	b	c
1.	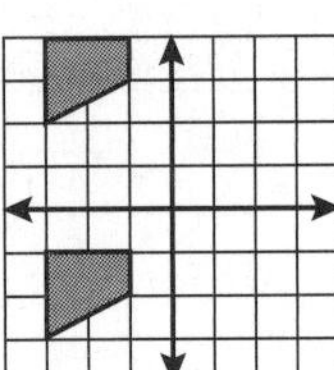 ____________	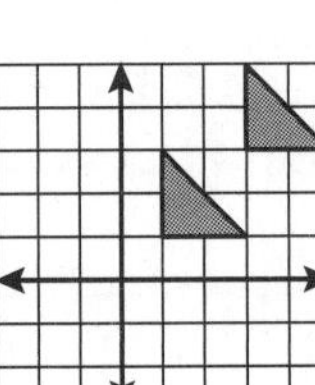 ____________	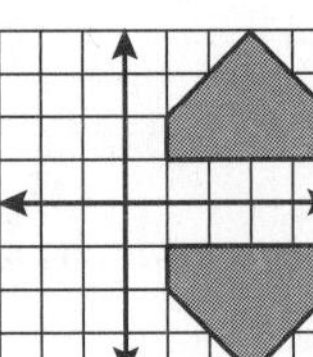 ____________
2.	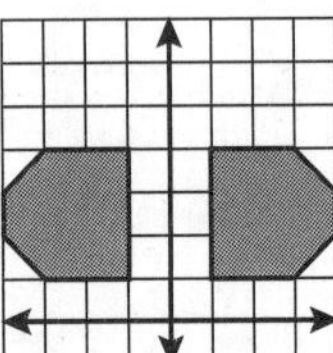 ____________	____________	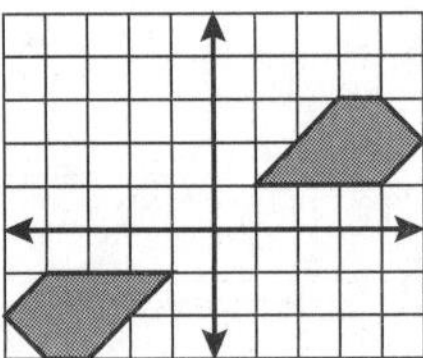 ____________
3.	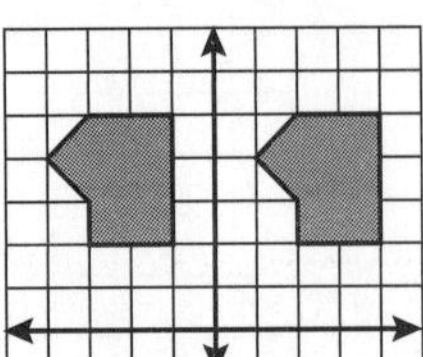 ____________	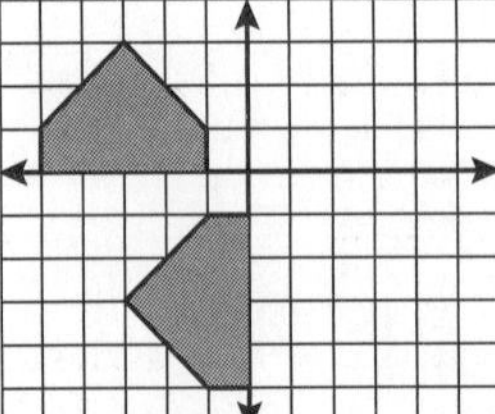 ____________	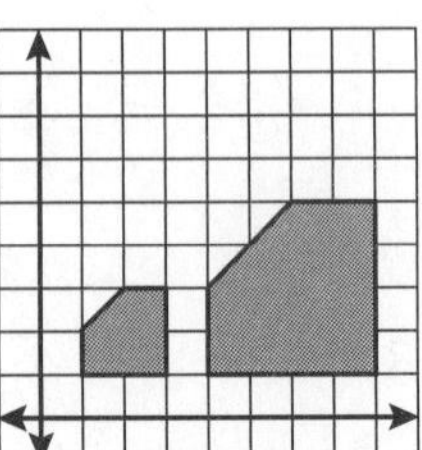 ____________

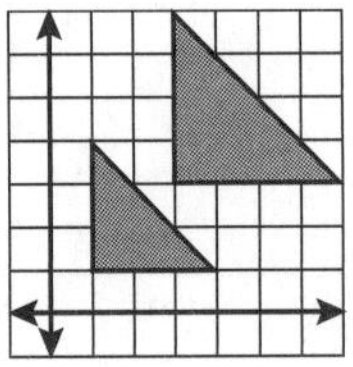

NAME ____________________

Check What You Learned

Geometry

Identify the following.

	a	b	c
1.		• P	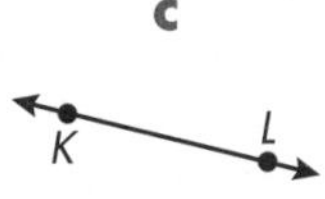
	____________	____________	____________
2.	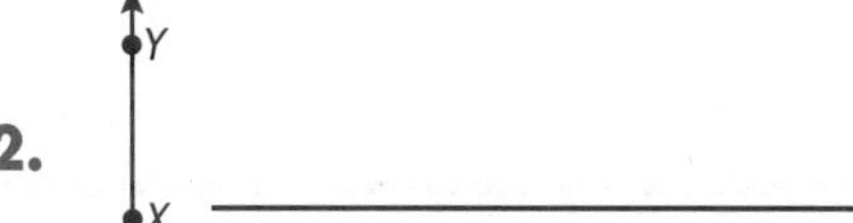	R S	
	____________	____________	____________

Name the angle, rays, and vertex.

3. 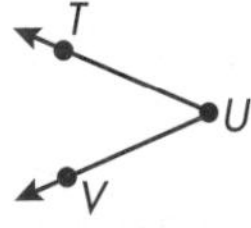

angle: ____________ rays: ____________ vertex: ____________

4. 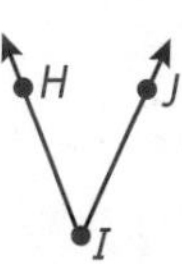

angle: ____________ rays: ____________ vertex: ____________

Use the figure to the right to complete the following.

5. What angle is vertical to ∠*6*? ____________

6. What angle is supplementary to ∠*11*? ____________

7. Which two lines are parallel? ____________

8. If ∠*11* is 70°, what is the measure of ∠*10*? ____________

9. Is ∠*10* acute, obtuse, or right? ____________

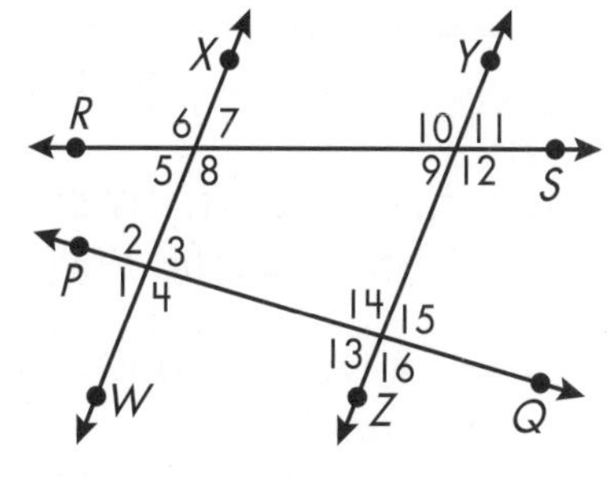

Name the transversal that forms each pair of angles. Write whether the angles are alternate interior, alternate exterior, or corresponding.

10. ∠*1* and ∠*15* ____________ ____________________

11. ∠*6* and ∠*10* ____________ ____________________

12. ∠*12* and ∠*14* ____________ ____________________

NAME ______________________

Check What You Learned

Geometry

Write whether each triangle is acute, right, or obtuse and equilateral, isosceles, or scalene.

	a	b	c
13.	 ______________	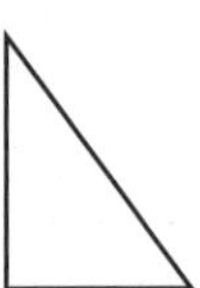 ______________	 ______________

Identify the following shapes. If more than one name applies, use the name that is most specific.

14.	 ______________	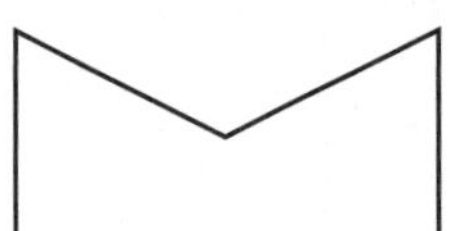 ______________	 ______________
15.	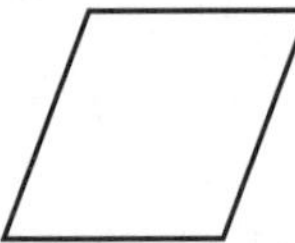 ______________	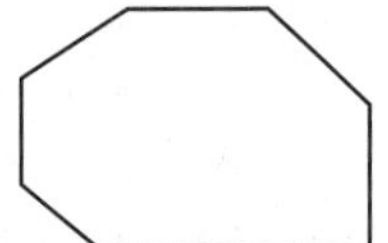 ______________	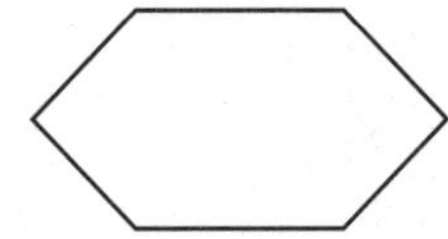 ______________

Use the grid at the right to answer the following.

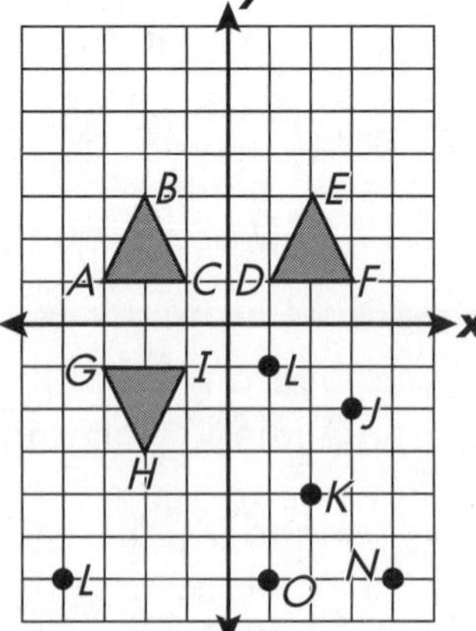

16. What type of transformation is represented by triangles *ABC* and *DEF*? ______________

17. What type of transformation is represented by triangles *DEF* and *GHI*? ______________

18. What are the coordinates of Point *J*? ______________

19. In which quadrant is Point *E*? ______________

20. What point is at coordinates $(-2, 3)$? ______________

21. What is the ordered pair of Point *A*? ______________

22. Are triangles *ABC* and *GHI* similar? ______________

If yes, write the ratios to show it. ______________

NAME ____________

Check What You Know

Perimeter, Area, and Volume

CHAPTER 11 PRETEST

Find the perimeter of each figure.

	a	b	c
1.	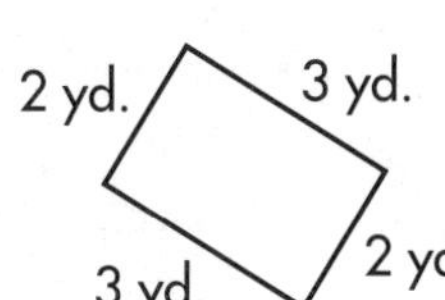	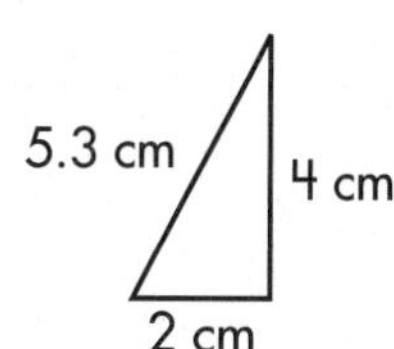	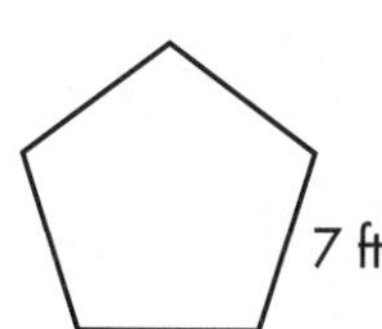
	________ yards	________ centimeters	________ feet
2.	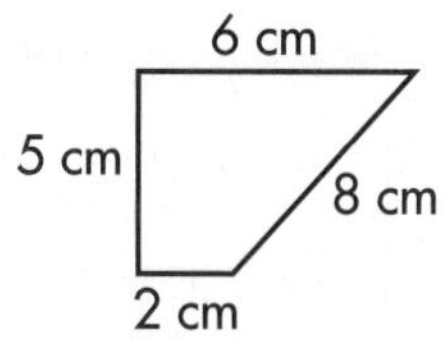		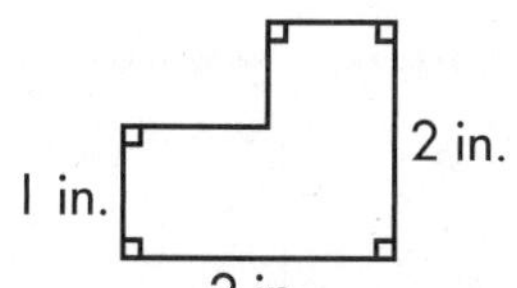
	________ centimeters	________ meters	________ inches

Find the circumference of each circle. Use 3.14 for pi.

3.	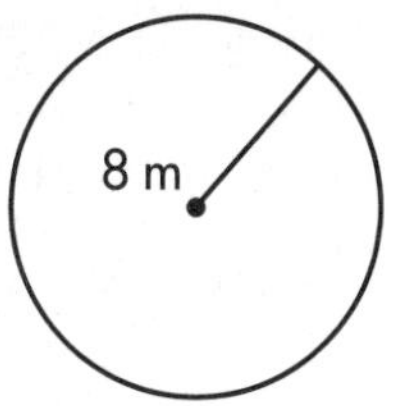	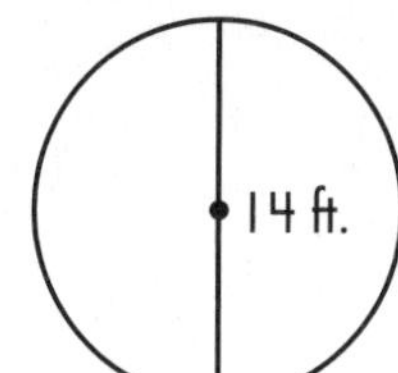	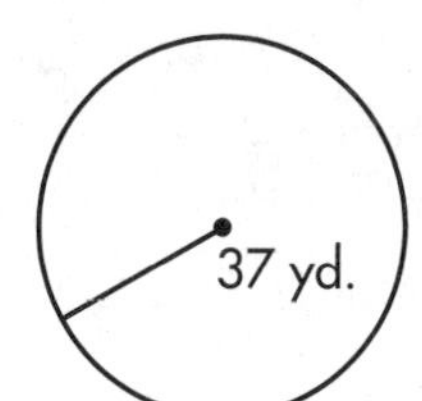
	________ meters	________ feet	________ yards

Find the area of each figure. Use 3.14 for pi.

4.	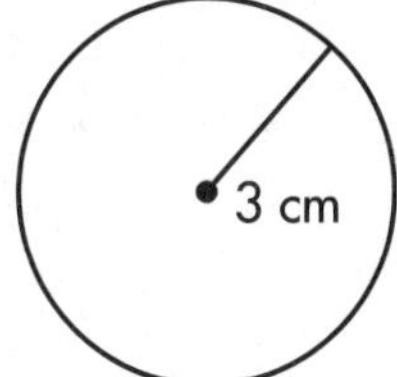	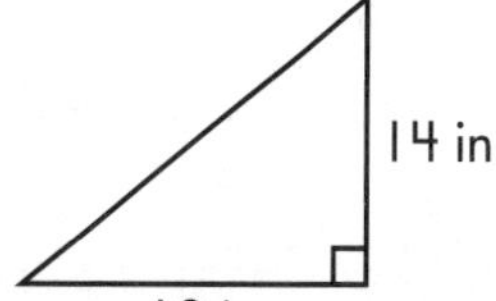	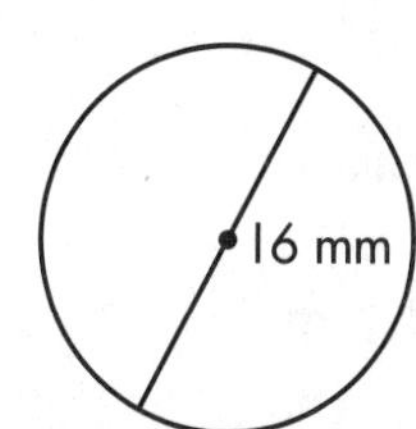
	______ square centimeters	______ square inches	______ square millimeters

NAME ___________________

Check What You Know

Perimeter, Area, and Volume

Complete the table for each rectangular solid.

	Length	Width	Height	Surface Area	Volume
5.	4 m	2 m	9 m	________ sq. m	________ cubic m
6.	14 in.	9 in.	3 in.	________ sq. in.	________ cubic in.
7.	8.5 cm	4 cm	2.5 cm	________ sq. cm	________ cubic cm
8.	32 ft.	11 ft.	8.5 ft.	________ sq. ft.	________ cubic ft.

Find the volume for each triangular solid.

9.

a

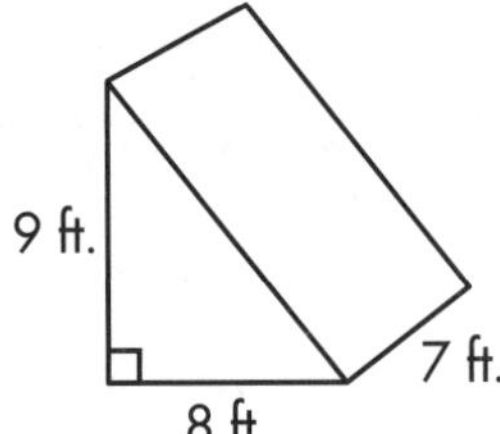

________ cubic feet

b

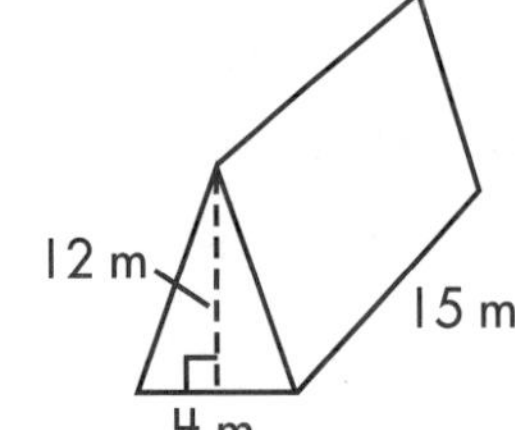

________ cubic meters

c

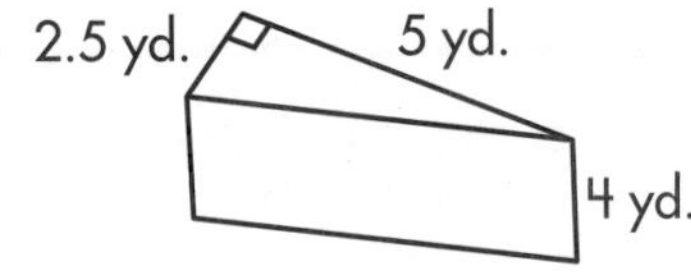

________ cubic yards

Complete the table for each cylinder. Use 3.14 for pi.

	Radius	Diameter	Height	Surface Area	Volume
10.	3 ft.	____ ft.	11 ft.	________ sq. ft.	________ cubic ft.
11.	____ cm	18 cm	5 cm	________ sq. cm	________ cubic cm
12.	2.5 m	____ m	16 m	________ sq. m	________ cubic m
13.	____ in.	38 in.	32 in.	________ sq. in.	________ cubic in.

NAME ____________________

Lesson 11.1 Perimeter

The **perimeter** of a figure is the sum of the lengths of its sides. If two or more sides are equal, the formula can be simplified with multiplication.

triangle	rectangle	square
$p = a + b + c$	$p = \ell + \ell + w + w$ $p = 2\ell + 2w$	$p = s + s + s + s$ $p = 4s$

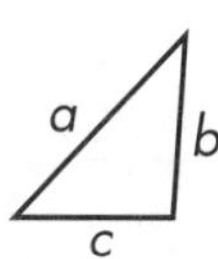

ℓ w w ℓ

s s s s

In the rectangle above, if the length is 6 cm and the width is 2 cm, the perimeter is $2(6) + 2(2) = 12 + 4 = 16$ cm.

Find the perimeter of each figure.

1.

a 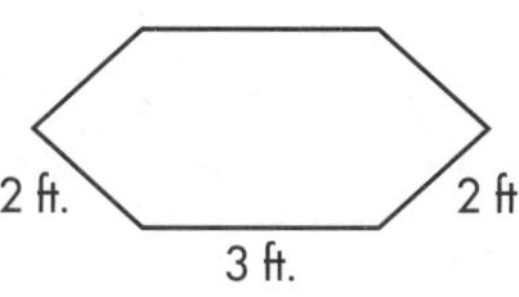

________ ft.

b 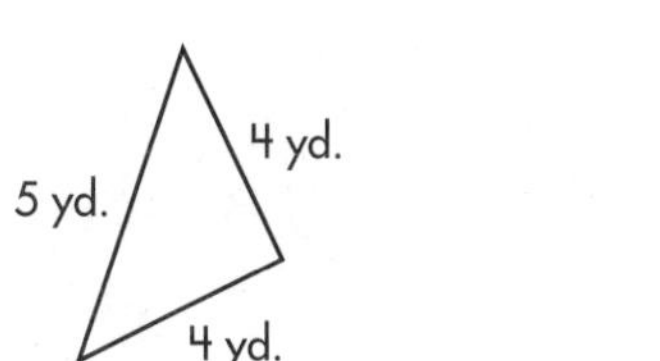

________ yd.

c 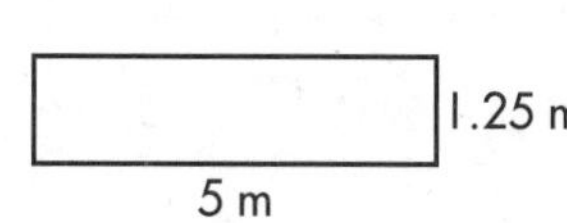

________ m

2.

a 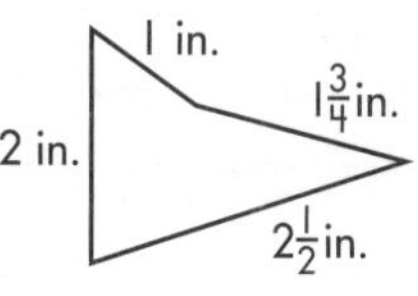

________ in.

b 

________ cm

c 9 yd. 9 yd. 9 yd.

________ yd.

3.

a 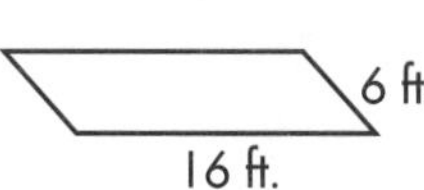

________ ft.

b 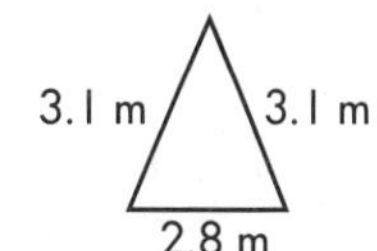

________ m

c 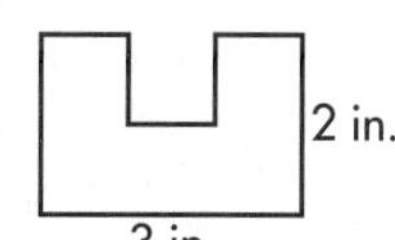

________ in.

4.

a 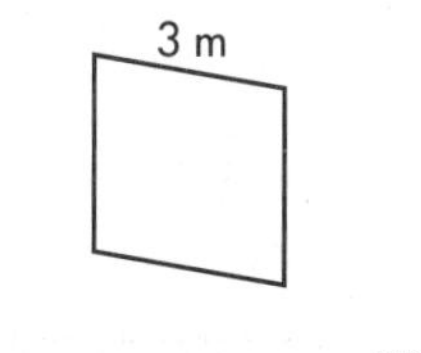

________ m

b 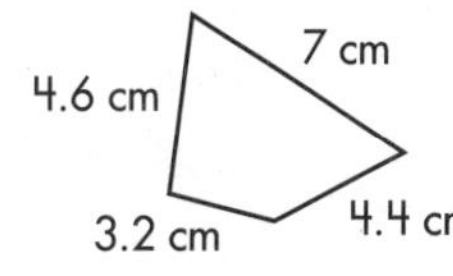

________ cm

c 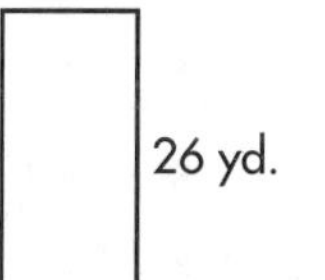

________ yd.

NAME ____________________

Lesson 11.2 Area of Rectangles

Area is the number of square units it takes to cover a figure. To find the area of a rectangle, multiply the length by the width.

length 7 units
width 2 units

$A = 7 \times 2$
$A = 14$ square units

8 units

$A = s \times s = 8 \times 8$
$A = 64$ square units

Find the area of each rectangle below.

	a	b	c

1.

a 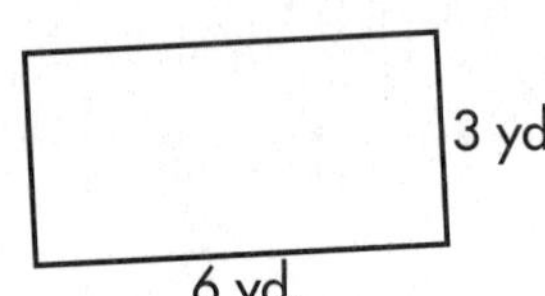

_______ square yards

b 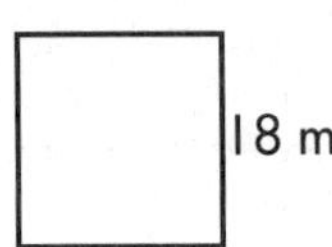

_______ square meters

c 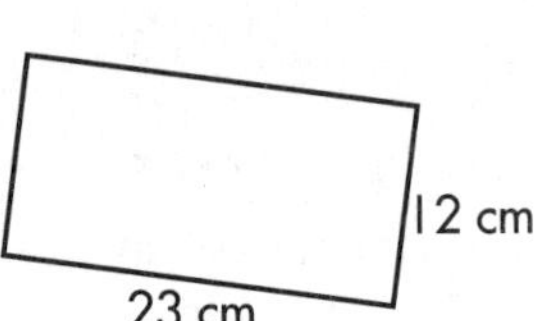

_______ square centimeters

2.

a 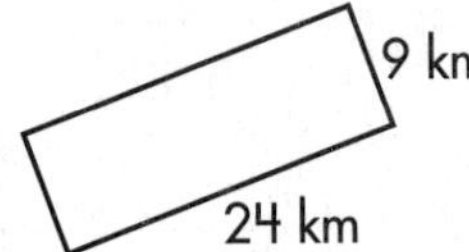

_______ square kilometers

b, c 

_______ square inches

_______ square feet

Find the length of each rectangle below.

3.

a 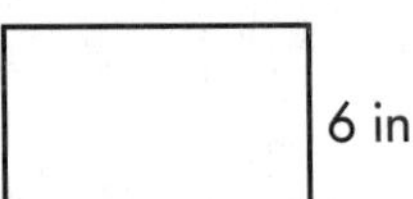

A = 54 sq. in.
ℓ = _______ in.

b 4.5 ft.

A = 58.5 sq. ft.
ℓ = _______ ft.

c 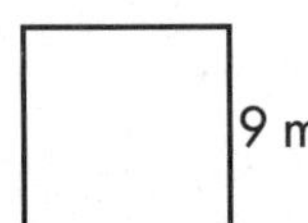

A = 81 sq. m
ℓ = _______ m

4.

a 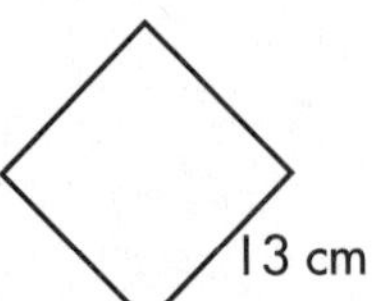

A = 169 sq. cm
ℓ = _______ cm

b 43 m

A = 3225 sq. m
ℓ = _______ m

c 16 yd.

A = 588.8 sq. yd.
ℓ = _______ yd.

NAME ____________________

Lesson 11.3 Area of Triangles

The area of a triangle is the product of $\frac{1}{2}$ of the base times the height. It is related to the area of a rectangle.

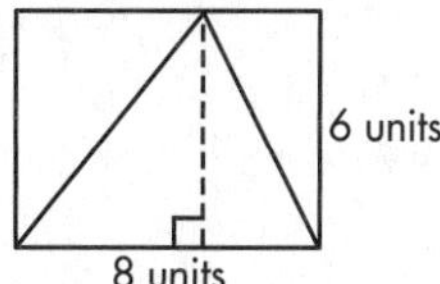

The dashed line indicates the height of the triangle.
rectangle: $A = 8 \times 6 = 48$ sq. units
triangle: $A = \frac{1}{2}(8)(6) = 24$ sq. units

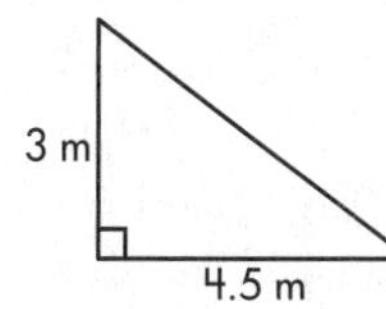

$A = \frac{1}{2}(4.5)(3) = 6\frac{3}{4}$ sq. m

Notice that in a right triangle the height is the length of one of the legs. This is not the case with acute and obtuse triangles.

Find the area of each triangle below.

	a	b	c
1.	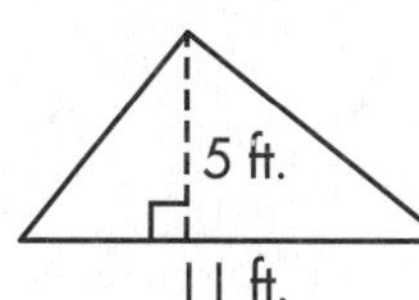 ________ sq. ft.	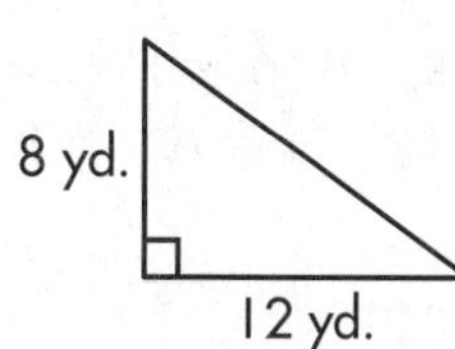 ________ sq. yd.	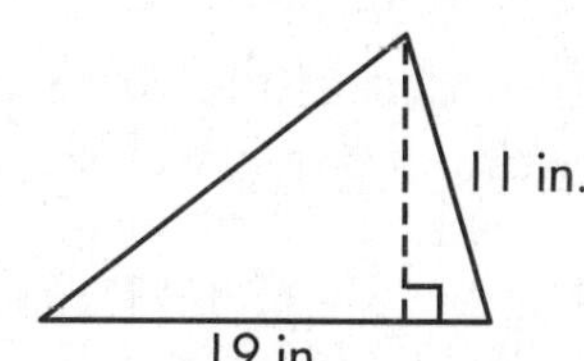 ________ sq. in.
2.	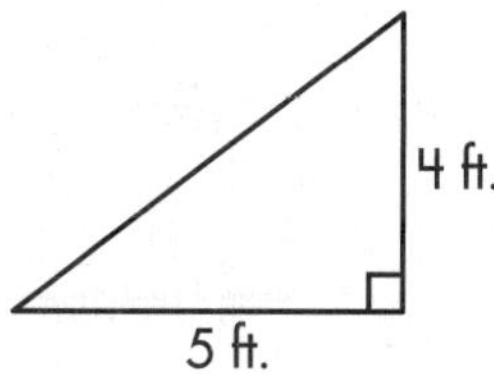 ________ sq. ft.	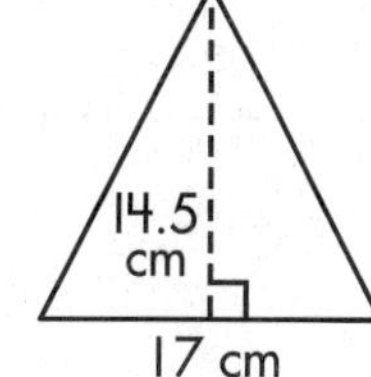 ________ sq. cm	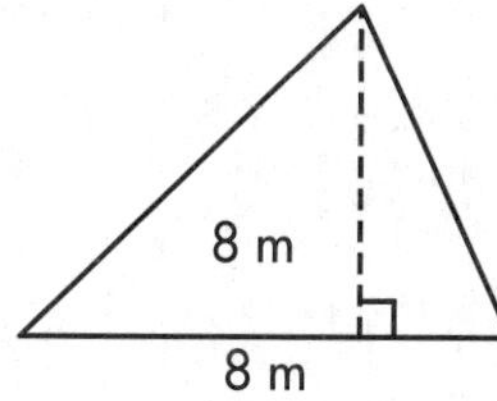 ________ sq. m
3.	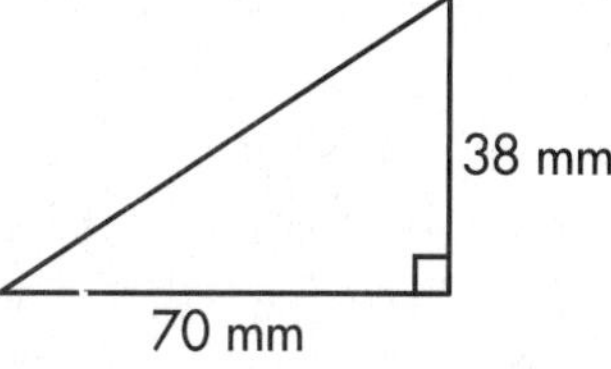 ________ sq. mm	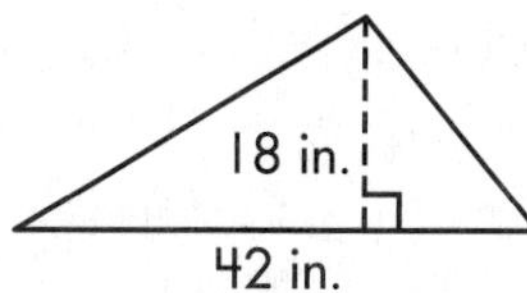 ________ sq. in.	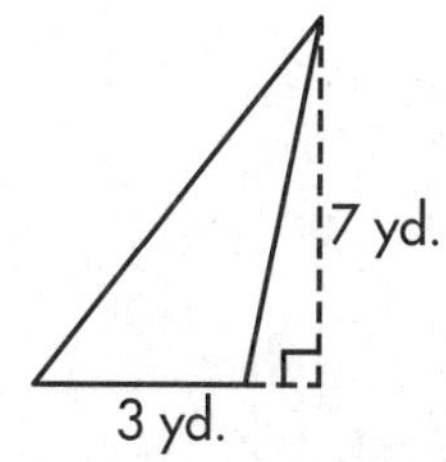 ________ sq. yd.

NAME ___________________________

Lesson 11.4 Problem Solving

SHOW YOUR WORK

Solve each problem.

1. The Robinsons want to put a fence around part of their yard. The width of the area is 22 feet and the length is 47 feet. What is the length of fence they will need?

They will need __________ feet of fence.

1.

2. Alicia made lasagna in a pan measuring 12 inches by 9 inches. What is the area of the lasagna?

The area of the lasagna is __________ square inches.

2.

3. Akira planted a garden in the shape of a triangle. The lengths of the sides of the garden are 3 meters, 4 meters, and 5 meters. What is the perimeter?

The perimeter of the garden is __________ meters.

3.

4. The area of the surface of a table is 1,836 inches. The width of the table is 34 inches. What is the length?

The length of the table is __________ inches.

4.

5. Josie is using a triangular piece of cloth to make a scarf. The base is 62 centimeters and the height is 41 centimeters. What is the area of the cloth?

The area of the piece of cloth is __________ square centimeters.

5.

6. Becky is buying a new countertop. The length is $4\frac{1}{4}$ feet and the width is $2\frac{1}{2}$ feet. What is the area?

The area of the countertop is __________ square feet.

6.

7. Rob made brownies in a square baking pan. The area of the brownies is 64 square inches. What are the length and width of the pan?

The length is ______ inches and the width is ______ inches.

7.

NAME ____________________

Lesson 11.5 Circumference of Circles

A **circle** is a set of points that are all the same distance from a given point, called the **center**. The perimeter of a circle is called the **circumference**. The **diameter** is a segment that passes through the center of the circle and has both endpoints on the circle. The **radius** is a segment that has as its endpoints the circle and the center. The relationship between the circumference (C) and the diameter (d) is $C \div d = \pi$. Pi (π) is approximately $3\frac{1}{7}$ or 3.14. To find the circumference, diameter, or radius of a circle, use the formulas $C = \pi \times d$ or $C = 2 \times \pi \times r$.

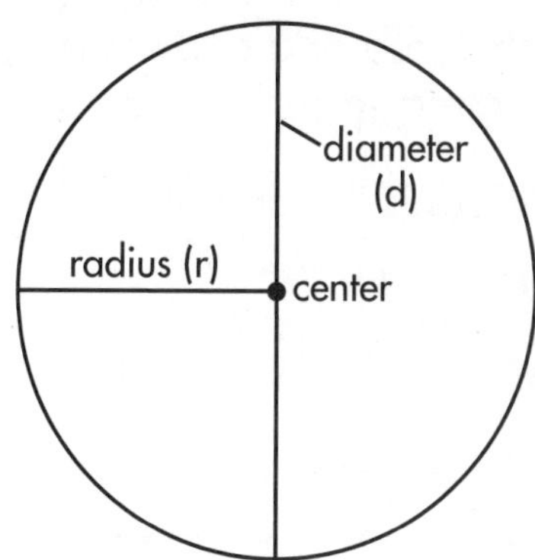

Complete the table. Use 3.14 for pi.

	a **Diameter**	b **Radius**	c **Circumference**
1.	________ feet	________ feet	4.71 feet
2.	3.5 meters	________ meters	________ meters
3.	________ inches	3.25 inches	________ inches
4.	________ yards	________ yards	26.69 yards
5.	7.5 centimeters	________ centimeters	________ centimeters
6.	________ inches	15 inches	________ inches
7.	________ meters	________ meters	7.85 meters
8.	5 kilometers	________ kilometers	________ kilometers
9.	________ feet	________ feet	31.4 feet
10.	________ centimeters	45 centimeters	________ centimeters
11.	4 yards	________ yards	________ yards
12.	________ miles	________ miles	9.42 miles

NAME ______________________

Lesson 11.6 Area of Circles

The area of a circle is found by using the formula $A = \pi \times r \times r$. Remember, π can be expressed as $3\frac{1}{7}$ or as 3.14. If you know the diameter of a circle, divide by 2 to find the radius.

What is the area if $r = 6$?	What is the area if $d = 8$?
$A = \frac{22}{7}(6)(6)$	$A = 3.14 \times \frac{8}{2} \times \frac{8}{2}$
$A = 113\frac{1}{7}$ square units	$A = 3.14 \times 4 \times 4$
	$A = 50.24$ square units

Find the area of each circle below. Use 3.14 for pi. Round your answer to the nearest tenth.

a **b** **c**

1.

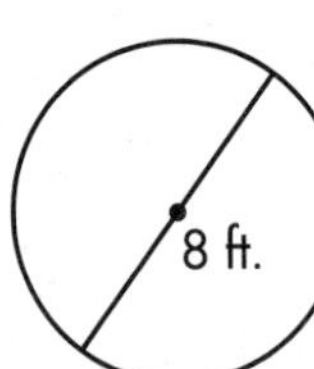

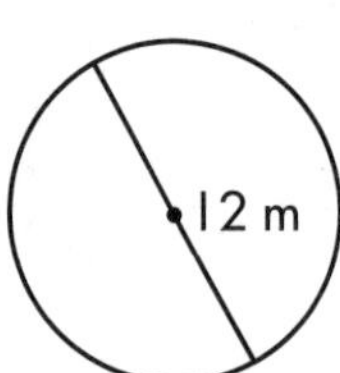

______ square feet ______ square meters ______ square centimeters

2.

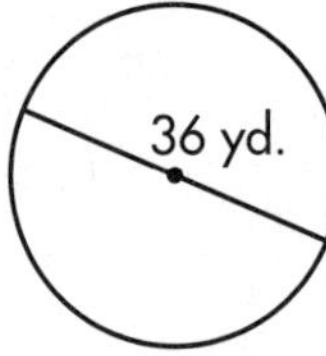

12 km

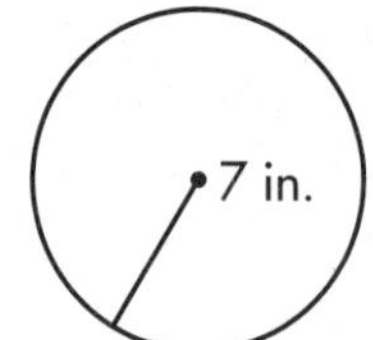

______ square yards ______ square kilometers ______ square inches

Complete the table. Use 3.14 for pi. Round your answer to the nearest tenth.

	Diameter	Radius	Area
3.	______ inches	3 inches	______ square inches
4.	18 feet	______ feet	______ square feet
5.	17 meters	______ meters	______ square meters
6.	______ centimeters	32 centimeters	______ square centimeters
7.	30 kilometers	______ kilometers	______ square kilometers
8.	______ yards	6 yards	______ square yards

Lesson 11.7 Area of Irregular Shapes

To find the area of irregular shapes, separate the shapes into figures for which you can find the area.

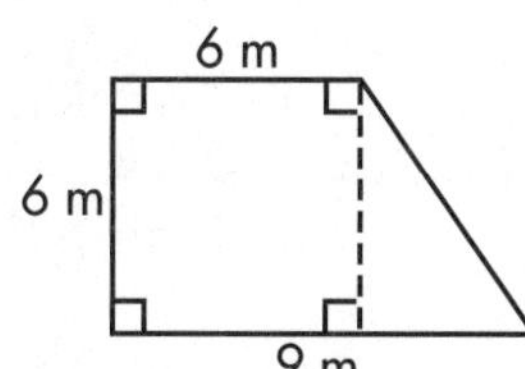

This figure can be divided into a square and a triangle.

area of square
$A = 6 \times 6 = 36$

area of triangle
$A = \frac{1}{2} \times 3 \times 6 = 9$

The area of the figure is $36 + 9 = 45$ square meters.

Find the area of each figure.

a **b** **c**

1.

a

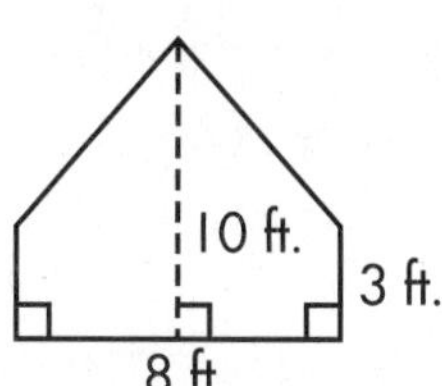

__________ square feet

b

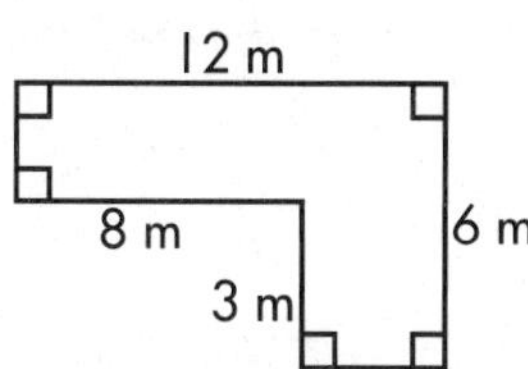

__________ square meters

c

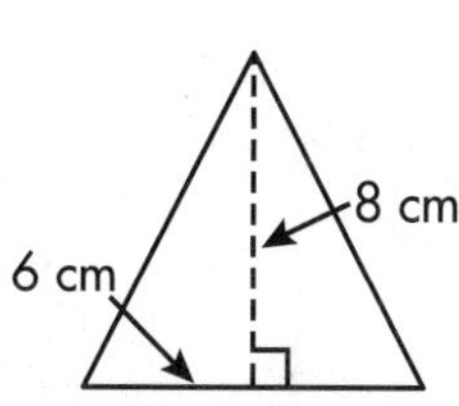

__________ square centimeters

2.

a

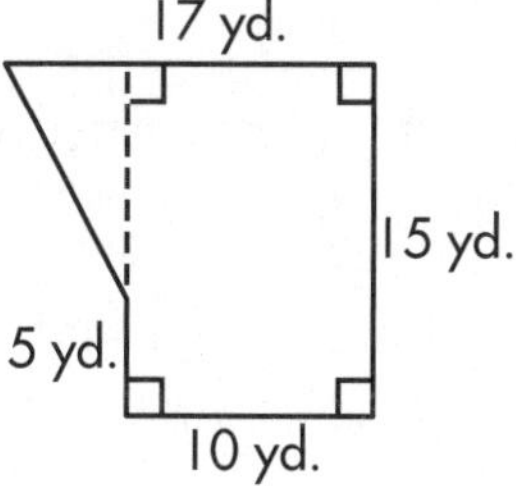

__________ square yards

b

4 mi.
3 mi.
2 mi.

__________ square miles

c

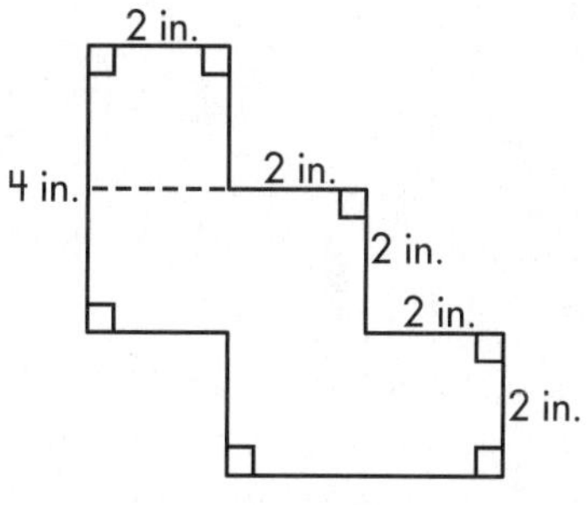

__________ square inches

3.

a

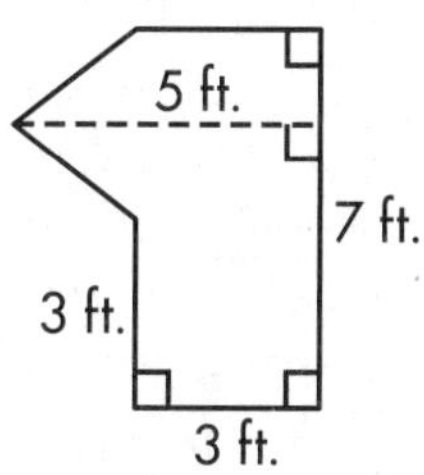

__________ square feet

b

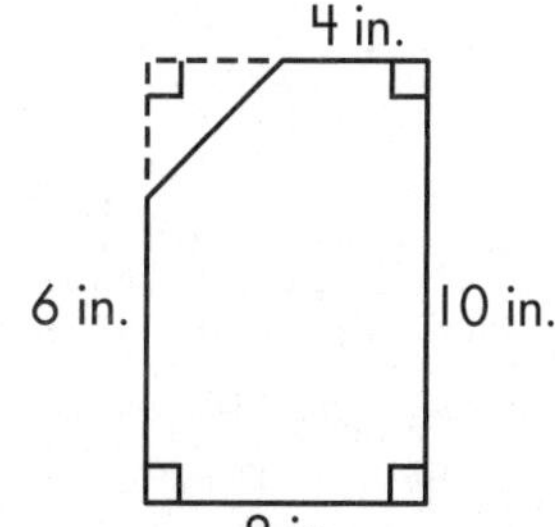

__________ square inches

c

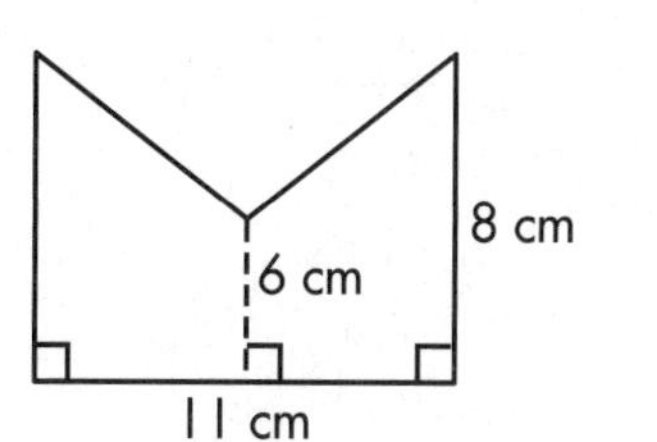

__________ square centimeters

NAME ______________________

Lesson 11.8 Surface Area (Rectangular Solids)

The **surface area** of a solid is the sum of the areas of all the faces (or surfaces of the solid). The surface area of a rectangular solid can be found by the formula $SA = 2\ell w + 2\ell h + 2wh$.

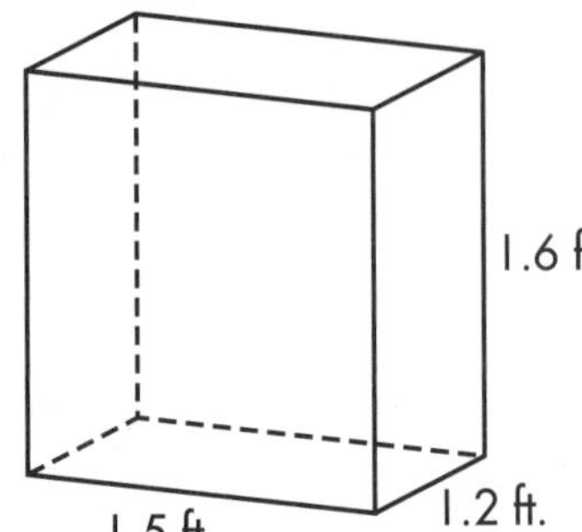

$SA = 2(1.5)(1.2) + 2(1.5)(1.6) + 2(1.2)(1.6)$

$SA = 3.6 \quad + 4.8 \quad + 3.84$

$SA = 12.24$ square feet

Find the surface area of each figure.

	a	b	c
1.	  2 in., 5 in., 3 in. ______ square inches	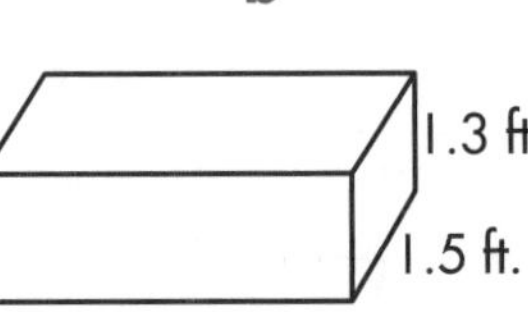 1.3 ft., 1.5 ft., 8 ft. ______ square feet	 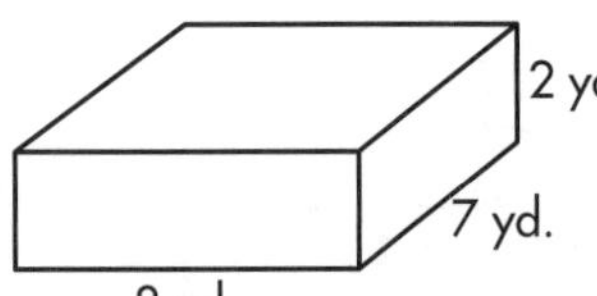 2 yd., 7 yd., 8 yd. ______ square yards
2.	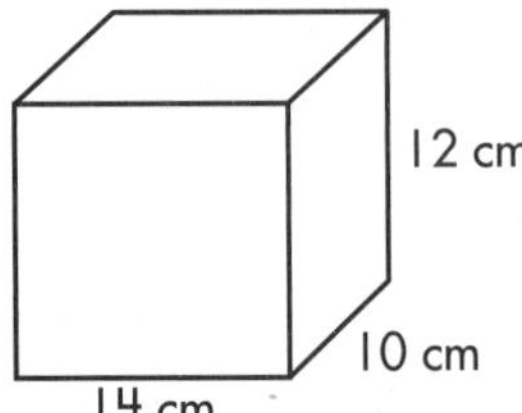 12 cm, 10 cm, 14 cm ______ square centimeters	5 m, 6 m, 2 m ______ square meters	6 in., 2 in., 14 in. ______ square inches
3.	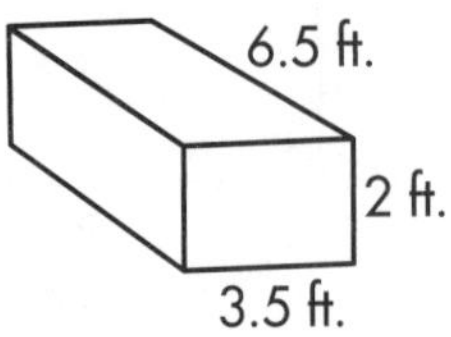 6.5 ft., 2 ft., 3.5 ft. ______ square feet	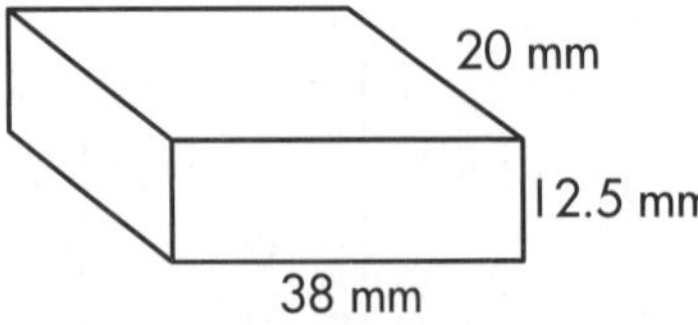 20 mm, 12.5 mm, 38 mm ______ square millimeters	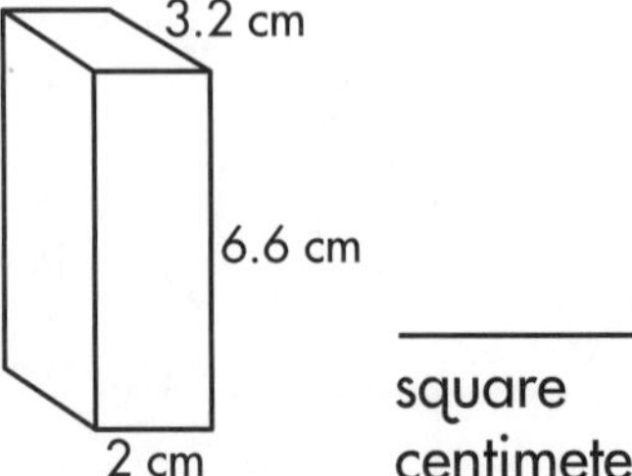 3.2 cm, 6.6 cm, 2 cm ______ square centimeters

NAME ____________________

Lesson 11.9 Volume of Rectangular Solids

The **volume** of a rectangular solid is the product of the length times width times height. The product of the length times width is the base. The formula for the volume is $V = B \times h$. Volume is expressed in cubic units.

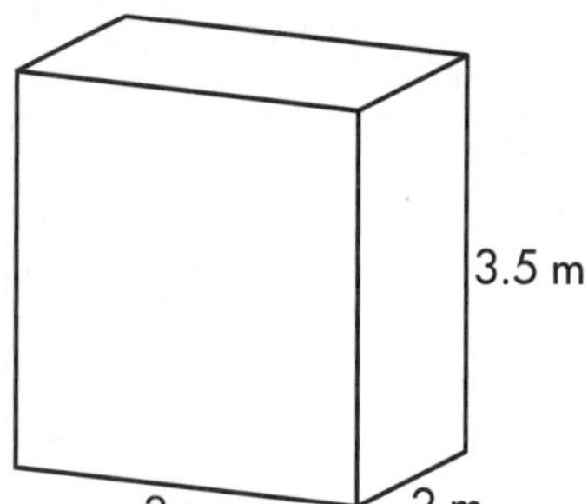

$B = 3 \times 2 = 6$

$V = B \times h = 6 \times 3.5$

$V = 21$ cubic meters

Find the volume of each figure.

	a	b	c
1.	 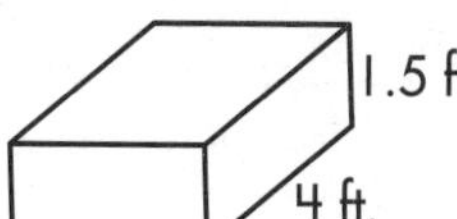 1.5 ft., 4 ft., 3 ft.	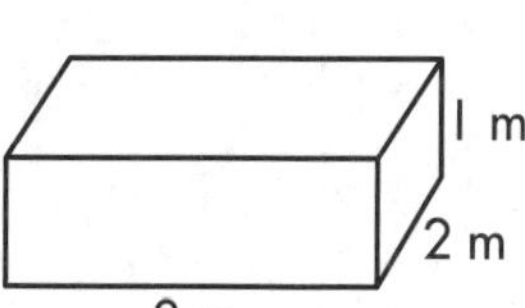 1 m, 2 m, 8 m	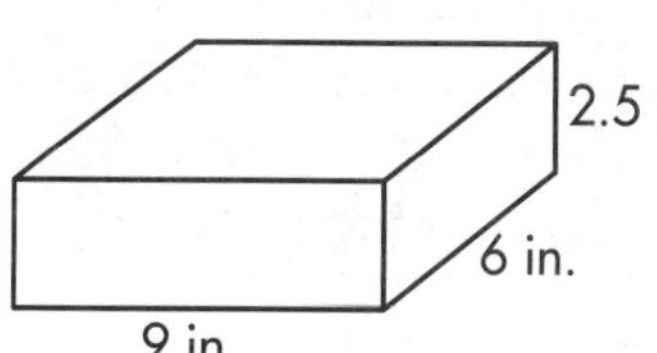 2.5 in., 6 in., 9 in.
	________ cubic feet	________ cubic meters	________ cubic inches
2.	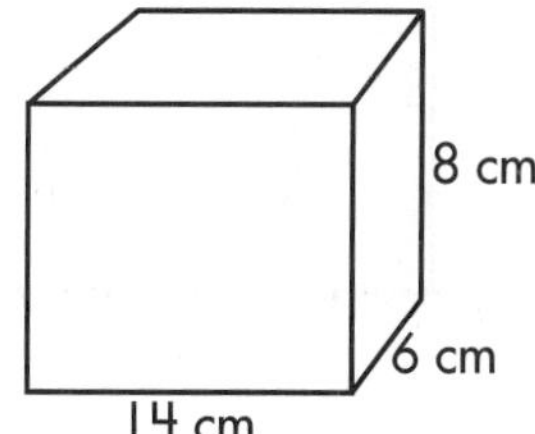 8 cm, 6 cm, 14 cm	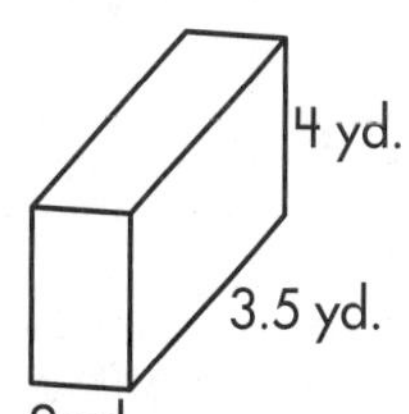 4 yd., 3.5 yd., 2 yd.	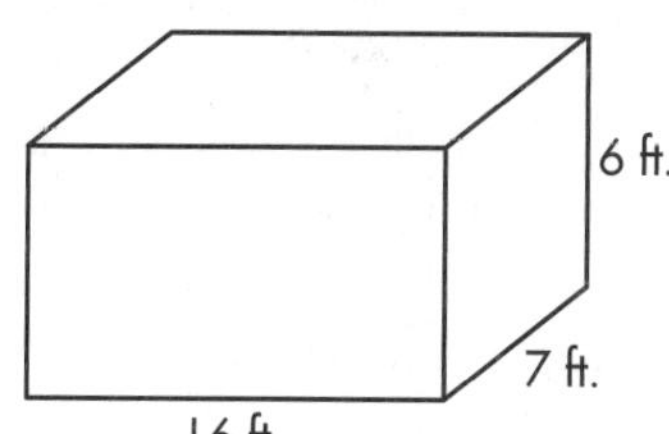 6 ft., 7 ft., 16 ft.
	________ cubic centimeters	________ cubic yards	________ cubic feet
3.	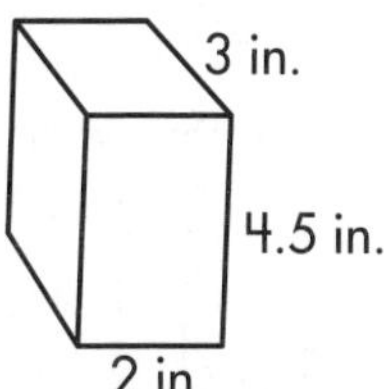 3 in., 4.5 in., 2 in.	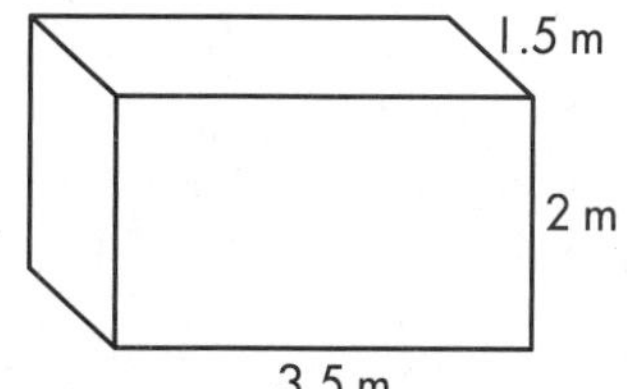 1.5 m, 2 m, 3.5 m	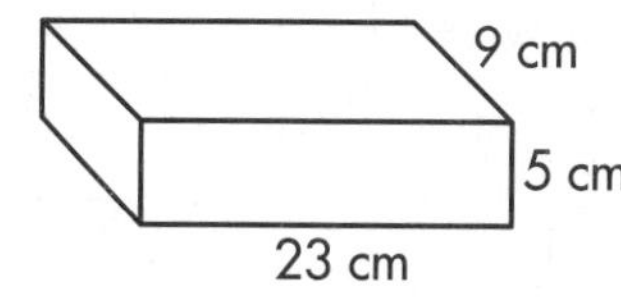 9 cm, 5 cm, 23 cm
	________ cubic inches	________ cubic meters	________ cubic centimeters

NAME ___________________________

Lesson 11.10 Problem Solving

SHOW YOUR WORK

Solve each problem.

1. The radius of a glass is 1.25 inches. What is the circumference? Use 3.14 for pi.

The circumference of the glass is __________ inches.

1.

2. Juan left a garbage can on the lawn, and the grass underneath it died. The diameter of the can is 54 centimeters. What is the area of the grass that died? Use 3.14 for pi.

The area of the grass is __________ square centimeters.

2.

3. A drawing of a house is made up of a rectangle for the walls and a triangle for the roof. The base of the drawing is 9 inches wide. The height of the walls is 7 inches. And the height to the top of the roof is 10 inches. What is the area of the house in the drawing?

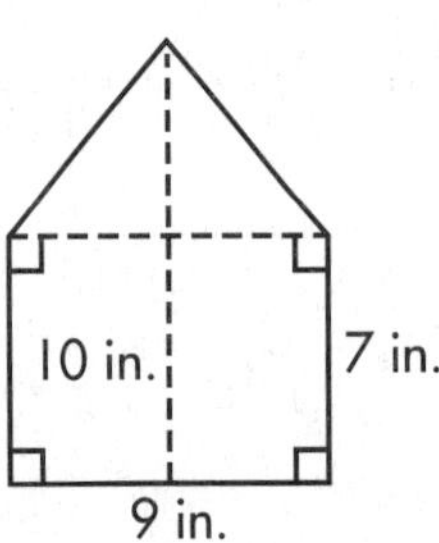

The area of the drawing is __________ square inches.

3.

4. A building with a flat roof is 11 meters long, 8 meters wide, and 6 meters high. What is the surface area?

The surface area of the building is __________ square meters.

4.

5. An aquarium is 50 centimeters long, 20 centimeters wide, and 30 centimeters high. How many cubic centimeters of water can it hold?

The aquarium can hold __________ cubic centimeters of water.

5.

6. Opal needs to wrap a box. The box is 12 inches by 8 inches by 1.5 inches. If she wants to wrap it with no overlap, how much paper does she need?

Opal needs __________ square inches of paper.

6.

NAME ____________________

Lesson 11.11 Volume of Triangular Solids

The bases of a triangular solid are triangles. To find the volume, multiply the area of one base times the height.

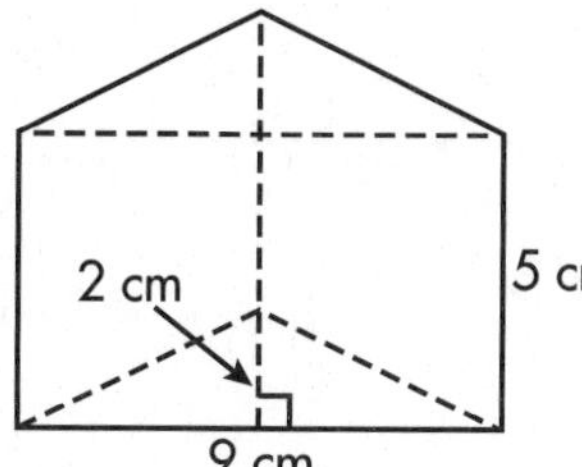

$B = \frac{1}{2}bh = \frac{1}{2}(9)(2) = 9$

$V = B \times h$

$V = 9 \times 5$

$V = 45$ cubic centimeters

Find the volume of each figure.

	a	b	c
1.	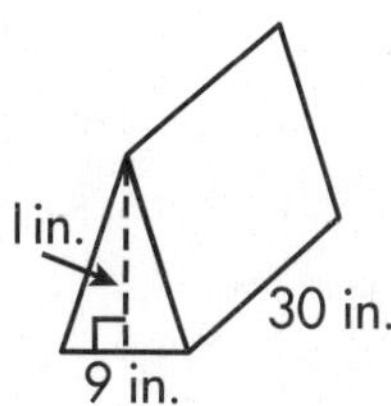	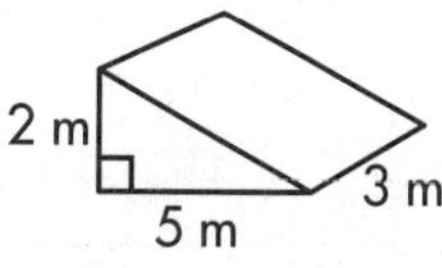	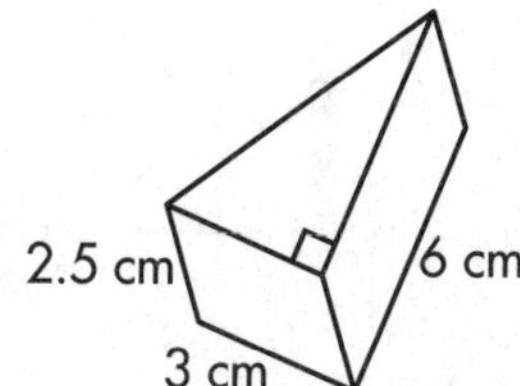
	________ cubic inches	________ cubic meters	________ cubic centimeters
2.	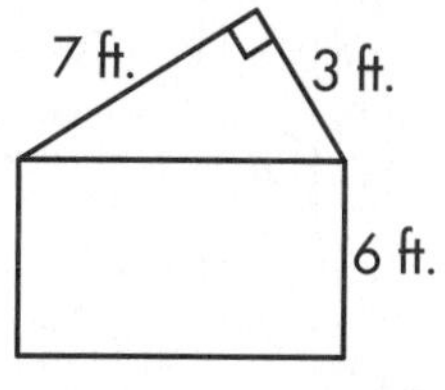	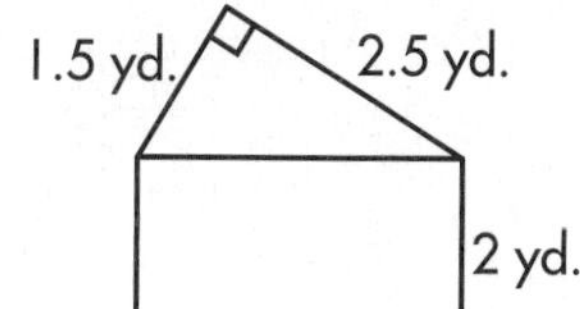	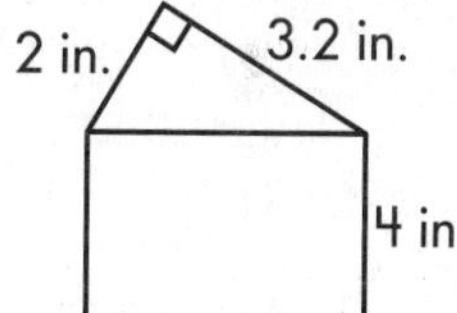
	________ cubic feet	________ cubic yards	________ cubic inches
3.	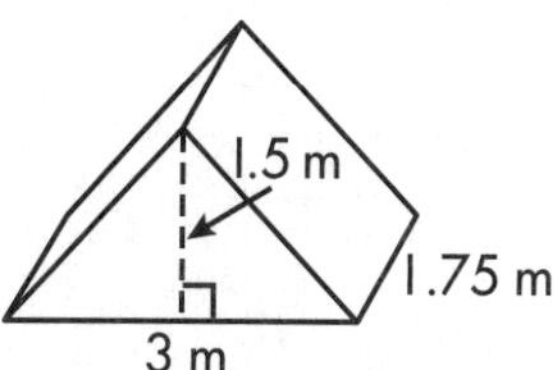	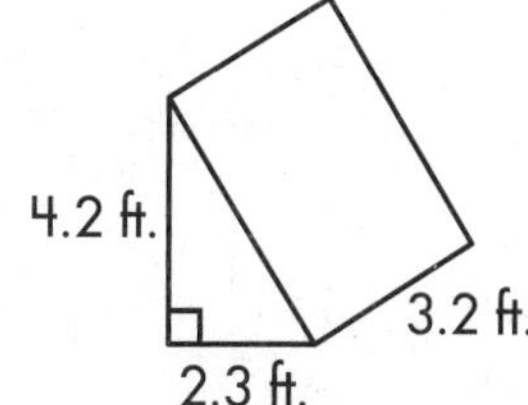	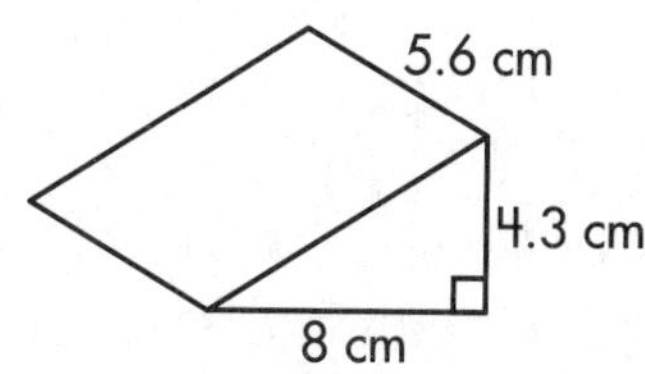
	________ cubic meters	________ cubic feet	________ cubic centimeters

Lesson 11.12 Surface Area (Cylinders)

A cylinder can be represented on a flat surface as two circles for the bases and a rectangle. The height of the cylinder is the width of the rectangle. The circumference of the base is the length. The surface area is the sum of the area of these three surfaces. It is found by the formula $2\pi r^2 + 2\pi rh$.

$SA = 2(3.14)(8)(8) + 2(3.14)(8)(30)$

$SA = 401.92 \qquad + 1507.2$

$SA = 1909.12$ square centimeters

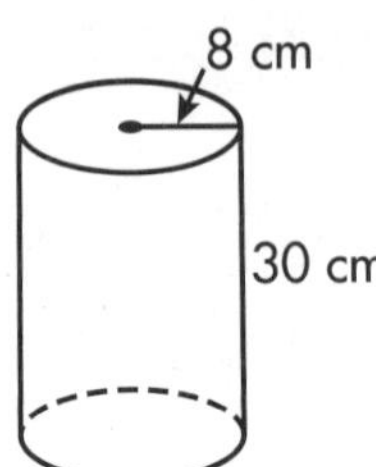

Find the surface area of each cylinder. Use 3.14 for π.

	a	b	c
1.	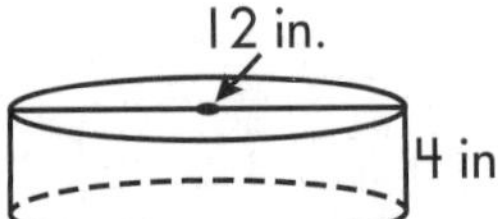	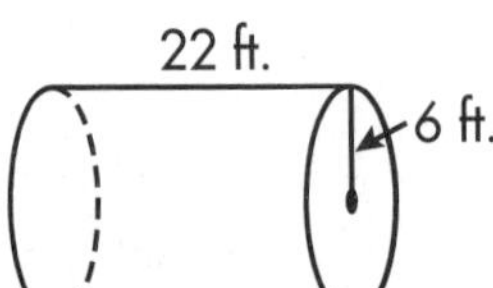	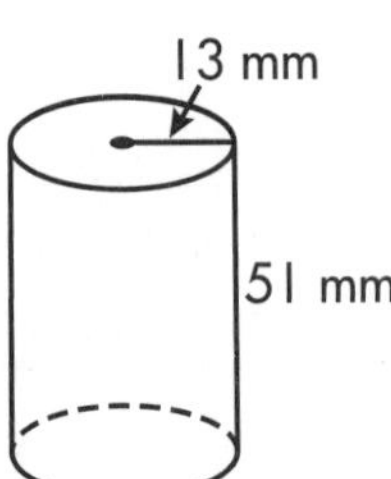
	______ square inches	______ square feet	______ square millimeters
2.	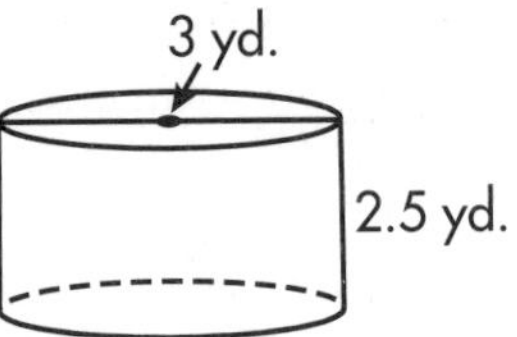	5 cm 14 cm	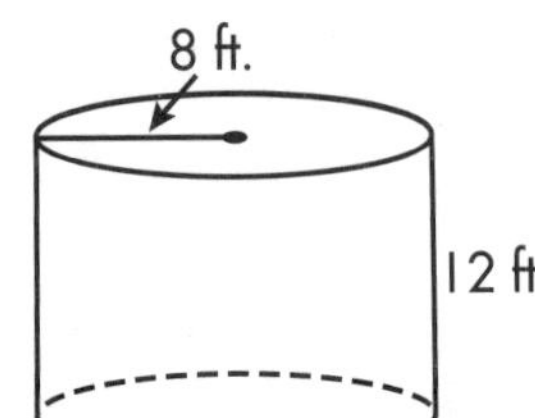
	______ square yards	______ square centimeters	______ square feet
3.	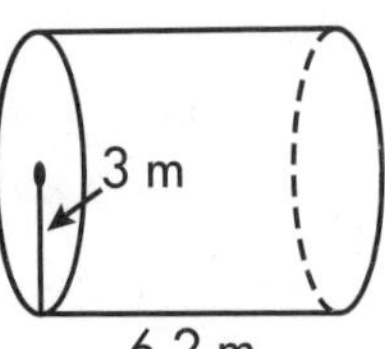	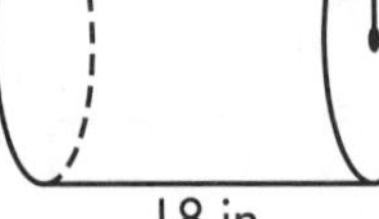	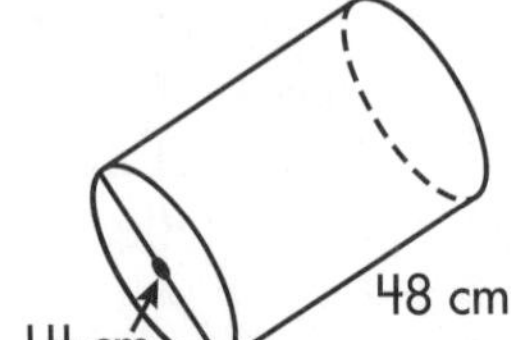
	______ square meters	______ square inches	______ square centimeters

NAME ____________________

Lesson 11.13 Volume of Cylinders

The volume of a cylinder is the product of the area of the base *(B)* times the height. The formula for the volume of a cylinder is $V = B \times h$.

$B = \pi r^2 = (3.14)(8)(8) = 200.96$

$V = 200.96 \times 10$

$V = 2009.6$ cubic feet

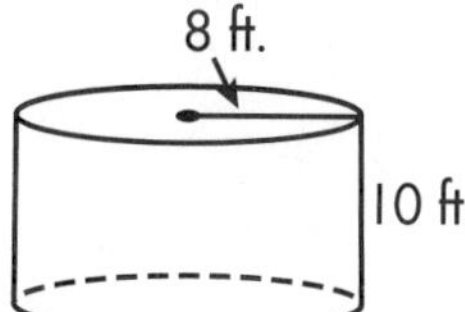

Find the volume of each cylinder. Use 3.14 for π.

	a	b	c
1.	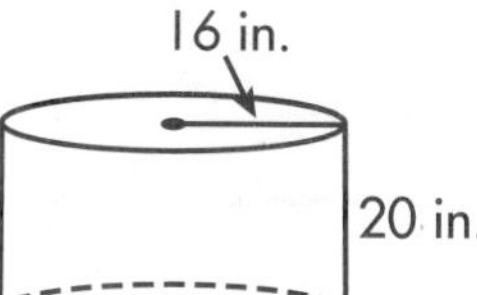 ______ cubic inches	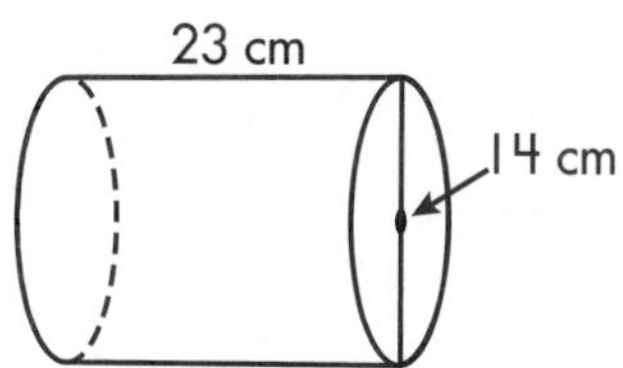 ______ cubic centimeters	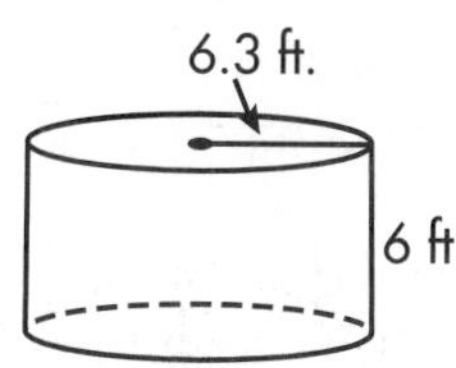 ______ cubic feet
2.	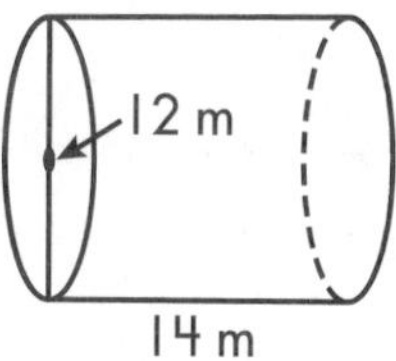 ______ cubic meters	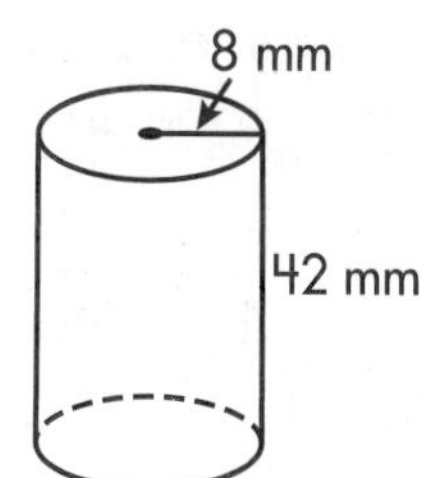 ______ cubic millimeters	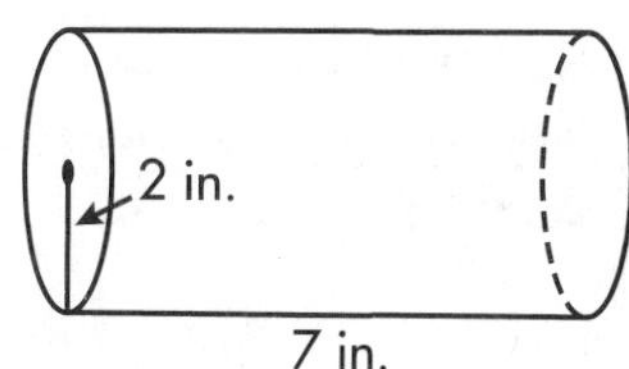 ______ cubic inches
3.	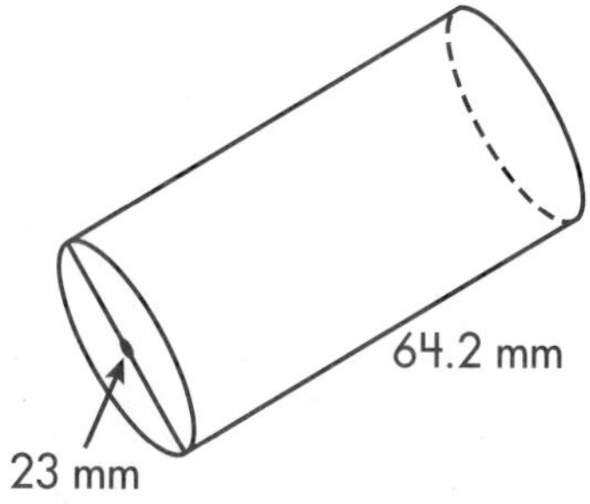 ______ cubic millimeters	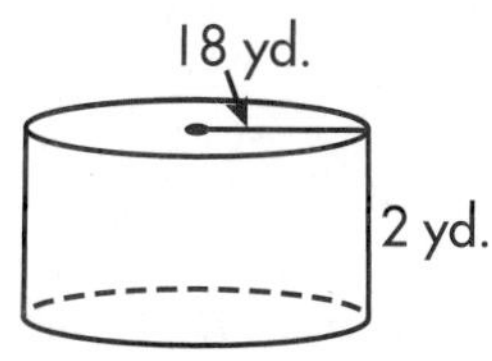 ______ cubic yards	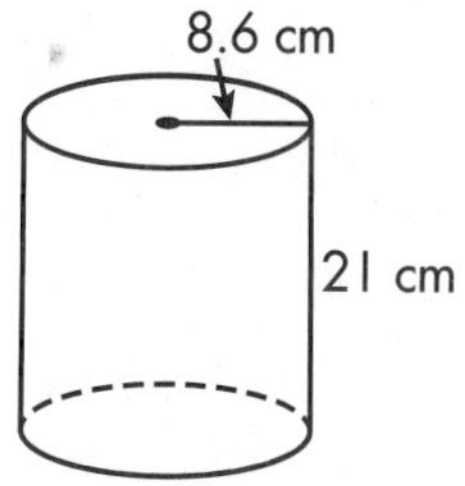 ______ cubic centimeters

NAME ______________________

Lesson 11.14 Problem Solving

SHOW YOUR WORK

Solve each problem.

1. When a certain tent is pitched, it forms a triangular pyramid. It is 2 meters high. The width is 3 meters, and the length is 4.5 meters. What is the volume of the tent?

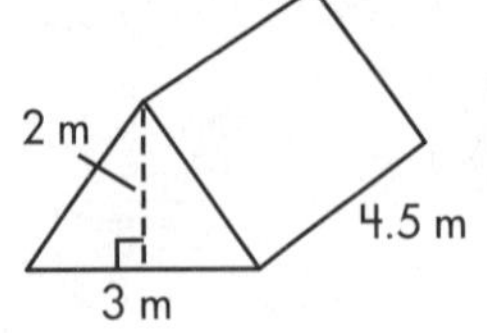

The volume of the tent is __________ cubic meters.

2. A triangular wedge of cheese has the dimensions shown in the figure. What is the volume?

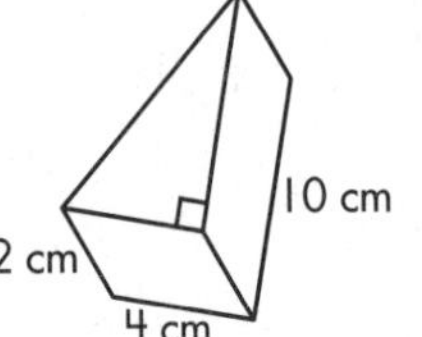

The volume of the cheese is __________ cubic centimeters.

3. A wooden block is cut in the shape of a triangular solid. Its volume is 3 cubic inches and the area of its base is 1.5 square inches. What is its height?

The block is __________ inches high.

4. A peanut butter jar is 16.5 centimeters tall and has a diameter of 9 centimeters. What is its surface area? What is its volume?

The surface area of the jar is __________ square centimeters.

The volume of the jar is __________ cubic centimeters.

5. A can of paint is 8 inches high and has a radius of 3.5 inches. What is its surface area? What is its volume?

The surface area of the can is ________ square inches.

The volume of the can is ________ cubic inches.

6. A holding tank in a manufacturing plant is 6.3 meters tall and has a diameter of 4 meters. What is its surface area? What is its volume?

The surface area of the tank is ________ square meters.

The volume of the tank is ________ cubic meters.

1.
2.
3.
4.
5.
6.

NAME ____________________

Check What You Learned

Perimeter, Area, and Volume

Find the perimeter of each figure.

	a	b	c
1.	4 m, 5 m, 3 m	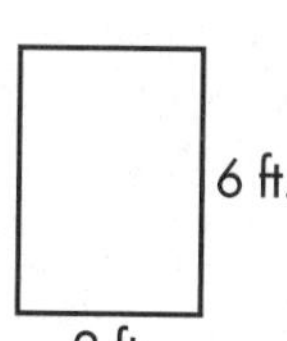	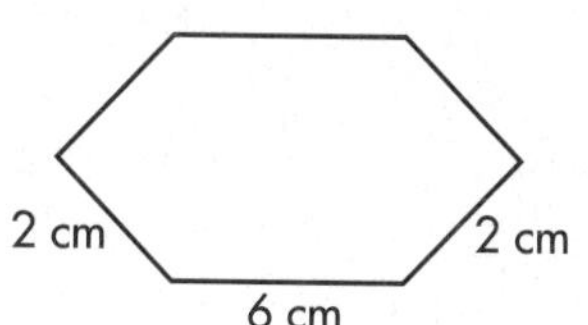
	________ meters	________ feet	________ centimeters
2.	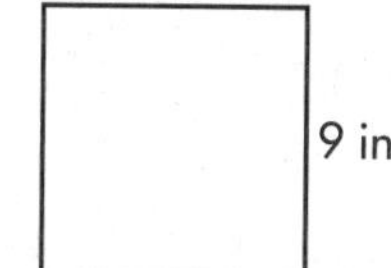	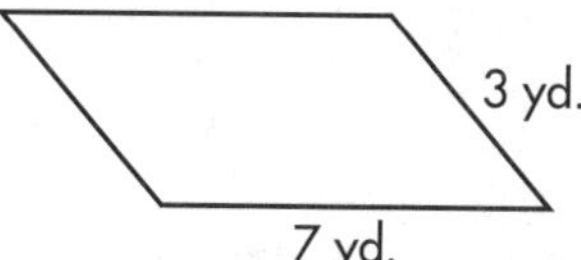	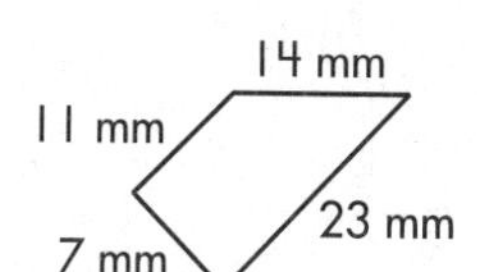
	________ inches	________ yards	________ millimeters

Find the circumference of each circle. Use 3.14 for pi.

3.	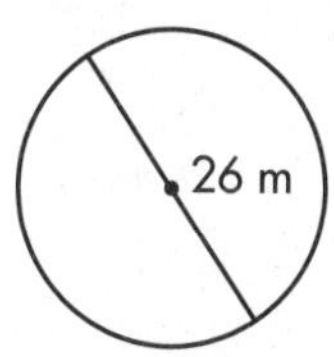	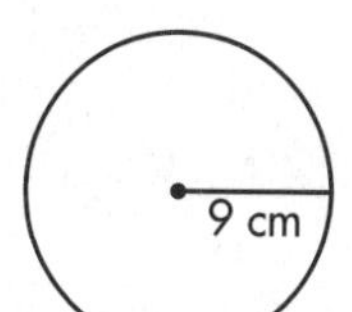	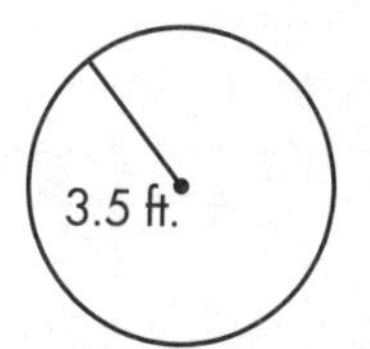
	________ meters	________ centimeters	________ feet

Find the area of each figure. Use 3.14 for pi.

4.		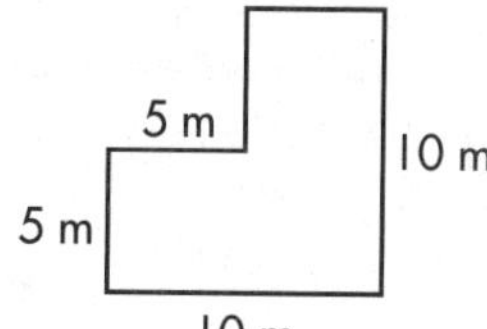	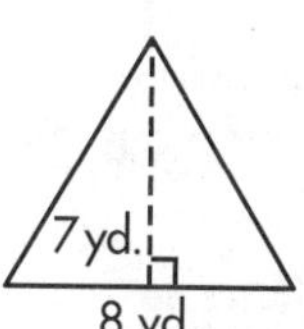
	________ square inches	________ square meters	________ square yards
5.	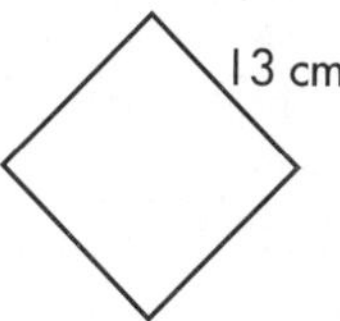	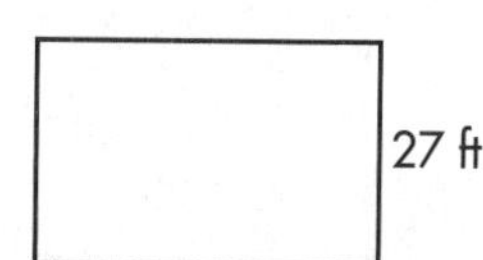	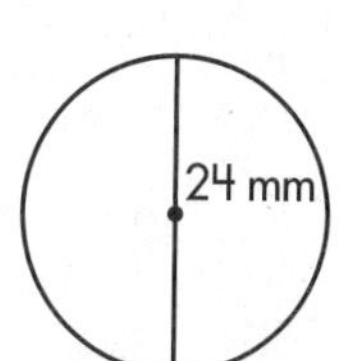
	________ square centimeters	________ square feet	________ square millimeters

NAME ____________________

Check What You Learned

Perimeter, Area, and Volume

Complete the table for each rectangular solid.

	Length	Width	Height	Surface Area	Volume
6.	4.5 yd.	2 yd.	8 yd.	________ sq. yd.	________ cubic yd.
7.	3 m	1.5 m	4 m	________ sq. m	________ cubic m
8.	23 mm	14 mm	18 mm	________ sq. mm	________ cubic mm
9.	5 in.	1.5 in.	6 in.	________ sq. in.	________ cubic in.

Find the volume for each triangular solid.

	a	b	c
10.	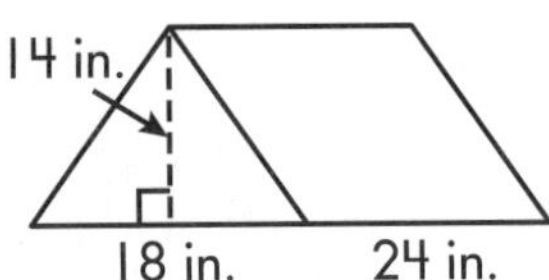	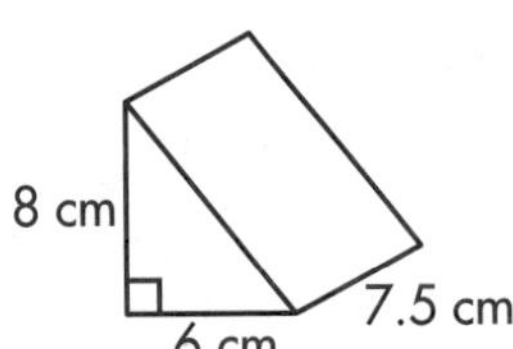	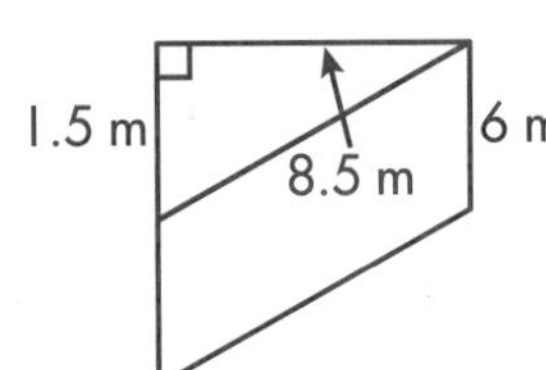
	________ cubic inches	________ cubic centimeters	________ cubic meters

Complete the table for each cylinder. Use 3.14 for pi.

	Radius	Diameter	Height	Surface Area	Volume
11.	_____ m	3 m	8 m	________ sq. m	________ cubic m
12.	2 yd.	_____ yd.	7 yd.	________ sq. yd.	________ cubic yd.
13.	_____ in.	22 in.	34 in.	________ sq. in.	________ cubic in.
14.	7 cm	_____ cm	3 cm	________ sq. cm	________ cubic cm

NAME ____________________

Check What You Know

Preparing for Algebra

CHAPTER 12 PRETEST

Write each phrase as a variable expression.

	a	b
1.	five less than n ________	eight more than b ________
2.	a number divided by six ________	the product of two and a number ________

Write each sentence as an equation.

3.	The sum of three and a number is twelve. ________	Six less than x is nineteen. ________
4.	Thirty divided by a number is three. ________	The product of five and n is fifteen. ________

Solve each equation.

	a	b	c
5.	$8 + d = 14$ ________	$s + 3 = 12$ ________	$9 + c = 21$ ________
6.	$25 = 10 + a$ ________	$13 = 9 + b$ ________	$26 = 4 + n$ ________
7.	$18 - x = 4$ ________	$31 - n = 19$ ________	$17 - b = 1$ ________
8.	$7 = 24 - y$ ________	$11 = 15 - b$ ________	$23 = 23 - n$ ________
9.	$3 \times a = 15$ ________	$2 \times n = 12$ ________	$5 \times d = 35$ ________
10.	$27 = 9 \times b$ ________	$24 = 6 \times n$ ________	$42 = 7 \times b$ ________
11.	$n \div 9 = 4$ ________	$b \div 6 = 7$ ________	$d \div 7 = 2$ ________
12.	$6 = b \div 3$ ________	$3 = a \div 20$ ________	$8 = c \div 9$ ________

NAME ____________________

Check What You Know

Preparing for Algebra

Find the value of each expression. Round to five decimal places if necessary.

	a	b	c
13.	$20 \div (5 - 1) =$ ______	$3 \times (6 + 2) =$ ______	$2 + 3 \times 6 =$ ______
14.	$9 + 2 - 3 =$ ______	$4 + (16 \div 4) =$ ______	$(4 + 16) \div 4 =$ ______
15.	$-3 + 2 =$ ______	$3 + (-2) =$ ______	$7 + (-4) =$ ______
16.	$-8 + (-3) =$ ______	$-7 + 6 =$ ______	$-4 + (-9) =$ ______
17.	$6 - 12 =$ ______	$3 - (-4) =$ ______	$-2 - 4 =$ ______
18.	$-8 - (-3) =$ ______	$7 - (-2) =$ ______	$-6 - (-5) =$ ______
19.	$7 \times (-6) =$ ______	$3 \times (-4) =$ ______	$-5 \times (-2) =$ ______
20.	$-4 \times 5 =$ ______	$-8 \times (-2) =$ ______	$6 \times (-4) =$ ______
21.	$12 \div (-4) =$ ______	$-15 \div (-5) =$ ______	$-21 \div 7 =$ ______
22.	$-24 \div (-8) =$ ______	$20 \div (-4) =$ ______	$6 \div (-2) =$ ______
23.	$3^2 \times 3^3 =$ ______	$2^2 \times 2^4 =$ ______	$4^2 \times 4^1 =$ ______
24.	$5^4 \div 5^2 =$ ______	$8^6 \div 8^4 =$ ______	$4^5 \times 4 =$ ______
25.	$2^{-2} \times 2^{-2} =$ ______	$3^{-3} \times 3^2 =$ ______	$5^{-3} \times 5^{-1} =$ ______
26.	$3^{-4} \div 3^{-2} =$ ______	$6^{-3} \div 6^2 =$ ______	$2^{-5} \div 2^{-3} =$ ______

NAME ____________________

Lesson 12.1 Variables, Expressions, and Equations

An **expression** is a way of naming a number.

A **numerical expression** contains only numbers. $2 + 5$

A **variable expression** contains numbers and variables. $2 + c$

An **equation** is a mathematical sentence that states that two expressions are equal.
$2 + 5 = 7$
$2 + c = 7$

An **inequality** is a mathematical sentence that states that two expressions are not equal.
$2 + 5 > 6$
$2 + 5 < 9$

Write whether each of the following is a numerical expression, a variable expression, an equation, or an inequality.

	a	b	c
1.	$r - 17$	$b + 12 = 15$	$s - 11 < 52$
	____________	____________	____________
2.	12×3	$15 - 9 > y$	$47 - 19 = 28$
	____________	____________	____________

Write each phrase as a numerical or variable expression.

	a	b
3.	three more than *d* ____________	the product of eight and *w* ____________
4.	seven less than twelve ____________	two more than a number ____________
5.	a number divided by six ____________	nine more than fifteen ____________

Write each sentence as an equation or inequality.

6. The sum of five and six is eleven. ____________ | Twelve divided by *s* equals 4. ____________

7. Three less than *t* is greater than five. ____________ | The product of two and *b* is greater than four. ____________

8. The product of five and three is *y*. ____________ | Twenty divided by a number is five. ____________

NAME ______________________

Lesson 12.2 Number Properties

Commutative Property: The order in which numbers are added does not change the sum. The order in which numbers are multiplied does not change the product.
$a + b = b + a$
$a \times b = b \times a$

Associative Property: The grouping of addends does not change the sum. The grouping of factors does not change the product.
$a + (b + c) = (a + b) + c$
$a \times (b \times c) = (a \times b) \times c$

Identity Property: The sum of an addend and 0 is the addend. The product of a factor and 1 is the factor.
$a + 0 = a$
$a \times 1 = a$

Properties of Zero: The product of a factor and 0 is 0. The quotient of the dividend 0 and any divisor is 0.
$a \times 0 = 0$
$0 \div a = 0$

Write the name of the property shown by each equation.

	a	b
1.	$3 + s = s + 3$ ____________	$3 \times (2 \times r) = (3 \times 2) \times r$ ____________
2.	$15 \times 1 = 15$ ____________	$12 \times p = p \times 12$ ____________
3.	$(6+t)+37 = 6+(t+37)$ ____________	$35 \times 0 = 0$ ____________
4.	$346 + 0 = 346$ ____________	$65 + 93 = 93 + 65$ ____________
5.	$0 \div 76 = 0$ ____________	$(8 \times 9) \times 12 = 8 \times (9 \times 12)$ ____________

Rewrite each expression using the property indicated.

6.	associative: $(3 + 7) + y =$ ____________	identity: $642 + 0 =$ ____________
7.	commutative: $15 \times z =$ ____________	zero: $16 \times 0 =$ ____________
8.	identity: $12a \times 1 =$ ____________	associative: $14 \times (3 \times p) =$ ____________
9.	zero: $0 \div 68 =$ ____________	commutative: $49 + 16 =$ ____________
10.	commutative: $3 + d =$ ____________	associative: $(6 \times 4) \times n =$ ____________

NAME ______________________

Lesson 12.3 The Distributive Property

The **distributive property** combines multiplication with addition or subtraction. The property states:

$a \times (b + c) = (a \times b) + (a \times c)$	$3 \times (6 + 4) = (3 \times 6) + (3 \times 4)$
$a \times (b - c) = (a \times b) - (a \times c)$	$3 \times (10) = (18) + (12)$
	$30 = 30$

Rewrite each expression using the distributive property.

	a	b
1.	$(a \times 4) + (a \times 3) =$ ______	$b \times (6 + 12) =$ ______
2.	$4 \times (a + b) =$ ______	$(3 \times a) + (3 \times b) =$ ______
3.	$(d \times 5) - (d \times 2) =$ ______	$5 \times (8 + p) =$ ______
4.	$d \times (8 - h) =$ ______	$12 \times (s - 10) =$ ______
5.	$r \times (16 + s) =$ ______	$(35 \times t) + (35 \times y) =$ ______
6.	$(8 \times a) + (b \times 8) =$ ______	$r \times (q - s) =$ ______
7.	$(6 \times 12) - (w \times 6) =$ ______	$p \times (15 + z) =$ ______
8.	$15 \times (y + 0) =$ ______	$(d \times d) + (d \times b) =$ ______
9.	$(a \times 2) + (a \times 3) + (a \times 4) =$ ______	$p \times (a + b + 4) =$ ______
10.	$(a \times b) + (a \times c) - (a \times d) =$ ______	$8 \times (a + b + c) =$ ______

NAME ______________________

Lesson 12.4 Order of Operations

If an expression contains two or more operations, they must be completed in a specified order. The order of operations is as follows.

1. Complete operations within grouping symbols, such as parentheses.
2. Multiply and divide in order from left to right.
3. Add and subtract in order from left to right.

$23 - (2 + 3) \times 2$	$= 23 - 5 \times 2$	Add $(2 + 3)$.
	$= 23 - 10$	Multiply 5×2.
	$= 13$	Subtract $23 - 10$.

Find the value of each expression.

	a	b	c
1.	$6 + 2 \times 5 =$ ____	$18 - (3 + 4) =$ ____	$18 - 3 + 4 =$ ____
2.	$3 \times 3 + 8 =$ ____	$3 \times (3 + 8) =$ ____	$12 \div (2 \times 3) =$ ____
3.	$12 \div 2 + 3 =$ ____	$8 + (5 \times 4) =$ ____	$8 + 5 \times 4 =$ ____
4.	$3 \times (2 \times 6) =$ ____	$15 \div (3 + 2) =$ ____	$15 \div 3 + 2 =$ ____
5.	$12 + 8 - 6 =$ ____	$2 + 6 \div 2 =$ ____	$(2 + 6) \div 2 =$ ____
6.	$3 \times 2 \div 6 =$ ____	$6 \div 3 \times 2 =$ ____	$8 - (2 + 4) =$ ____
7.	$30 \div 5 + 1 =$ ____	$30 \div (5 + 1) =$ ____	$7 + 12 \div 4 =$ ____
8.	$23 - 15 \div 3 =$ ____	$(32 - 7) \div 5 =$ ____	$48 - (12 \div 4) =$ ____
9.	$2 + 2 \times 3 - 1 =$ ____	$(2 + 2) \times 3 - 1 =$ ____	$3 + 4 \times 3 + 2 =$ ____
10.	$3 + 8 \div 2 - 1 =$ ____	$(4 + 8) \div (5 - 1) =$ ____	$12 \div (2 + 2) + 2 =$ ____
11.	$9 + 18 \div 6 - 3 =$ ____	$(9 + 18) \div (6 - 3) =$ ____	$3 + 2 \times 8 \div 4 =$ ____
12.	$10 - 8 \times 3 \div 6 =$ ____	$3 + 6 + 9 \div 3 =$ ____	$3 + (6 + 9) \div 3 =$ ____
13.	$12 - 10 + 2 \times 7 =$ ____	$(4 \times 3) + (4 \times 5) =$ ____	$4 \times (3 + 4) \times 5 =$ ____
14.	$8 + 2 \times 5 - 7 =$ ____	$(8 + 2) \times 5 - 7 =$ ____	$12 + 3 \times 10 \div 6 =$ ____

NAME ______________________

Lesson 12.5 Solving Addition and Subtraction Equations

Subtraction Property of Equality: When two expressions are equal, if you subtract the same number from both expressions, the differences will also be equal.

$a = b$
$a - c = b - c$

Addition Property of Equality: When two expressions are equal, if you add the same number to both expressions, the sums will also be equal.

$a = b$
$a + c = b + c$

Use these properties to solve equations.

$a + 3 = 14$	$b - 11 = 6$
$a + 3 - 3 = 14 - 3$	$b - 11 + 11 = 6 + 11$
$a = 11$	$b = 17$

Solve each equation.

	a	b	c
1.	$9 + d = 16$ ________	$y + 3 = 9$ ________	$12 + a = 27$ ________
2.	$18 - b = 4$ ________	$23 - c = 21$ ________	$w - 11 = 11$ ________
3.	$n + 8 = 41$ ________	$7 + m = 20$ ________	$9 + s = 9$ ________
4.	$t - 18 = 5$ ________	$36 - a = 36$ ________	$15 - b = 0$ ________
5.	$17 = c + 3$ ________	$29 = 5 + b$ ________	$36 = 35 + n$ ________
6.	$2 = d - 4$ ________	$19 = 25 - a$ ________	$12 = t - 12$ ________

Write an equation for each problem. Then, solve the equation.

7. Ruben read 37 pages in his history book over the weekend. He read 21 pages on Saturday. How many pages did he read on Sunday?

______________________ He read ________ pages on Sunday.

8. The Garcias ate 9 pieces of toast for breakfast. If there are 33 slices of bread left, how many slices were in the loaf of bread?

______________________ There were ________ slices in the loaf of bread.

9. In a 25-kilometer triathlon, competitors swim 2 kilometers, run 5 kilometers, and bike the rest. How far do they bike?

______________________ They bike ________ kilometers.

NAME ____________________

Lesson 12.6 Solving Multiplication and Division Equations

Division Property of Equality: When two expressions are equal, if they are divided by the same number, the quotients will also be equal.

$a = b$
$a \div c = b \div c$
$\frac{a}{c} = \frac{b}{c}$

Multiplication Property of Equality: When two expressions are equal, if they are multiplied by the same number, the products will also be equal.

$a = b$
$a \times c = b \times c$

Use these properties to solve equations.

$3 \times n = 15$	$n \div 6 = 8$
$\frac{3 \times n}{3} = \frac{15}{3}$	$n \div 6 \times 6 = 8 \times 6$
$n = 5$	$n = 48$

Solve each equation.

	a	b	c
1.	$2 \times d = 18$ ________	$a \times 4 = 20$ ________	$5 \times n = 30$ ________
2.	$y \div 3 = 4$ ________	$t \div 9 = 3$ ________	$\frac{a}{5} = 3$ ________
3.	$8 \times s = 64$ ________	$p \times 16 = 16$ ________	$7 \times r = 42$ ________
4.	$\frac{n}{5} = 10$ ________	$n \div 3 = 12$ ________	$a \div 8 = 6$ ________
5.	$25 = 5 \times d$ ________	$0 = a \times 57$ ________	$32 = b \times 2$ ________
6.	$19 = \frac{x}{1}$ ________	$7 = b \div 4$ ________	$9 = \frac{c}{7}$ ________

Write an equation for each problem. Then, solve the equation.

7. Taryn practiced piano the same amount of time every day for 6 days. If she practiced a total of 12 hours, how many hours did she practice each day?

________________ She practiced ________ hours each day.

8. A group of friends decided to equally share a package of trading cards. If there were 48 cards in the package and each person received 12, how many friends were in the group?

________________ There were ________ friends in the group.

9. Twenty-five cars can take the ferry across the river at one time. If 150 cars took the ferry, and it was full each time, how many times did the ferry cross the river?

________________ The ferry crossed the river ________ times.

NAME ______________________________

Lesson 12.7 Adding and Subtracting Integers

The sum of two positive integers is positive.

$4 + 3 = 7$

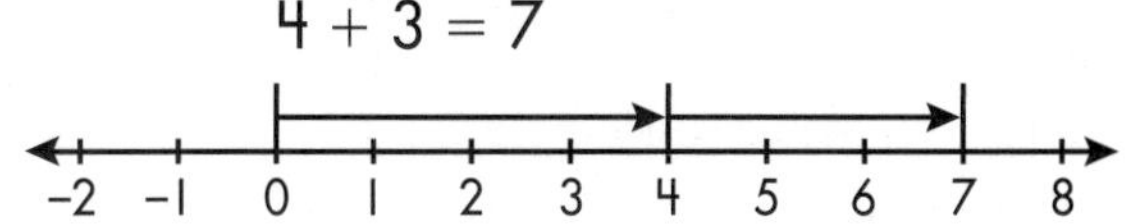

The sum of two negative integers is negative.

$-4 + (-3) = -7$

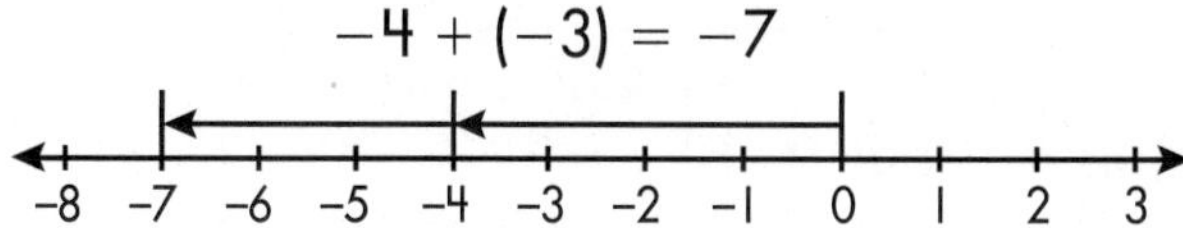

To find the sum of two integers with different signs, find their absolute values. **Absolute value** is the distance (in units) that a number is from 0 expressed as a positive quantity. Subtract the lesser number from the greater number. Absolute value is written as $|X|$.

The sum has the same sign as the integer with the larger absolute value.

$-4 + 3 = -1$

$|-4| = 4 \quad 4 - 3 = 1$

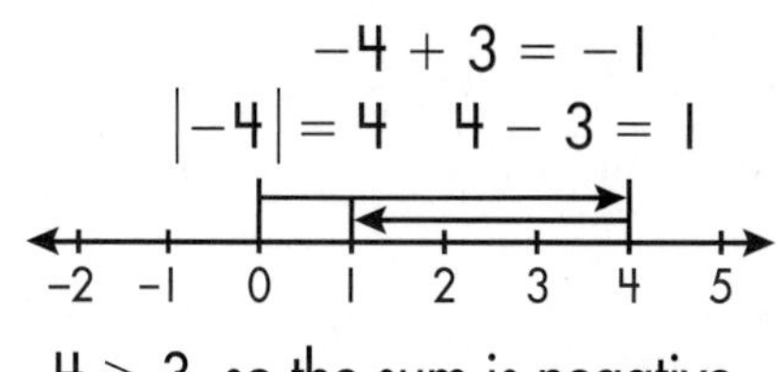

$4 > 3$, so the sum is negative.

To subtract an integer, add its opposite.

$5 - 7 = 5 + (-7) = -2$

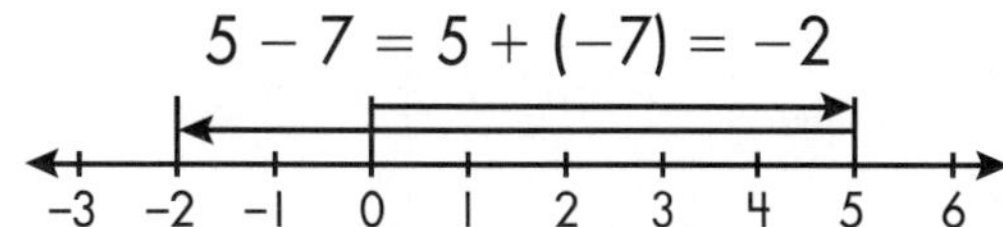

Add or subtract.

	a	b	c	d
1.	$6 + 2 =$ ______	$9 + (-4) =$ ______	$7 + (-9) =$ ______	$-3 + 8 =$ ______
2.	$3 - 11 =$ ______	$5 - 2 =$ ______	$-4 - 6 =$ ______	$8 - (-2) =$ ______
3.	$-4 + 7 =$ ______	$-3 + (-6) =$ ______	$-12 + 11 =$ ______	$-16 + (-7) =$ ______
4.	$-12 - 3 =$ ______	$-5 - (-6) =$ ______	$14 - 19 =$ ______	$7 - 18 =$ ______
5.	$-16 + 0 =$ ______	$13 + (-24) =$ ______	$-6 + 8 =$ ______	$-3 + (-2) =$ ______
6.	$4 - 19 =$ ______	$-11 - (-1) =$ ______	$16 - (-27) =$ ______	$7 - 22 =$ ______
7.	$0 + (-9) =$ ______	$-1 + 2 =$ ______	$1 + (-2) =$ ______	$8 + (-8) =$ ______
8.	$-6 - (-6) =$ ______	$-11 - 0 =$ ______	$-2 - 2 =$ ______	$1 - 2 =$ ______
9.	$-4 + 4 =$ ______	$3 + (-6) =$ ______	$7 + (-17) =$ ______	$6 + 5 =$ ______
10.	$8 - 1 =$ ______	$8 - (-1) =$ ______	$-13 - 3 =$ ______	$-4 - (-8) =$ ______

NAME ______________________

Lesson 12.8 Multiplying and Dividing Integers

The product of two integers with the same sign is positive.	$3 \times 3 = 9$ $-3 \times -3 = 9$
The product of two integers with different signs is negative.	$3 \times (-3) = -9$ $-3 \times 3 = -9$
The quotient of two integers with the same sign is positive.	$8 \div 2 = 4$ $-8 \div (-2) = 4$
The quotient of two integers with different signs is negative.	$8 \div (-2) = -4$ $-8 \div 2 = -4$

Multiply or divide.

	a	b	c	d
1.	$3 \times 2 =$ ____	$-4 \times 6 =$ ____	$8 \times (-3) =$ ____	$-3 \times (-4) =$ ____
2.	$12 \div 4 =$ ____	$16 \div (-4) =$ ____	$-8 \div 4 =$ ____	$9 \div (-3) =$ ____
3.	$-8 \times 7 =$ ____	$6 \times (-5) =$ ____	$-3 \times (-8) =$ ____	$-4 \times 11 =$ ____
4.	$7 \div (-1) =$ ____	$-14 \div 7 =$ ____	$24 \div (-6) =$ ____	$28 \div 7 =$ ____
5.	$16 \times (-2) =$ ____	$-4 \times (-1) =$ ____	$8 \times (-11) =$ ____	$-7 \times (-10) =$ ____
6.	$81 \div (-3) =$ ____	$-63 \div 9 =$ ____	$-55 \div (-5) =$ ____	$18 \div 9 =$ ____
7.	$5 \times 8 =$ ____	$6 \times (-6) =$ ____	$-13 \times (-2) =$ ____	$-9 \times 9 =$ ____
8.	$21 \div (-7) =$ ____	$-38 \div 2 =$ ____	$-19 \div (-1) =$ ____	$-56 \div 8 =$ ____
9.	$17 \times (-1) =$ ____	$5 \times (-2) =$ ____	$-14 \times 3 =$ ____	$-7 \times (-5) =$ ____
10.	$12 \div (-12) =$ ____	$42 \div (-21) =$ ____	$-60 \div (-10) =$ ____	$54 \div (-6) =$ ____

NAME ______________________

Lesson 12.9 Multiplying and Dividing Powers

A **power** is a number that is expressed using an **exponent**. The **base** is the number that is multiplied, and the exponent tells how many times the base is used as a factor.

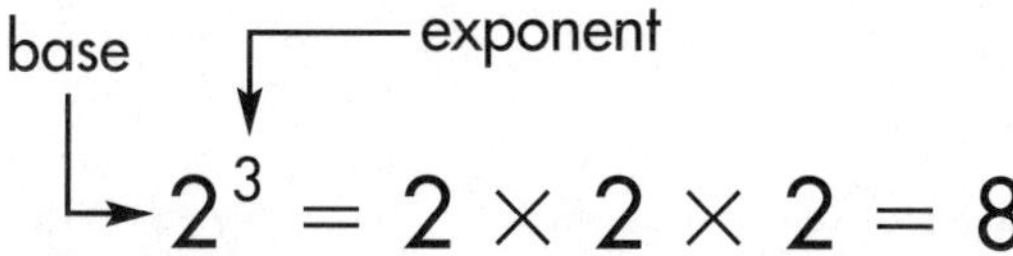

To multiply powers with the same base, combine bases, add the exponents, then simplify. $2^2 \times 2^3 = 2^{2+3} = 2^5 = 32$

To divide powers with the same base, combine bases, subtract the exponents, then simplify. $3^5 \div 3^2 = 3^{5-2} = 3^3 = 27$

Find the value of each expression.

	a	b	c
1.	$7^2 =$ ______	$8^3 =$ ______	$4^3 =$ ______
2.	$10^2 =$ ______	$9^4 =$ ______	$11^5 =$ ______
3.	$17^3 =$ ______	$5^6 =$ ______	$6^4 =$ ______
4.	$21^3 =$ ______	$16^4 =$ ______	$12^5 =$ ______

Rewrite each expression as one base and one exponent. Then, find the value.

5.	$8^2 \times 8^3 =$ 8^5; 32768	$3^3 \times 3^3 =$ ______	$2^2 \times 2^2 =$ ______
6.	$7^4 \div 7^2 =$ ______	$9^5 \div 9^3 =$ ______	$16^4 \div 16^2 =$ ______
7.	$6^4 \times 6^1 =$ ______	$4^4 \times 4^2 =$ ______	$3^2 \times 3^2 =$ ______
8.	$10^6 \div 10^4 =$ ______	$8^3 \div 8^2 =$ ______	$7^6 \div 7^3 =$ ______
9.	$5^3 \times 5^2 =$ ______	$10^3 \times 10^4 =$ ______	$15^2 \times 15^1 =$ ______
10.	$2^8 \div 2^3 =$ ______	$3^9 \div 3^7 =$ ______	$6^6 \div 6^3 =$ ______

NAME ______________________

Lesson 12.10 Negative Exponents

When a power includes a negative exponent, express the number as 1 divided by the base and change the exponent to positive.

$$4^{-2} = \frac{1}{4^2} = \frac{1}{16} = 0.0625$$

To multiply or divide powers with the same base, combine bases, add or subtract the exponents, then simplify.

$$2^{-3} \times 2^{-2} = 2^{-5} = \frac{1}{2^5} = 0.03125$$

$$2^{-4} \div 2^{-2} = 2^{-2} = \frac{1}{2^2} = 0.25$$

Rewrite each expression with a positive exponent. Then, solve. Round your answer to four decimal places.

	a	b	c
1.	$3^{-2} =$ ______	$6^{-3} =$ ______	$8^{-2} =$ ______
2.	$7^{-3} =$ ______	$3^{-3} =$ ______	$9^{-2} =$ ______
3.	$4^{-3} =$ ______	$5^{-2} =$ ______	$2^{-3} =$ ______
4.	$2^{-4} =$ ______	$10^{-3} =$ ______	$1^{-4} =$ ______

Find each product. Round your answer to five decimal places.

5.	$4^{-2} \times 4^{-3} =$ ______	$2^{-4} \times 2^{-1} =$ ______	$3^{-2} \times 3^{-3} =$ ______
6.	$6^{-2} \times 6^{-2} =$ ______	$5^{-2} \times 5^{-4} =$ ______	$3^{-2} \times 3^{-2} =$ ______
7.	$8^{-6} \times 8^{4} =$ ______	$7^{-5} \times 7^{2} =$ ______	$2^{-7} \times 2^{4} =$ ______

Find each quotient. Round your answer to five decimal places.

8.	$4^{-4} \div 4^{-2} =$ ______	$8^{-5} \div 8^{-3} =$ ______	$3^{-5} \div 3^{-2} =$ ______
9.	$2^{-8} \div 2^{-4} =$ ______	$5^{-6} \div 5^{-4} =$ ______	$6^{-7} \div 6^{-4} =$ ______
10.	$3^{-3} \div 3^{2} =$ ______	$4^{-3} \div 4^{1} =$ ______	$2^{-6} \div 2^{-3} =$ ______

NAME ______________________

Check What You Learned

Preparing for Algebra

Write each phrase as a numerical expression.

	a	b
1.	seven less than a number ______	eight more than a number ______
2.	the product of six and a number ______	a number divided by twelve ______

Write each sentence as an equation.

3.	The product of four and a number is sixteen. ______	Nine more than n is 11. ______
4.	Three less than a number is twenty. ______	Twenty-five divided by b is five. ______

Solve each equation.

	a	b	c
5.	$5 + n = 12$ ______	$n + 3 = 8$ ______	$4 + d = 25$ ______
6.	$18 = n + 6$ ______	$27 = 9 + b$ ______	$32 = 20 + c$ ______
7.	$5 - n = 0$ ______	$15 - b = 7$ ______	$23 - a = 12$ ______
8.	$9 = 10 - d$ ______	$26 = 30 - n$ ______	$7 = 42 \div s$ ______
9.	$2 \times b = 18$ ______	$7 \times f = 35$ ______	$r \times 6 = 30$ ______
10.	$45 = n \times 9$ ______	$62 = 2 \times b$ ______	$66 = 11 \times t$ ______
11.	$n \div 3 = 11$ ______	$b \div 6 = 9$ ______	$a \div 2 = 8$ ______
12.	$14 = b \div 2$ ______	$7 = c \div 3$ ______	$3 = n \div 8$ ______

CHAPTER 12 POSTTEST

NAME ____________________

Check What You Learned

Preparing for Algebra

Find the value of each expression. Round to five decimal places if necessary.

	a	b	c
13.	$30 \div (6 - 1) =$ ______	$(3 + 2) \times 3 =$ ______	$(6 - 2) \times 4 =$ ______
14.	$3 + 15 \div 3 =$ ______	$(3 + 15) \div 3 =$ ______	$10 - 4 \times 2 =$ ______
15.	$-6 + 4 =$ ______	$7 + (-3) =$ ______	$-5 + (-2) =$ ______
16.	$-9 + 12 =$ ______	$8 + (-11) =$ ______	$-4 + (-8) =$ ______
17.	$13 - 16 =$ ______	$9 - (-8) =$ ______	$-3 - 7 =$ ______
18.	$-7 - (-4) =$ ______	$12 - (-3) =$ ______	$-9 - 1 =$ ______
19.	$-3 \times 4 =$ ______	$6 \times (-3) =$ ______	$-2 \times (-8) =$ ______
20.	$-5 \times (-6) =$ ______	$7 \times (-9) =$ ______	$-6 \times (-1) =$ ______
21.	$-18 \div 9 =$ ______	$24 \div (-6) =$ ______	$-40 \div (-4) =$ ______
22.	$-6 \div 6 =$ ______	$17 \div (-1) =$ ______	$-46 \div 2 =$ ______
23.	$2^2 \times 2^2 =$ ______	$3^3 \times 3^2 =$ ______	$6^2 \times 6^1 =$ ______
24.	$7^5 \div 7^3 =$ ______	$8^6 \div 8^3 =$ ______	$5^5 \div 5^2 =$ ______
25.	$3^{-2} \times 3^{-1} =$ ______	$2^{-3} \times 2^{-2} =$ ______	$4^{-3} \times 4^1 =$ ______
26.	$3^{-2} \div 3^{-1} =$ ______	$7^{-6} \div 7^{-3} =$ ______	$2^2 \div 2^4 =$ ______

CHAPTER 12 POSTTEST

NAME ______________________

Final Test Chapters 1–12

Multiply or divide. Write answers in simplest form.

	a	b	c	d
1.	$\frac{1}{8} \times \frac{3}{5}$ ______	$\frac{2}{3} \times \frac{3}{7}$ ______	$3\frac{1}{7} \times \frac{5}{8}$ ______	$2\frac{1}{3} \times 1\frac{3}{8}$ ______
2.	$\frac{3}{8} \times 1\frac{5}{6}$ ______	$2\frac{1}{7} \times 1\frac{1}{3}$ ______	$6\frac{1}{2} \times 2\frac{1}{3}$ ______	$3\frac{5}{8} \times \frac{2}{9}$ ______
3.	$\frac{6}{7} \div \frac{1}{2}$ ______	$\frac{3}{5} \div \frac{7}{10}$ ______	$\frac{5}{8} \div \frac{1}{3}$ ______	$1\frac{2}{3} \div \frac{3}{5}$ ______
4.	$3\frac{4}{5} \div 1\frac{1}{2}$ ______	$4\frac{1}{4} \div 3\frac{3}{8}$ ______	$6\frac{1}{2} \div \frac{1}{5}$ ______	$2\frac{1}{3} \div 2$ ______

Complete the following table.

	Principal	Rate	Time	Interest	Total Amount
5.	\$350	4%	$1\frac{1}{2}$ years	______	______
6.	\$720	$5\frac{1}{4}$%	3 years	______	______
7.	\$1340	$8\frac{1}{2}$%	$\frac{1}{2}$ year	______	______
8.	\$600	3%	$4\frac{3}{4}$ years	______	______

Solve each of the following.

	a	b	c
9.	$\frac{3}{5} = \frac{n}{20}$ ______	$\frac{n}{6} = \frac{12}{18}$ ______	$\frac{4}{n} = \frac{10}{20}$ ______
10.	$\frac{5}{8} = \frac{15}{n}$ ______	$\frac{8}{25} = \frac{n}{100}$ ______	$\frac{12}{n} = \frac{1}{3}$ ______

CHAPTERS 1–12 FINAL TEST

NAME ___________________________

Final Test Chapters 1–12

Convert the following.

	a		b		c	
11.	$3\frac{1}{4}$ mi. = ________	yd.	5 ft. 3 in. = ________	in.	3.5 lb. = ________	oz.
12.	78 hr. = ________	days	223 min. = ___ hr. ___	min.	$1\frac{3}{4}$ gal. = ________	pt.
13.	340 m = ________	km	0.7 m = ________	cm	1.2 g = ________	mg
14.	350 L = ________	kL	1246 g = ________	kg	1382 mL = ________	L

Use this data set to complete the following.

Score on quiz: 9, 18, 12, 9, 13, 22, 8, 23, 16, 17, 22, 20, 22, 15, 10, 17, 21, 23, 14, 11

15. Make a stem-and-leaf plot.

16. Draw in the bars to complete the histogram.

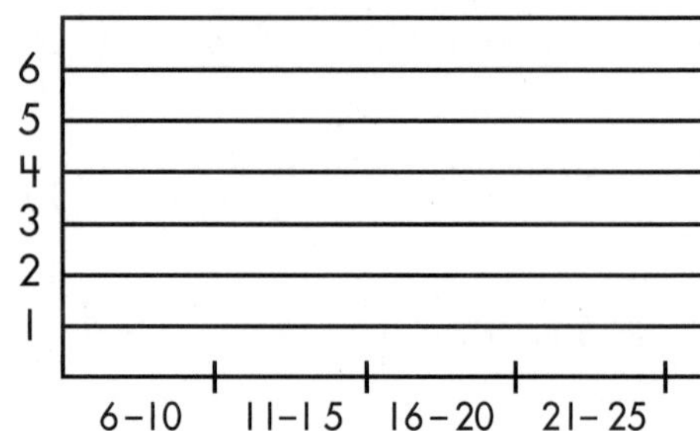

17. Find the mean, median, mode, and range of the data.

mean: ________ mode: ________

median: ________ range: ________

18. What percent of the people scored 16–20 points? ________%

19. What was the highest quiz score? ________

20. What was the lowest quiz score? ________

21. What percent of the scores are 21–25 points? ________%

NAME ______________________

Final Test Chapters 1–12

Find the perimeter of each figure.

	a	b	c
22.	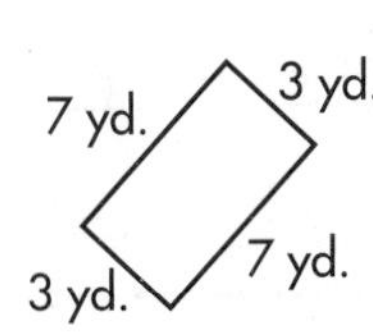	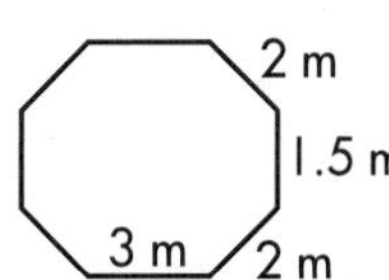	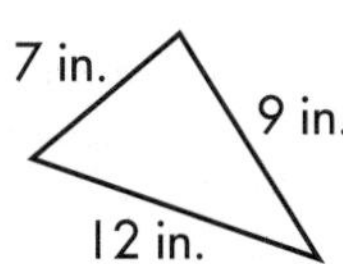
	________ yd.	________ m	________ in.

Find the area of each figure.

23.	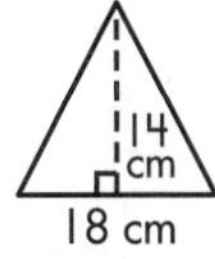	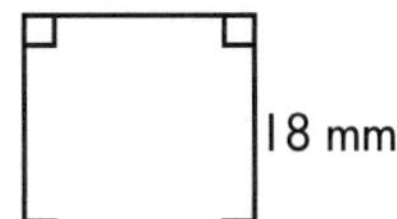	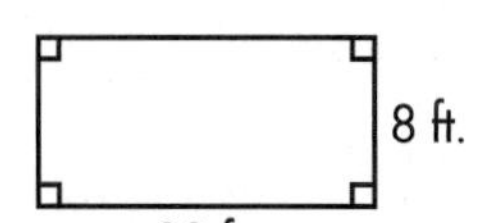
	________ sq. cm	________ sq. mm	________ sq. ft.

Find the circumference and area of each circle. Use 3.14 for pi.

24.	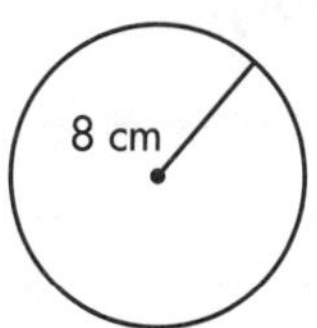	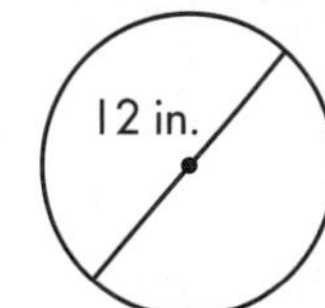	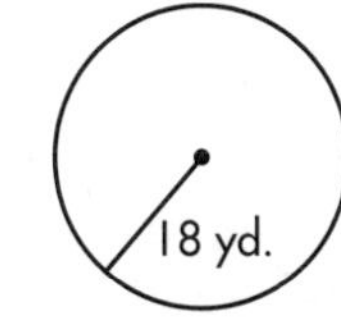
	circumference: ________ cm	________ in.	________ yd.
	area: ________ sq. cm	________ sq. in.	________ sq. yd.

Find the surface area of each figure. Use 3.14 for pi.

25.	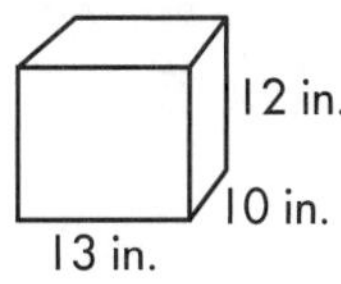	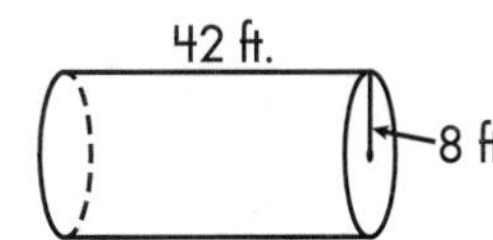	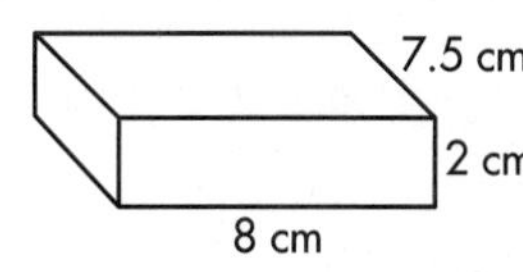
	________ sq. in.	________ sq. ft.	________ sq. cm

CHAPTERS 1–12 FINAL TEST

NAME ______________________

Final Test Chapters 1–12

Find the volume of each figure. Use 3.14 for pi.

26.

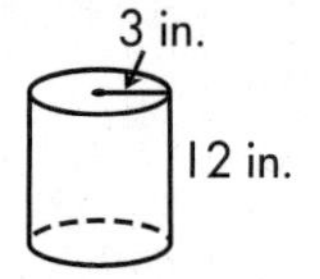

______ cubic in.

6 cm
11 cm
9.5 cm

______ cubic cm

2.5 m
8 m
3 m

______ cubic m

Solve each equation.

	a	b	c
27.	$6 + c = 23$ ______	$d + 11 = 15$ ______	$28 = a + 9$ ______
28.	$32 - r = 15$ ______	$p - 13 = 5$ ______	$7 = 15 - n$ ______
29.	$8 \times b = 48$ ______	$7 \times d = 21$ ______	$33 = 3 \times t$ ______
30.	$a \div 5 = 5$ ______	$n \div 8 = 5$ ______	$6 = m \div 10$ ______

Find the value of each expression. Round to five decimal places if necessary.

31.	$(3 + 2) \times 10 =$ ______	$24 \div (8 - 4) =$ ______	$6 + 4 \times 7 =$ ______
32.	$-4 + 2 =$ ______	$3 + (-8) =$ ______	$2 + (-3) =$ ______
33.	$-10 - 4 =$ ______	$-9 - (-6) =$ ______	$15 - (-11) =$ ______
34.	$6 \times (-2) =$ ______	$-4 \times 3 =$ ______	$-3 \times (-9) =$ ______
35.	$-8 \div 4 =$ ______	$12 \div (-6) =$ ______	$-14 \div (-2) =$ ______
36.	$2 + 3 \times (-4) =$ ______	$(-3 + 2) \times 5 =$ ______	$-4 \times 5 \div 2 =$ ______
37.	$2^2 \times 2^1 =$ ______	$3^2 \times 3^2 =$ ______	$2^3 \times 2^2 =$ ______
38.	$2^{-2} \div 2^3 =$ ______	$3^{-3} \div 3^{-2} =$ ______	$2^{-6} \div 2^{-4} =$ ______
39.	$20 \div (-5) + 3 =$ ______	$2 + (-3) + 1 =$ ______	$-3 \times 4 + 6 =$ ______
40.	$3^2 + 4 =$ ______	$2^3 - 4 =$ ______	$4^2 - 9 =$ ______

NAME ________________________________ DATE ____________

Scoring Record for Posttests, Mid-Test, and Final Test

		Performance			
Chapter Posttest	Your Score	Excellent	Very Good	Fair	Needs Improvement
1	___ of 36	34–36	30–33	23–29	22 or fewer
2	___ of 26	25–26	22–24	17–21	16 or fewer
3	___ of 30	29–30	25–28	19–24	18 or fewer
4	___ of 39	37–39	32–36	24–31	23 or fewer
5	___ of 40	38–40	33–37	25–32	24 or fewer
6	___ of 22	21–22	19–20	14–18	13 or fewer
7	___ of 68	57–60	49–56	37–48	36 or fewer
8	___ of 37	34–36	30–33	23–29	22 or fewer
9	___ of 20	20	17–19	13–16	12 or fewer
10	___ of 40	38–40	33–37	25–32	24 or fewer
11	___ of 38	36–38	31–35	24–30	23 or fewer
12	___ of 74	70–74	60–69	45–59	44 or fewer
Mid-Test	___ of 83	78–83	67–77	51–66	50 or fewer
Final Test	___ of 113	106–113	91–105	69–90	68 or fewer

Record your test score in the Your Score column. See where your score falls in the Performance columns. Your score is based on the total number of required responses. If your score is fair or needs improvement, review the chapter material.

Grade 7 Answers

Chapter 1

Pretest, page 1

	a	b	c	d	e
1.	145	999	8775	149795	1002996
2.	66	278	841	37368	165267
3.	476	26961	34758	42258	252711
4.	1591	135432	525586	1346235	979232
5.	7	247r2	761r2	12r2	21r8
6.	13r11	322	226r35	288r11	1413r2

Pretest, page 2

7. 138 **8.** 37 **9.** $1764 **10.** 587529
11. $117480 **12.** 154; 18

Lesson 1.1, page 3

	a	b	c	d	e
1.	392	178	943	15519	757609
2.	127	747	8056	79807	320840
3.	981	1240	4792	96064	869998
4.	178	898	8911	47693	819274
5.	119	980	7928	78850	776414

Lesson 1.2, page 4

	a	b	c	d	e
1.	31	594	4109	21116	82327
2.	16	187	6787	22296	582109
3.	85	294	3084	37611	791087
4.	8	291	4917	88912	44089
5.	59	149	916	57082	239981
6.	23	263	2691	58091	317818

Lesson 1.3, page 5

1. $3 **2.** 82206 **3.** 11729 **4.** $1050 **5.** 9430
6. 359 **7.** 1098

Lesson 1.4, page 6

	a	b	c	d
1.	148	4774	1578	10865
2.	2438	18424	27072	414143
3.	1972	121401	195415	1718412
4.	17316	196176	1146140	585044

Lesson 1.5, page 7

	a	b	c	d	e
1.	6r1	29	53r3	68	778
2.	9r2	37r1	85r2	543r3	172r5
3.	14	17r4	175r1	2064r1	1930r3

Lesson 1.6, page 8

	a	b	c	d	e
1.	34r1	27r20	3r30	7r14	11r48
2.	26r22	6r42	38r6	3r16	7
3.	18r28	23	6r5	33r13	26r29

Lesson 1.6, page 9

	a	b	c	d	e
1.	273r5	94r71	606	1259r47	635r56
2.	176r17	237	211r25	2281r18	6428r3
3.	249	107r53	376r42	1014r59	447

Lesson 1.7, page 10

1. 6; 39 **2.** 9450 **3.** 427 **4.** 118990 **5.** 47
6. 670560 **7.** 6; 16

Posttest, page 11

	a	b	c	d	e
1.	173	1573	14048	212666	1172870
2.	84	443	1604	15991	377917
3.	2992	70176	7968	17232	37944
4.	7553	360240	282576	708876	1288686
5.	12r1	222r3	1917r1	24r8	13r5
6.	94r5	278r16	111r21	406r85	351

Posttest, page 12

7. 1626 **8.** 792 **9.** 11; 17 **10.** 1635
11. 3650 **12.** 2851

Chapter 2

Pretest, page 13

	a	b	c	d
1.	$4\frac{11}{12}$	$5\frac{9}{14}$	$6\frac{19}{24}$	$4\frac{18}{35}$
2.	$4\frac{1}{12}$	$\frac{1}{8}$	$2\frac{1}{2}$	$2\frac{1}{14}$
3.	$\frac{1}{8}$	$\frac{10}{21}$	$\frac{2}{9}$	$\frac{21}{320}$
4.	$3\frac{5}{24}$	$6\frac{7}{8}$	$6\frac{2}{7}$	$2\frac{1}{6}$
5.	$3\frac{9}{11}$	$\frac{23}{42}$	$2\frac{1}{2}$	$\frac{16}{19}$

Pretest, page 14

6. $10\frac{1}{24}$ **7.** $26\frac{1}{6}$ **8.** $6\frac{1}{4}$ **9.** $6\frac{1}{2}$ **10.** $21\frac{2}{3}$ **11.** $9\frac{7}{24}$

Lesson 2.1, page 15

1. 1, 2, 7, 14
1, 3, 7, 21; 1, 7; 7
2. 1, 2, 3, 4, 6, 12
1, 2, 4, 5, 10, 20; 1, 2, 4; 4
3. 1, 2, 5, 10
1, 2, 3, 4, 6, 12; 1, 2; 2
4. 1, 2, 3, 4, 6, 8, 12, 24
1, 2, 3, 4, 6, 9, 12, 18, 36; 1, 2, 3, 4, 6, 12; 12
5. 1, 3, 9
1, 3, 5, 15; 1, 3; 3
6. 1, 2, 3, 6
1, 2, 4, 8; 1, 2; 2
7. 1, 2, 3, 6, 9, 18
1, 2, 4, 5, 10, 20; 1, 2; 2

Grade 7 Answers

Lesson 2.2, page 16

	a	b	c
1.	$\frac{9}{10}$	$3\frac{3}{4}$	$\frac{5}{19}$
2.	$\frac{1}{2}$	$\frac{9}{10}$	$9\frac{2}{3}$
3.	$\frac{3}{4}$	$7\frac{1}{3}$	$\frac{3}{4}$
4.	$8\frac{3}{4}$	$6\frac{1}{4}$	$4\frac{5}{7}$
5.	$4\frac{1}{5}$	$\frac{1}{2}$	$2\frac{3}{13}$

Lesson 2.3, page 17

	a	b
1.	$\frac{5}{30}$ and $\frac{12}{30}$	$\frac{9}{24}$ and $\frac{8}{24}$
2.	$\frac{21}{28}$ and $\frac{4}{28}$	$\frac{2}{12}$ and $\frac{9}{12}$
3.	$\frac{4}{8}$ and $\frac{5}{8}$	$\frac{5}{20}$ and $\frac{6}{20}$
4.	$\frac{9}{45}$ and $\frac{20}{45}$	$\frac{8}{20}$ and $\frac{5}{20}$
5.	$\frac{5}{15}$ and $\frac{9}{15}$	$\frac{3}{18}$ and $\frac{4}{18}$

Lesson 2.4, page 18

	a	b	c	d
1.	$\frac{29}{8}$	$\frac{9}{1}$	$\frac{17}{7}$	$\frac{11}{2}$
2.	$\frac{9}{8}$	$\frac{33}{4}$	$\frac{14}{1}$	$\frac{23}{6}$
3.	$\frac{13}{3}$	$\frac{43}{9}$	$\frac{7}{5}$	$\frac{47}{1}$
4.	$3\frac{1}{3}$	$2\frac{7}{8}$	$1\frac{1}{2}$	$5\frac{4}{7}$
5.	$3\frac{3}{4}$	$5\frac{2}{3}$	$1\frac{1}{2}$	$6\frac{2}{3}$
6.	$1\frac{8}{11}$	$4\frac{1}{5}$	$9\frac{2}{5}$	$4\frac{8}{11}$

Lesson 2.5, page 19

	a	b	c	d
1.	$1\frac{3}{8}$	$\frac{5}{6}$	$1\frac{3}{20}$	$\frac{1}{2}$
2.	$1\frac{7}{40}$	$\frac{4}{5}$	$\frac{11}{12}$	$1\frac{9}{20}$
3.	$\frac{5}{8}$	$\frac{29}{35}$	$1\frac{1}{56}$	$\frac{13}{15}$
4.	$\frac{7}{20}$	$\frac{1}{5}$	$\frac{3}{8}$	$\frac{7}{15}$
5.	$\frac{1}{2}$	$\frac{7}{15}$	$\frac{11}{24}$	$\frac{1}{5}$
6.	$\frac{1}{12}$	$\frac{1}{18}$	$\frac{1}{6}$	$\frac{41}{99}$

Lesson 2.6, page 20

	a	b	c	d
1.	$3\frac{7}{12}$	$10\frac{7}{8}$	$6\frac{13}{21}$	$4\frac{7}{10}$
2.	$7\frac{7}{9}$	$2\frac{33}{40}$	$5\frac{19}{24}$	$3\frac{22}{35}$
3.	$5\frac{3}{4}$	$4\frac{7}{18}$	$4\frac{47}{70}$	$6\frac{5}{6}$
4.	$1\frac{11}{72}$	$1\frac{11}{12}$	$\frac{3}{4}$	$1\frac{43}{56}$
5.	$1\frac{49}{88}$	$4\frac{4}{15}$	$2\frac{5}{6}$	$1\frac{23}{42}$
6.	$2\frac{1}{9}$	$1\frac{9}{20}$	$2\frac{17}{24}$	$1\frac{3}{8}$

Lesson 2.7, page 21

1. $\frac{3}{4}$ **2.** $13\frac{31}{40}$ **3.** $9\frac{7}{12}$ **4.** $\frac{3}{4}$ **5.** $3\frac{31}{56}$; $1\frac{17}{56}$ **6.** $2\frac{11}{24}$

Lesson 2.8, page 22

	a	b	c	d
1.	$\frac{3}{8}$	$\frac{8}{15}$	$\frac{9}{16}$	$\frac{1}{10}$
2.	$\frac{21}{40}$	$\frac{1}{5}$	$\frac{3}{35}$	$\frac{6}{25}$
3.	$\frac{15}{64}$	$\frac{1}{3}$	$\frac{5}{9}$	$\frac{4}{21}$
4.	$\frac{1}{9}$	$\frac{1}{5}$	$\frac{16}{105}$	$\frac{5}{48}$
5.	$\frac{3}{32}$	$\frac{1}{8}$	$\frac{3}{14}$	$\frac{1}{12}$
6.	$\frac{3}{35}$	$\frac{1}{30}$	$\frac{7}{60}$	$\frac{3}{8}$

Lesson 2.9, page 23

	a	b	c
1.	$3\frac{6}{7}$	$7\frac{1}{2}$	$3\frac{11}{18}$
2.	$13\frac{1}{2}$	$6\frac{11}{24}$	$2\frac{6}{7}$
3.	$31\frac{1}{2}$	$17\frac{1}{2}$	$94\frac{7}{8}$
4.	$2\frac{2}{9}$	$3\frac{25}{48}$	$4\frac{1}{2}$
5.	$1\frac{11}{16}$	$3\frac{1}{18}$	$3\frac{2}{3}$
6.	$12\frac{4}{7}$	$1\frac{2}{3}$	$\frac{35}{36}$

Lesson 2.10, page 24

	a	b	c	d	e	f
1.	$\frac{3}{2}$	$\frac{8}{9}$	$\frac{2}{7}$	$\frac{4}{13}$	$\frac{12}{9}$	$\frac{5}{2}$
2.	$\frac{8}{7}$	$\frac{3}{10}$	$\frac{5}{8}$	$\frac{1}{12}$	$\frac{7}{3}$	2
3.	10	$\frac{5}{3}$	$\frac{7}{15}$	$\frac{11}{3}$	$\frac{8}{19}$	$\frac{1}{4}$
4.	$\frac{8}{3}$	$\frac{7}{2}$	$\frac{9}{4}$	$\frac{4}{7}$	$\frac{12}{7}$	$\frac{14}{3}$
5.	$\frac{17}{2}$	15	$\frac{20}{13}$	$\frac{9}{20}$	$\frac{1}{3}$	$\frac{7}{25}$
6.	$\frac{1}{5}$	$\frac{2}{5}$	$\frac{5}{3}$	$\frac{12}{13}$	$\frac{11}{14}$	$\frac{16}{3}$
7.	$\frac{7}{17}$	$\frac{1}{20}$	$\frac{9}{8}$	$\frac{16}{53}$	$\frac{8}{17}$	16

Lesson 2.11, page 25

	a	b	c	d
1.	$5\frac{1}{4}$	$2\frac{8}{15}$	$1\frac{1}{2}$	$21\frac{1}{3}$
2.	$11\frac{2}{3}$	$1\frac{9}{16}$	$2\frac{6}{7}$	$\frac{3}{5}$
3.	$11\frac{1}{4}$	$\frac{3}{5}$	$3\frac{1}{3}$	$2\frac{1}{6}$
4.	10	$10\frac{15}{16}$	51	98
5.	$2\frac{1}{45}$	$1\frac{47}{63}$	$\frac{4}{5}$	$\frac{14}{15}$

Lesson 2.11, page 26

	a	b	c	d
1.	$2\frac{1}{2}$	$1\frac{81}{119}$	$1\frac{15}{26}$	$1\frac{3}{4}$
2.	$\frac{8}{17}$	$9\frac{3}{4}$	6	$\frac{14}{15}$
3.	$2\frac{2}{11}$	$1\frac{11}{12}$	$1\frac{19}{22}$	30

4.	$1\frac{20}{33}$	28	$\frac{9}{10}$	$5\frac{5}{7}$
5.	$6\frac{1}{14}$	$\frac{17}{22}$	$1\frac{11}{16}$	$2\frac{5}{14}$
6.	$\frac{7}{24}$	30	$2\frac{14}{15}$	$3\frac{13}{15}$

Lesson 2.12, page 27

	a	b	c	d
1.	$\frac{1}{8}$	$\frac{14}{39}$	$\frac{12}{35}$	$\frac{1}{8}$
2.	$\frac{5}{24}$	$\frac{10}{27}$	$\frac{5}{168}$	$\frac{1}{5}$
3.	$\frac{7}{10}$	$1\frac{29}{56}$	$1\frac{1}{8}$	$4\frac{41}{96}$
4.	$\frac{5}{6}$	$3\frac{19}{24}$	$12\frac{6}{7}$	$11\frac{47}{56}$
5.	$2\frac{1}{10}$	$1\frac{1}{2}$	$1\frac{1}{24}$	$8\frac{1}{3}$
6.	4	$5\frac{1}{4}$	$\frac{104}{119}$	$1\frac{5}{8}$
7.	$1\frac{29}{45}$	$1\frac{43}{78}$	$\frac{1}{5}$	$2\frac{4}{27}$

Lesson 2.13, page 28

1. $\frac{2}{3}$ **2.** $14\frac{7}{12}$ **3.** 5 **4.** $\frac{1}{4}$ **5.** $3\frac{1}{3}$ **6.** $14\frac{5}{8}$
7. $74\frac{2}{3}$

Posttest, page 29

	a	b	c	d
1.	$2\frac{5}{56}$	$5\frac{7}{12}$	$4\frac{17}{24}$	$7\frac{1}{8}$
2.	$3\frac{5}{12}$	$\frac{3}{8}$	$2\frac{31}{70}$	$2\frac{5}{12}$
3.	$\frac{3}{10}$	$\frac{3}{14}$	$\frac{5}{27}$	$\frac{1}{48}$
4.	$2\frac{3}{56}$	$3\frac{15}{28}$	$6\frac{13}{18}$	$10\frac{1}{2}$
5.	$2\frac{55}{144}$	$\frac{11}{24}$	$3\frac{13}{14}$	6

Posttest, page 30

6. $2\frac{1}{24}$ **7.** $3\frac{1}{4}$ **8.** 6; $\frac{3}{7}$ **9.** $1\frac{1}{2}$ **10.** $5\frac{7}{12}$ **11.** $13\frac{3}{4}$

Chapter 3

Pretest, page 31

	a	b	c	d
1.	8.94	27.763	9.244	9.1360
2.	2.8	13.103	12.764	3.9133
3.	6.24	7.038	2.52604	8.74698
4.	0.52	.305	.834	3.4187
5.	4	2400	38.6	12000
6.	4.2	3.11	8.6	14.4

Pretest, page 32

7. 2.45 **8.** 353.8 **9.** $3.02 **10.** $12.38
11. 91.75 **12.** 183.875

Lesson 3.1, page 33

	a	b	c
1.	1.6	2.25	0.240
2.	2.5	5.24	2.046
3.	5.8	1.35	6.628
4.	6.2	2.90	3.720
5.	3.7420	4.1120	1.5148
6.	$\frac{3}{10}$	$1\frac{3}{5}$	$3\frac{7}{10}$
7.	$\frac{3}{4}$	$5\frac{43}{50}$	$1\frac{13}{100}$
8.	$\frac{387}{1000}$	$2\frac{147}{250}$	$3\frac{9}{100}$
9.	$\frac{5329}{10000}$	$6\frac{4273}{10000}$	$5\frac{233}{400}$

Lesson 3.2, page 34

	a	b	c	d	e
1.	1.1	4.0	4.3	7.7	13.3
2.	0.91	3.45	3.57	7.62	1.94
3.	0.499	4.327	6.237	5.513	9.717
4.	4.245	2.314	22.427	3.8600	7.8239
5.	5.7047	14.0272	65.437	3.281	7.3883
6.	4.938	3.8366	6.3361	7.417	4.6694

Lesson 3.3, page 35

	a	b	c	d	e
1.	0.5	0.88	0.94	2.181	2.881
2.	0.16	0.067	1.68	0.696	0.801
3.	0.114	1.873	20.567	2.069	39.329
4.	8.295	17.513	26.44	6.863	0.281
5.	0.173	2.813	29.22	2.14	2.693
6.	46.407	0.873	2.62	1.029	5.558

Lesson 3.4, page 36

1. 0.347 **2.** $25.12 **3.** $4.02 **4.** 115.84
5. $22.42 **6.** 1.433 **7.** 0.705

Lesson 3.5, page 37

	a	b	c	d	e
1.	3.6	2.44	6.96	3.636	65.4
2.	5.55	17.472	2.8721	2.6334	4.48100
3.	5.566	1.4602	30.102	5.139	4.41234
4.	18.21	2.3304	2.12403	3.48	44.5278

Lesson 3.6, page 38

	a	b	c	d
1.	0.12	3.8	0.35	3.01
2.	0.909	0.411	5.008	0.6774
3.	0.0032	0.77	0.807	0.514
4.	0.116	0.902	0.0211	1.0907

Grade 7 Answers

Lesson 3.7, page 39

	a	b	c	d
1.	140	50	600	100
2.	30	4	400	7000
3.	5	200	1500	2000
4.	120	1600	44000	172000

Lesson 3.8, page 40

	a	b	c	d
1.	1520	12	4.4	3.75
2.	3.9	63	36.5	6.282
3.	31.55	243	6.335	4.225
4.	0.65	21.7	17.5	1.4

Lesson 3.9, page 41

	a	b	c	d
1.	0.26	11.362	1.8855	6.34524
2.	53.94	0.30702	14.0196	0.71706
3.	0.12	0.91	0.09	0.006
4.	2.06	4.009	2.711	0.6015
5.	90	30	90	300
6.	36	1.3	33.8	23.7
7.	60000	3.8	2.55	37

Lesson 3.10, page 42

1. $14.95 **2.** 14.5 **3.** 17.5 **4.** 127.75
5. $64.93 **6.** 0.806 **7.** 0.88

Posttest, page 43

	a	b	c	d
1.	1.13	79.41	11.845	57.7984
2.	10.8363	32.2458	2.9	26.29
3.	26.983	5.092	2.414	4.2634
4.	2.48	8.6315	47.0352	4.43597
5.	1.36	1.793	260	475
6.	18.91	6	0.39	13.9

Posttest, page 44

7. $36.65 **8.** 9 **9.** 0.238 **10.** $3.53 **11.** 8.8
12. 29.16

Chapter 4

Pretest, page 45

	a	b	c
1.	82%	35%	60%
2.	350%	725%	30%
3.	0.2	0.38	1.27
4.	0.125	0.076	0.2225
5.	$\frac{1}{4}$	$\frac{2}{5}$	$3\frac{1}{5}$
6.	1.6	14	2.4
7.	99	0.04	60
8.	32	200	35
9.	17.5	4	30
10.	25%	80%	200%
11.	15%	2%	20%

Pretest, page 46

12. $4.31 **13.** $763.50 **14.** $37.40 **15.** $108.75
16. $2.34 **17.** $0.48

Lesson 4.1, page 47

1.	$\frac{7}{100}$	0.07
2.	$\frac{13}{100}$	0.13
3.	$\frac{12}{25}$	0.48
4.	$\frac{71}{100}$	0.71
5.	$\frac{27}{100}$	0.27
6.	$\frac{1}{50}$	0.02
7.	$\frac{3}{20}$	0.15
8.	$\frac{39}{100}$	0.39
9.	$\frac{1}{10}$	0.10
10.	$\frac{31}{50}$	0.62
11.	$\frac{3}{4}$	0.75
12.	$\frac{97}{100}$	0.97
13.	$\frac{53}{100}$	0.53
14.	$\frac{41}{50}$	0.82

Lesson 4.2, page 48

	a	b	c
1.	$13\% < \frac{2}{5}$	$0.35 > \frac{1}{8}$	$\frac{1}{4} = 0.25$
2.	$87\% > 0.79$	$18 > 18\%$	$\frac{1}{2} > 0.42$
3.	$\frac{9}{10} > 9\%$	$40\% < \frac{4}{5}$	$0.72 > \frac{2}{3}$
4.	$0.82 = \frac{41}{50}$	$63\% > \frac{1}{2}$	$14\% > 0.014$
5.	$\frac{1}{3} < 50\%$	$\frac{4}{5} = 80\%$	$0.07 < \frac{1}{10}$
6.	$\frac{250}{100} = 2.5$	$0.25 < \frac{1}{3}$	$318 > 3.18\%$
7.	$50\% < \frac{2}{3}$	$93\% = 0.93$	$22\% < \frac{1}{4}$
8.	$0.67 > \frac{3}{5}$	$\frac{1}{2} > 20\%$	$642\% = 6.42$
9.	$0.08 < 80\%$	$50\% < \frac{3}{4}$	$\frac{1}{2} > 0.050$
10.	$\frac{2}{5} < 2.5$	$70\% = \frac{7}{10}$	$\frac{147}{100} > 14\%$
11.	$\frac{45}{100} < 55\%$	$1238\% = 12.38$	$16\frac{2}{5} > 16.25$
12.	$3.75 = 375\%$	$0.15 < \frac{1}{5}$	$7.5 > \frac{3}{4}$
13.	$\frac{13}{25} > 49\%$	$0.45 > \frac{7}{20}$	$3\% = 0.03$
14.	$25\% > \frac{11}{50}$	$12\frac{1}{5} = 12.2$	$18\% < \frac{1}{4}$

Grade 7 Answers

Lesson 4.3, page 49

	a	b
1.	13%, $\frac{1}{4}$, $\frac{1}{3}$, 0.35	0.02, 0.34, 72%, $\frac{3}{4}$
2.	0.25, $\frac{1}{3}$, $\frac{2}{5}$,45%	1%, $\frac{1}{10}$, $\frac{11}{100}$, 0.15
3.	$\frac{14}{100}$, $\frac{14}{25}$, 143%, 14.5	0.55, $\frac{3}{5}$, 0.63, 68%
4.	$3\frac{1}{2}$, 320%, 35%, $\frac{3}{100}$	0.5, 0.4, 30%, $\frac{1}{4}$, $\frac{1}{5}$
5.	$\frac{7}{8}$, $\frac{3}{4}$, 0.625, 60%	1.7, 17%, $\frac{1}{7}$, 0.017
6.	4.1, 406%, $\frac{4}{5}$, $\frac{40}{100}$	$5\frac{2}{5}$, $\frac{16}{5}$, 32%, 16%

Lesson 4.4, page 50

	a	b	c	d
1.	$\frac{3}{4}$	28	32	$\frac{49}{50}$
2.	$\frac{14}{25}$	$\frac{12}{25}$	240	930
3.	62	45	$\frac{3}{25}$	$4\frac{1}{4}$
4.	760	$\frac{3}{20}$	225	$\frac{31}{100}$
5.	$\frac{3}{5}$	20	50	$\frac{18}{25}$
6.	375	$1\frac{7}{20}$	$\frac{2}{5}$	56
7.	85	$62\frac{1}{2}$	$\frac{13}{20}$	$\frac{1}{10}$
8.	$\frac{1}{20}$	1016	$\frac{1}{2}$	335

Lesson 4.5, page 51

	a	b	c
1.	0.85	147	0.17
2.	38	0.0832	69
3.	0.27	5	0.021
4.	150	0.15	42.6
5.	0.335	65	0.0925
6.	3.9	0.526	485
7.	0.055	22.5	0.0625
8.	0.5	5.25	70
9.	0.001	10	6320

Lesson 4.5, page 52

	a	b	c
1.	0.2525	0.035	0.027
2.	0.1505	0.632	0.1268
3.	0.0575	0.113	0.4275
4.	0.175	0.224	0.7545
5.	0.096	0.1808	0.5225
6.	0.0338	0.391	0.8348
7.	0.152	0.7916	0.2775
8.	0.3895	0.089	0.9372
9.	0.4866	0.034	0.817
10.	0.505	0.145	0.4575

Lesson 4.6, page 53

	a	b	c
1.	12.5	19.5	19.25
2.	14.6	1.6	5.64
3.	3.5	41.85	1.875
4.	3.12	0.88	82.4
5.	1.24	0.36	3.822
6.	2.94	3.48	33.75
7.	0.15	3.3	50.4
8.	8	118.75	48
9.	0.8	10.355	52.25
10.	47.25	395.5	2.45

Lesson 4.6, page 54

	a	b	c
1.	25	25	50
2.	24	200	150
3.	15	140	30
4.	40	75	80
5.	17.25	20	5
6.	20	10	5
7.	1	7.5	55
8.	12.5	25	62.5
9.	85	5	120
10.	500	12.5	100

Lesson 4.6, page 55

	a	b	c
1.	64	35	125
2.	2.5	332	40
3.	300	15	50
4.	290	200	50
5.	19.3	0.5	100
6.	50	15	25
7.	45	78	95
8.	46	56	100
9.	500	73	2
10.	342	15	20

Lesson 4.7, page 56

1. \$2.25 **2.** \$4.84 **3.** \$4.95; \$94.95 **4.** 20%
5. \$8000 **6.** 40%

Posttest, page 57

	a	b	c
1.	40	90	15
2.	42	130	1
3.	0.53	2.5	0.08
4.	0.0775	0.292	0.051
5.	$4\frac{3}{4}$	$\frac{3}{5}$	$1\frac{11}{20}$
6.	2	3.8	72
7.	112	0.3	0.008
8.	400	75	15

9.	0.5	30	50
10.	13.75	5	8
11.	20	1000	165

Posttest, page 58

12. $4.19 **13.** $3.57 **14.** $2.47 **15.** 20%
16. 15.625% **17.** $379.50

Chapter 5

Pretest, page 59

1. $31.50; $556.50
2. $30.40; $410.40
3. $85.68; $799.68
4. $87.50; $1,337.50
5. $135.00; $635.00
6. $84.50; $734.50
7. $90.20; $910.20
8. $139.50; $439.50
9. $33.75; $1,033.75
10. $50.05; $570.05
11. $1,323.00; $5,523.00
12. $267.75; $1,967.75
13. $2.00; $52.00
14. $131.25; $1,531.25
15. $4.55; $284.55

Pretest, page 60

16. $51.00; $531.00
17. $15,750.00; $35,750.00
18. $3.15; $123.15
19. $8.25; $58.25
20. $86.80; $706.80

Lesson 5.1, page 61

1. $19.50 **2.** $14.00 **3.** $16.00
4. $8.75 **5.** $17.50 **6.** $19.50
7. $16.60 **8.** $15.94 **9.** $21.75
10. $59.50 **11.** $46.00 **12.** $46.25
13. $21.82 **14.** $96.60

Lesson 5.1, page 62

1. $45.00 **2.** $26.00 **3.** $2.08 **4.** $105.00
5. $9.00 **6.** $33.10 **7.** $325.00

Lesson 5.2, page 63

1. $105.00; $605.00
2. $180.00; $930.00
3. $161.50; $586.50
4. $153.00; $753.00
5. $168.00; $518.00
6. $73.50; $773.50
7. $416.50; $1,266.50
8. $225.50; $1,250.50
9. $190.00; $990.00
10. $195.00; $1,695.00
11. $337.50; $2,587.50
12. $207.75; $1,592.75

Lesson 5.2, page 64

1. $96.25; $596.25
2. $31.50; $211.50
3. $105.30; $825.30
4. $110.50; $760.50
5. $257.40; $842.40
6. $370.00; $1,970.00
7. $5.25; $65.25
8. $136.50; $836.50
9. $519.75; $2,719.75
10. $614.25; $1,964.25
11. $276.00; $676.00
12. $607.50; $5,607.50

Lesson 5.3, page 65

1. $31.50; $731.50
2. $11.25; $511.25
3. $17.00; $867.00
4. $19.50; $1,219.50
5. $12.75; $437.75
6. $18.00; $218.00
7. $131.25; $2,631.25
8. $41.25; $3,041.25
9. $0.75; $50.75
10. $59.40; $779.40

Lesson 5.3, page 66

1. $10.00; $510.00
2. $65.25; $425.25
3. $147.00; $747.00
4. $51.75
5. $4,462.50; $19,462.50

Posttest, page 67

1. $36.00; $486.00
2. $31.50; $661.50
3. $11.00; $286.00
4. $35.73; $631.23
5. $39.60; $399.60
6. $138.60; $558.60
7. $262.50; $1,012.50
8. $56.55; $636.55
9. $182.00; $1,482.00
10. $225.25; $1,285.25
11. $57.75; $657.75
12. $177.45; $697.45

Grade 7 Answers

13. $28.05; $908.05
14. $30.00; $1,530.00
15. $5.25; $705.25

Posttest, page 68

16. $59.40; $719.40
17. $19.50; $1,219.50
18. $258.75; $1,008.75
19. $189.75; $1,109.75
20. $26.70; $916.70

Chapter 6

Pretest, page 69

	a	b	c
1.	45	1	8
2.	24	5	9
3.	10	16	1
4.	36	3	4
5.	8	11	7

Pretest, page 70

6. 160 **7.** 12 **8.** 105 **9.** 35 **10.** 56
11. 150 **12.** 72

Lesson 6.1, page 71

	a	b	c
1.	($\frac{1}{3}, \frac{2}{6}$)	$\frac{3}{8}, \frac{1}{4}$	($\frac{3}{5}, \frac{9}{15}$)
2.	($\frac{3}{4}, \frac{9}{12}$)	($\frac{1}{2}, \frac{4}{8}$)	($\frac{5}{6}, \frac{15}{18}$)
3.	$\frac{5}{8}, \frac{4}{7}$	$\frac{1}{2}, \frac{1}{4}$	($\frac{4}{3}, \frac{16}{12}$)
4.	($\frac{6}{18}, \frac{2}{6}$)	($\frac{3}{25}, \frac{6}{50}$)	$\frac{1}{8}, \frac{2}{10}$
5.	$\frac{1}{4}, \frac{2}{4}$	($\frac{5}{10}, \frac{3}{6}$)	($\frac{4}{24}, \frac{7}{42}$)
6.	$\frac{3}{5}, \frac{5}{3}$	($\frac{7}{8}, \frac{21}{24}$)	$\frac{8}{23}, \frac{9}{46}$
7.	($\frac{7}{4}, \frac{28}{16}$)	($\frac{3}{9}, \frac{1}{3}$)	$\frac{16}{20}, \frac{9}{10}$
8.	$\frac{8}{100}, \frac{80}{50}$	$\frac{8}{12}, \frac{10}{14}$	($\frac{15}{20}, \frac{3}{4}$)
9.	$\frac{9}{2}, \frac{12}{3}$	($\frac{6}{3}, \frac{8}{4}$)	($\frac{1}{3}, \frac{11}{33}$)
10.	($\frac{12}{7}, \frac{36}{21}$)	$\frac{10}{12}, \frac{15}{20}$	$\frac{3}{4}, \frac{9}{16}$

Lesson 6.2, page 72

	a	b	c
1.	8	16	1
2.	9	1	10
3.	21	2	21
4.	64	11	15
5.	15	36	10

Lesson 6.3, page 73

	a	b	c
1.	1	9	8
2.	4	16	5
3.	8	6	6
4.	49	5	10
5.	70	9	10

Lesson 6.4, page 74

1. 64 **2.** 30 **3.** 36 **4.** 7 **5.** 36 **6.** 10; 69

Lesson 6.5, page 75

1. 440 **2.** 8 **3.** 32 **4.** 36

Lesson 6.6, page 76

1. 14 **2.** 3 **3.** 12 **4.** 3 **5.** 8 **6.** $10 **7.** 315

Posttest, page 77

	a	b	c
1.	9	2	24
2.	4	25	112
3.	8	6	72
4.	1	3	25
5.	30	16	4

Posttest, page 78

6. 96 **7.** 72 **8.** 39 **9.** 18 **10.** 36
11. 32 **12.** 98

Mid-Test

Page 79

	a	b	c	d
1.	525	2210	$13\frac{1}{6}$	$6\frac{11}{40}$
2.	274	361	$2\frac{35}{36}$	$3\frac{1}{14}$
3.	15400	2808	58378	243852
4.	$\frac{5}{24}$	$\frac{1}{4}$	$1\frac{13}{63}$	$\frac{1}{5}$
5.	9	20r4	118r11	169
6.	$1\frac{1}{6}$	$4\frac{1}{5}$	$5\frac{1}{3}$	$2\frac{10}{27}$

Page 80

	a	b	c	d
7.	5355	389023	7.542	34.9562
8.	578441	24092	26.196	6.321
9.	2168.2	1.68	9.1182	289.556
10.	39.2	2368	63.1935	550.68
11.	4	1200	0.8	0.708
12.	5.2	6.15	7.3	3.5

Page 81

	a	b	c
13.	15%	80%	28%
14.	0.3	0.7225	3.46
15.	$\frac{3}{4}$	$\frac{1}{5}$	$1\frac{2}{5}$
16.	2.7	1.2	19.8
17.	82	3	80

18.	25%	4%	95%

19. $93.60; $813.60
20. $96.25; $596.25
21. $1.80; $61.80
22. $315.00; $795.00

Page 82

23. 70 **24.** $60.75; $510.75 **25.** 7
26. $4.05; $184.05 **27.** $384 **28.** $139.50; 18%

Chapter 7

Pretest, page 83

	a	b	c
1.	42	7480	13200
2.	30	27	$1\frac{1}{8}$
3.	50	87	5600
4.	4.575	5 ft. 9 in.	1512
5.	5.5	13	5.125
6.	2.25	53	13 qt. 1 pt.
7.	86	12	22 pt.
8.	9 pt. 1 c.	3 gal. 1 qt.	22 qt.
9.	1.5	1.2	88
10.	12500	208	0.75
11.	3.1	0.75	5200
12.	1 lb. 2 oz.	2 lb. 8 oz.	4
13.	330	$6\frac{1}{3}$	900
14.	4.5	1.2	8 days 12 hr.
15.	9 min. 20 sec.	78	1380
16.	3600	0.75	900

Pretest, page 84

17. English: 7 hr. 23 min. Science: 8 hr. 47 min.
History: 7 hr. 54 min. Spanish: 7 hr. 18 min.
Math: 6 hr. 22 min. Total: 1 day 13 hr. 44 min.
18. 228 oz.; 14.25 lb.
19. 28.5 qt.; 7.125 gal.
20. 3 yd. 1 ft. 6 in.
21. 1.9 mi.

Lesson 7.1, page 85

	a	b	c
1.	51	42240	3
2.	7.8	14960	59
3.	120	37	21120
4.	7222	161	12672
5.	9 yd. 4 in.	73216	12.5
6.	772.8	199584	10871

7. 440 **8.** 200 **9.** 2816 yd.; 8448 ft.

Lesson 7.2, page 86

	a	b	c
1.	6.5	10	14
2.	4.5	9	21.6
3.	24	34	2 gal. 3 qt.
4.	8	84	13 pt. 1 c.
5.	4.75	19	4 gal. 1 pt.

6. 8 **7.** 7 **8.** 168 qt.; 336 pt.

Lesson 7.3, page 87

1. 18 c.; 4.5 qt.; 1.125 gal.
2. 3520 yd.; 10560 ft.; 2 mi.
3. 4 ft. 10 in.; 4 ft. 9 in.; 4 ft. 6 in.; Bill
4. 1.4375 **5.** 6 pt.; 12 c.

Lesson 7.4, page 88

	a	b	c
1.	7000 lb.	4.5 lb.	12 oz.
2.	4.5 T.	2 T.	$26\frac{7}{8}$
3.	5 T. 689 lb.	52 oz.	1.9 T.
4.	158 oz.	12.35 T.	13600 lb.
5.	32 lb. 7 oz.	104 oz.	26000 lb.

6. 1.6 T. **7.** 204.8 oz. **8.** 108 oz.; 6.75 lb.

Lesson 7.5, page 89

	a	b	c
1.	0.2 hr.	15 min.	210 min.
2.	192 hr.	420 sec.	3.5 days
3.	5 hr. 20 min.	315 min.	6.6 min.
4.	6 days 6 hr.	$\frac{1}{2}$ hr.	390 min.
5.	1008 hr.	195 min.	225 sec.

6. 1.6 min. **7.** 1.5 hr. **8.** 9 days; 12 hr.

Lesson 7.6, page 90

1. 5 min. 24 sec.; 5 min. 48 sec.; 5 min. 22 sec.; Will
2. 11.25 lb.
3. 4.125 gal.; 33 pt.; 66 c.
4. 29000 lb. **5.** 5.75 days **6.** 67.2 oz.

Posttest, page 91

	a	b	c
1.	24 yd.	1.5 ft.	2112 yd.
2.	37.5 ft.	3.75 mi.	20 yd. 2 ft.
3.	80 in.	114 ft.	2.25 mi.
4.	5820 yd.	390 in.	27 yd. 2 ft.
5.	8.5 qt.	3 pt.	10.25 gal.
6.	14 c.	11 qt.	53 c.
7.	6 pt. 1 c.	1.75 gal.	4 gal.
8.	4.25 qt.	26 pt.	19 qt.
9.	1.75 lb.	7000 lb.	40 oz.
10.	4.1 T.	179 oz.	3.375 lb.
11.	3 lb. 8 oz.	14500 lb.	2 lb.

12.	73.6 oz.	5500 lb.	84 oz.
13.	84 hr.	263 min.	375 sec.
14.	3.5 min.	3 days 16 hr.	5.25 hr.
15.	0.75 hr.	192 sec.	0.5 days
16.	402 sec.	8 days 18 hr.	390 min.

Posttest, page 92

17. 3 T. 820 lb. **18.** 2640 yd.; 7920 ft.
19. 180 qt.; 720 c. **20.** 36 c.; 9 qt.; 2.25 gal.
21. 2 hr. 15 min. **22.** 666 in.; 55 ft. 6 in.

Chapter 8

Pretest, page 93

	a	b
1.	4800 m	120 cm
2.	700 mm	2.475 km
3.	30 mm	0.682 m
4.	80.4 cm	13100 m
5.	5.2 m	0.480 km
6.	2400 mg	6.8 MT
7.	12000 g	0.46 g
8.	4860 kg	2700 g
9.	0.743 kg	800 mg
10.	0.375 MT	2.162 g
11.	710 L	0.56 L
12.	0.087 kL	8940 mL
13.	1.720 kL	0.346 L
14.	2.635 L	500000 L
15.	630 mL	0.5 kL

Pretest, page 94

16. 4 cans **17.** 1130 g **18.** 4.458 km
19. 14.7 cm **20.** 4.557 kL **21.** 25
22. 0.723 kg; 723000 mg

Lesson 8.1, page 95

	a	b	c
1.	3500 m	400 cm	1100 mm
2.	2.5 km	5.2 m	130 mm
3.	40 m	500000 mm	2.3 m
4.	327 cm	0.0016 km	1800 cm
5.	7.2 m	86 cm	750 m

6. 136 mm **7.** 11.32 km

Lesson 8.2, page 96

	a	b
1.	2500 L	17000 mL
2.	0.560 kL	820 mL
3.	0.427 L	1340 L
4.	1.826 kL	0.038 L
5.	7480 mL	0.075 kL

6. 50 **7.** 3.68 kL

Lesson 8.3, page 97

	a	b
1.	750 g	3.41 MT
2.	0.827 kg	8450 kg
3.	6200 mg	1300 g
4.	0.25 MT	0.63 g
5.	9000 g	800 mg

6. 2.75 kg; 2750 g **7.** 1.316 MT

Lesson 8.4, page 98

1. 3225 m; 3.225 km **2.** 270 **3.** 3600 kg
4. 1.93 m **5.** 1 bottle **6.** 57.12 g
7. 1 m 55 cm 4 mm; 1 m 54 cm 8 mm; Pablo

Posttest, page 99

	a	b
1.	6.23 m	0.346 km
2.	21.1 cm	8700 m
3.	13 mm	0.512 m
4.	200 mm	3.864 km
5.	3600 m	882 cm
6.	0.422 MT	5.847 g
7.	0.394 kg	240 mg
8.	2910 kg	3120 g
9.	8200 g	0.643 g
10.	9600 mg	3.425 MT
11.	510 mL	0.832 kL
12.	6.235 L	26000L
13.	4.807 kL	0.918L
14.	0.036 kL	6470 mL
15.	680 L	0.39 L

Posttest, page 100

16. 50 **17.** 1 giant box **18.** 50 **19.** 3.5
20. 1.2 kL **21.** 2.844 km **22.** 9.945 L

Chapter 9

Pretest, page 101

1.

Stem	Leaves
6	6 7 8 8 9
7	2 3 3 3 4 9
8	1 2 2 5

Key: 6 | 7 = 67

Grade 7 Answers

2.

Temperature	Frequency	Cumulative Frequency	Relative Frequency
66–70	5	5	33.33%
71–75	5	10	33.33%
76–80	1	11	6.67%
81–85	4	15	26.67%

3.

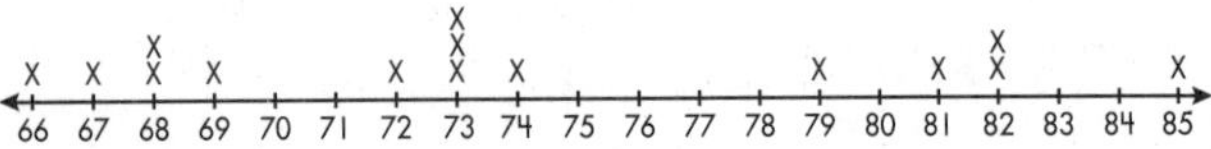

4.

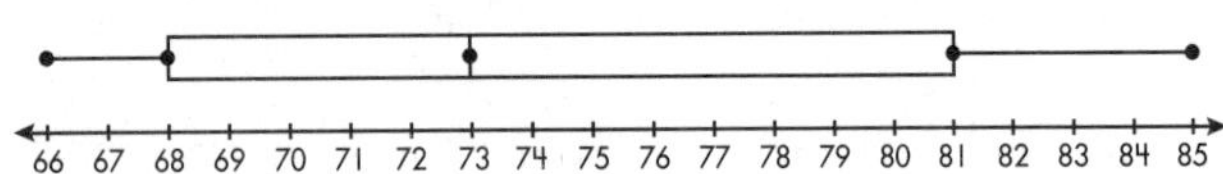

	a	b
5.	74.1	19
	73	85
	73	66

Pretest, page 102

6.

Thin crust — mushroom, onion, pepperoni, sausage

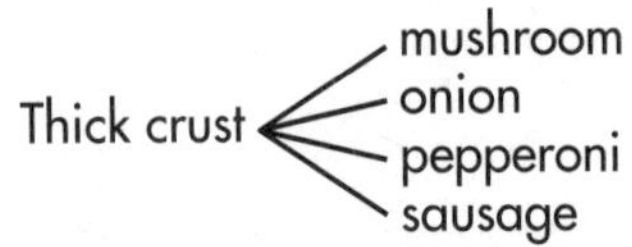

7. 8 **8.** $\frac{1}{2}$ **9.** $\frac{1}{4}$ **10.** $\frac{1}{8}$ **11.** Saturday and Sunday

12. Thursday **13.** 4 **14.** 90°

15. **Day People Go Grocery Shopping**

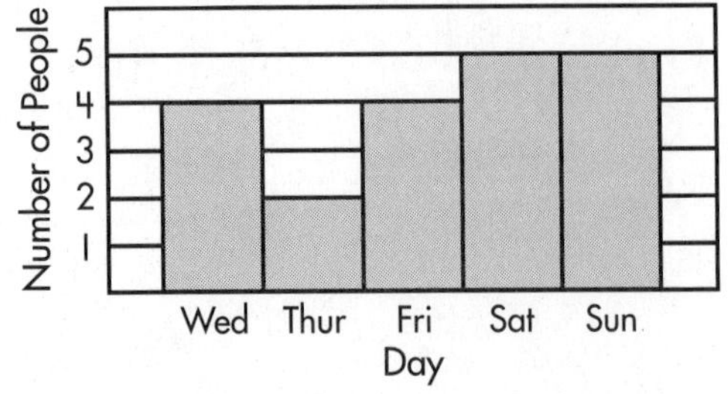

Lesson 9.1, page 103

1. 85 **2.** 42; 43 **3.** 6 **4.** 11 **5.** 1
6. 6 **7.** cat **8.** fish **9.** 10

Lesson 9.2, page 104

1. 11 **2.** 1–5; 21–25; 1 **3.** 11–15 **4.** 2
5. Jan. **6.** $11\frac{1}{2}$ in. **7.** $3\frac{1}{2}$ in. **8.** 2 in.

Lesson 9.3, page 105

1. 36 **2.** 18 **3.** 9 **4.** 2 **5.** 4, 8 **6.** 1, 3
7. strikeouts **8.** 1

Lesson 9.4, page 106

1. bubblegum **2.** 40 **3.** 100 **4.** fruit
5. cinnamon and fruit **6.** 120 **7.** 36°
8. 90° **9.** 108°

Lesson 9.5, page 107

1.

15	16	17	18	18	20	21	22	23	24
75	70	75	65	80	75	80	85	80	85

2. negative; no relationship; positive

3.

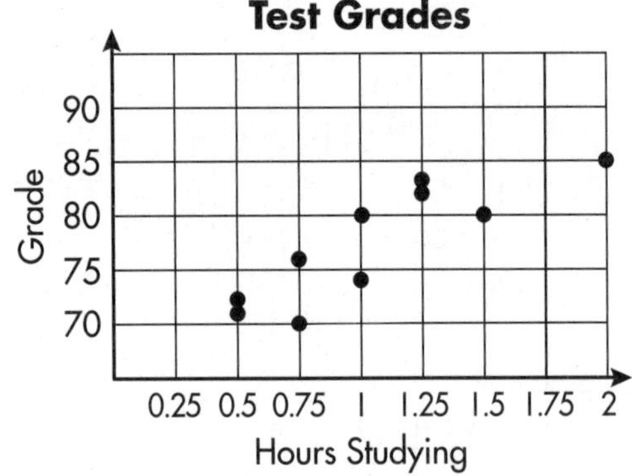

Note: student answers may vary depending on intervals for axis labels.

Lesson 9.6, page 108

	a	b
1.	8	37.1
	9	42.15
	9	23.1
	10	33.6
2.	174.6	516.9
	171	546.25
	171	349
	92	715

Grade 7 Answers

Lesson 9.7, page 109

1.

a

Stem	Leaves
1	2 4 6 7 7 8
2	0 1 2 4
3	0 1 3 5

Key: 1 | 2 = 12

b

Stem	Leaves
12	0 2 2
13	0 1 2 3 5 5
14	2 3 8

Key: 12 | 0 = 120

2.

Stem	Leaves
2	1 2
3	2 3
4	5 6
5	1
6	5

Key: 2 | 1 = 21

Stem	Leaves
7	3 8
8	2 6
9	3 5
10	9 9
11	2

Key: 7 | 3 = 73

3.

Stem	Leaves
12	8
13	5 7
14	6
15	0 2
16	4 7

Key: 12 | 8 = 128

Stem	Leaves
32	7 9
33	9
34	2 6 6
35	1
36	8

Key: 32 | 7 = 327

Lesson 9.8, page 110

	Frequency	Cumulative Frequency	Relative Frequency
1.	3	3	15%
	3	6	15%
	2	8	10%
	4	12	20%
	1	13	5%
	1	14	5%
	2	16	10%
	4	20	20%

2. 4 **3.** 1 **4.** 8 **5.** 7 **6.** 20% **7.** 15%

Lesson 9.9, page 111

1. 15 **2.** 1; 9 **3.** 5 **4.** 9 **5.** 19 **6.** $1\frac{1}{2}$; 3
7. 12 **8.** 0 **9.** 2 or more

Lesson 9.10, page 112

1. 8 **2.** 5; 13 **3.** 63 **4.** 25% **5.** 11 **6.** 18
7. 25% **8.** 22 **9.** 41

Lesson 9.11, page 113

1.

Lemonade — small, medium, large, jumbo
Fruit Punch — small, medium, large, jumbo
Apple Cider — small, medium, large, jumbo

12

2.

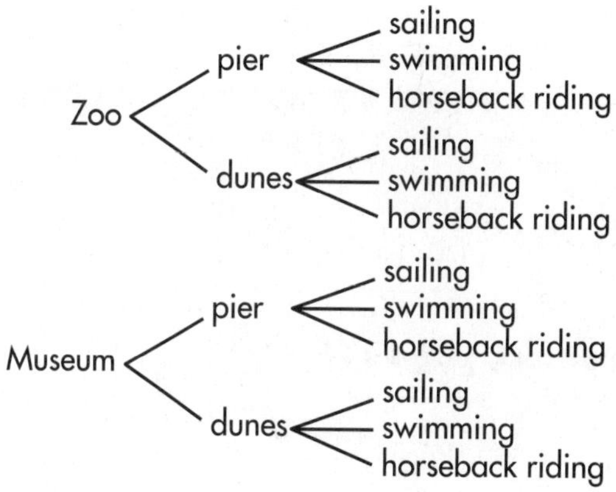

Zoo
- pier — sailing, swimming, horseback riding
- dunes — sailing, swimming, horseback riding

Museum
- pier — sailing, swimming, horseback riding
- dunes — sailing, swimming, horseback riding

12

Lesson 9.12, page 114

1. $\frac{3}{10}$ **2.** $\frac{2}{5}$ **3.** $\frac{1}{5}$ **4.** $\frac{1}{10}$ **5.** $\frac{1}{2}$ **6.** $\frac{1}{3}$ **7.** $\frac{1}{6}$
8. $\frac{1}{6}$ **9.** $\frac{1}{6}$ **10.** $\frac{1}{3}$

Posttest, page 115

1.

Stem	Leaves
9	1 2 3 6 7 7 8
10	1 3 4 5 8
11	1 2 5

Key: 9 | 1 = 91

Grade 7 Answers

2. Note: Answers will vary depending on intervals chosen in column 1. Here is one possible answer.

Cars	Frequency	Cumulative Frequency	Relative Frequency
91–95	3	3	20%
96–100	4	7	26.67%
101–105	4	11	26.67%
106–110	1	12	6.67%
111–115	3	15	20%

3.

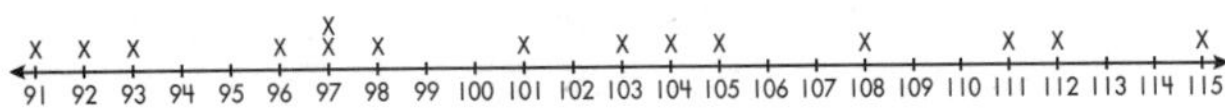

4.

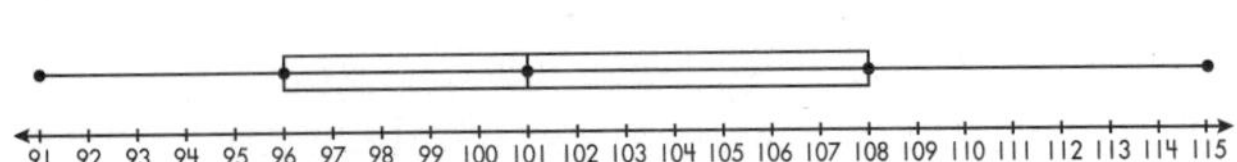

	a	b
5.	101.5	24
	101	108
	97	96

Posttest, page 116

6.

Racing — red, black, silver

Mountain — red, black, silver

7. 6 **8.** $\frac{1}{2}$ **9.** $\frac{1}{3}$ **10.** $\frac{1}{6}$ **11.** 4 **12.** 72°

13. 4–6 **14.** 0–3

15.

Weekly Exercise

Number of People: 4, 8, 12, 16

Hours: 0–3, 4–6, 7–9, 10–12

Chapter 10

Pretest, page 117

	a	b	c
1.	point T	$\overline{RS}$ or $\overline{SR}$	$\overleftrightarrow{XY}$ or $\overleftrightarrow{YX}$
2.	$\overrightarrow{DC}$	$\overleftrightarrow{JK}$ or $\overleftrightarrow{KJ}$	$\overline{QR}$ or $\overline{RQ}$
3.	$\angle RST$ or $\angle TSR$	$\overrightarrow{SR}$, $\overrightarrow{ST}$	S
4.	$\angle ABC$ or $\angle CBA$	$\overrightarrow{BA}$, $\overrightarrow{BC}$	B

5. $\overleftrightarrow{AB}$ and $\overleftrightarrow{CD}$

6. 60° **7.** acute **8.** $\angle 9$ **9.** $\angle 5$ or $\angle 7$

10. $\overleftrightarrow{RS}$; alternate exterior

11. $\overleftrightarrow{TU}$; alternate interior

12. $\overleftrightarrow{AB}$; alternate exterior

13. $\overleftrightarrow{TU}$; corresponding

Pretest, page 118

	a	b	c
14.	right, isosceles	acute, equilateral	obtuse, scalene
15.	trapezoid	octagon	rectangle
16.	pentagon	hexagon	parallelogram

17. reflection **18.** (4, −1) **19.** (−4, 5) **20.** U

21. N **22.** III **23.** yes

Lesson 10.1, page 119

	a	b
1.	RS; SR	$\overleftrightarrow{RS}$; $\overleftrightarrow{SR}$
2.	PQ; QP	$\overleftrightarrow{PQ}$; $\overleftrightarrow{QP}$
3.	MN; NM	$\overleftrightarrow{MN}$; $\overleftrightarrow{NM}$

	a	b	c
4.	XY; YX	$\overline{XY}$; $\overline{YX}$	X; Y
5.	AB; BA	$\overline{AB}$; $\overline{BA}$	A; B
6.	CD; DC	$\overline{CD}$; $\overline{DC}$	C; D

7–9 Answers will vary. Sample answers are shown.

	a	b
7.	$\overleftrightarrow{TU}$	$\overleftrightarrow{OP}$
8.	$\overline{GH}$	$\overleftrightarrow{JK}$
9.	$\overline{XY}$	$\overline{WX}$

Grade 7 Answers

Lesson 10.2, page 120

	a	b
1.	AB ; $\overrightarrow{AB}$	A
2.	CD ; $\overrightarrow{CD}$	C
3.	FE ; $\overrightarrow{FE}$	F
4.	GHI ; IHG	∠GHI ∠IHG
	$\overrightarrow{HG}$; $\overrightarrow{HI}$	H
5.	JKL ; LKJ	∠JKL ∠LKJ
	$\overrightarrow{KJ}$; $\overrightarrow{KL}$	K
6.	MNO ; ONM	∠MNO ∠ONM
	$\overrightarrow{NM}$; $\overrightarrow{NO}$	N

7.

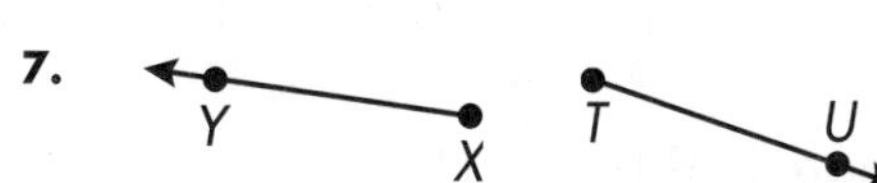

8.

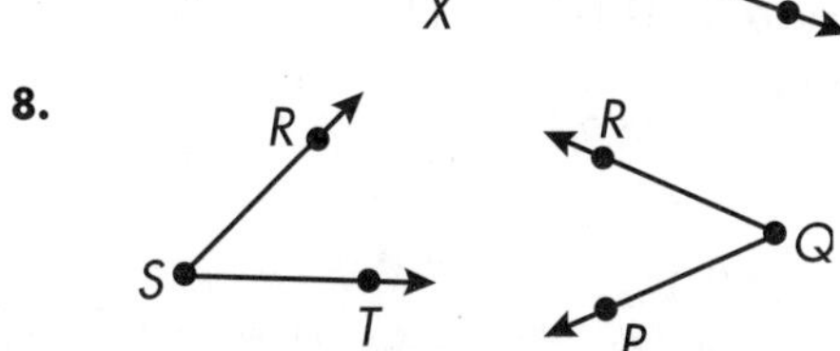

Lesson 10.3, page 121

	a	b
1.	60°; acute	90°; right
2.	120°; obtuse	30°; acute
3.	140°; obtuse	80°; acute

Lesson 10.4, page 122

1. ∠GHJ or ∠GHM
2. ∠FHG
3. ∠JMK or ∠IMH
4. $\overrightarrow{ML}$
5. ∠CFD
6. ∠GFE
7. 77°
8. 68°
9. 52°; 104°

Lesson 10.5, page 123

1. $\overleftrightarrow{RS}$; corresponding
2. $\overleftrightarrow{AB}$; alternate interior
3. $\overleftrightarrow{RS}$; corresponding
4. $\overleftrightarrow{TU}$; alternate exterior
5. $\overleftrightarrow{TU}$; alternate interior
6. $\overleftrightarrow{CD}$; alternate exterior
7. $\overleftrightarrow{TU}$; alternate exterior
8. $\overleftrightarrow{TU}$; corresponding
9. $\overleftrightarrow{AB}$; alternate interior
10. $\overleftrightarrow{CD}$; alternate interior
11. $\overleftrightarrow{RS}$; corresponding
12. $\overleftrightarrow{TU}$; corresponding

Lesson 10.6, page 124

	a	b	c
1.	acute	right	acute
2.	obtuse	obtuse	right
3.	obtuse	acute	right
4.	right	obtuse	acute

Lesson 10.7, page 125

	a	b	c
1.	scalene	equilateral	scalene
2.	isosceles	scalene	isosceles
3.	equilateral	scalene	isosceles

Lesson 10.8, page 126

1. rectangle and square
2. rhombus and square
3. no
4. yes
5. yes
6. no
7. yes

	a	b
8.	trapezoid	square, rhombus, rectangle, parallelogram
9.	parallelogram	rectangle, parallelogram

Lesson 10.9, page 127

	a	b
1.	heptagon	decagon
2.	nonagon	pentagon
3.	octagon	hexagon
4.	heptagon	nonagon

Lesson 10.10, page 128

	a	b
1.	$\frac{AB}{XY}=\frac{BC}{YZ}$ $\frac{1}{2}=\frac{1}{2}$ similar	$\frac{AB}{WX}=\frac{BC}{XY}$ $\frac{2.3}{1.5}\neq\frac{1.5}{1}$ not similar
2.	$\frac{AB}{TU}=\frac{BC}{UV}=\frac{CD}{VW}=\frac{DE}{WX}=\frac{EA}{XT}$ $\frac{2}{3}=\frac{2}{3}\neq\frac{1}{2}\neq\frac{1}{1}\neq\frac{1}{2}$ not similar	$\frac{AB}{WX}=\frac{BC}{XY}=\frac{CD}{YZ}=\frac{DA}{ZW}$ $\frac{6}{3}=\frac{12}{6}=\frac{10}{5}=\frac{5}{2.5}$ similar

Lesson 10.11, page 129

	a	b
1.	*D*	*A*
2.	*E*	*C*
3.	*F*	*B*
4.	(−4, 3)	(−4, −2)
5.	(−2, −3)	(1, −3)
6.	(2, 1)	(2, 3)

7–9. See grid for points A, B, C, D, E, and F.

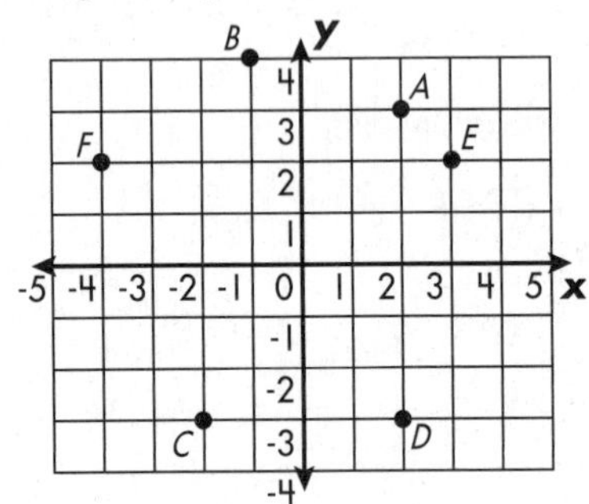

Lesson 10.12, page 130

	a	b	c
1.	translation	translation	reflection
2.	reflection	dilation	rotation
3.	translation	rotation	dilation

Posttest, page 131

	a	b	c
1.	$\overline{MN}$ or $\overline{NM}$	point *P*	$\overleftrightarrow{KL}$ or $\overleftrightarrow{LK}$
2.	$\overrightarrow{XY}$	$\overline{RS}$ or $\overline{SR}$	$\overrightarrow{FG}$
3.	∠*TUV* or ∠*VUT*	$\overrightarrow{UT}$, $\overrightarrow{UV}$	*U*
4.	∠*HIJ* or ∠*JIH*	$\overrightarrow{IH}$, $\overrightarrow{IJ}$	*I*

5. ∠8 **6.** ∠10 or ∠12

7. $\overleftrightarrow{WX}$ and $\overleftrightarrow{YZ}$

8. 110° **9.** obtuse

10. $\overleftrightarrow{PQ}$; alternate exterior

11. $\overleftrightarrow{RS}$; corresponding

12. $\overleftrightarrow{YZ}$; alternate interior

Posttest, page 132

	a	b	c
13.	acute, isosceles	right, scalene	obtuse, scalene
14.	square	pentagon	decagon
15.	rhombus	heptagon	hexagon

16. slide **17.** rotation **18.** (3, −2) **19.** *l*

20. *B* **21.** (−3, 1)

22. yes; $\frac{AB}{GH} = \frac{BC}{HI} = \frac{CA}{IG}$

Chapter 11

Pretest, page 133

	a	b	c
1.	10 yd.	11.3 cm	35 ft.
2.	21 cm	12 m	8 in.
3.	50.24 m	43.96 ft.	232.36 yd.
4.	28.26 sq. cm	133 sq. in.	200.96 sq. mm

Pretest, page 134

5. 124 sq. m; 72 cubic m

6. 390 sq. in.; 378 cubic in.

7. 130.5 sq. cm; 85 cubic cm

8. 1435 sq. ft.; 2992 cubic ft.

	a	b	c
9.	252 cubic ft.	360 cubic m	25 cubic yd.

10. 6 ft.; 263.76 sq. ft.; 310.86 cubic ft.

11. 9 cm; 791.28 sq. cm; 1271.7 cubic cm

12. 5 m; 290.45 sq. m; 314 cubic m

13. 19 in.; 6085.32 sq. in.; 36273.28 cubic in.

Lesson 11.1, page 135

	a	b	c
1.	14 ft.	13 yd.	12.5 m
2.	$7\frac{1}{4}$	64 cm	45 yd.
3.	44 ft.	9 m	12 in.
4.	12 m	19.2 cm	80 yd.

Lesson 11.2, page 136

	a	b	c
1.	18 sq. yd.	324 sq. m	276 sq. cm
2.	216 sq. km	529 sq. in.	48 sq. ft.
3.	9 in.	13 ft.	9 m
4.	13 cm	75 m	36.8 yd.

Lesson 11.3, page 137

	a	b	c
1.	27.5 sq. ft.	48 sq. yd.	104.5 sq. in.
2.	10 sq. ft.	123.25 sq. cm	32 sq. m
3.	1330 sq. mm	378 sq. in.	10.5 sq. yd.

Grade 7 Answers

Lesson 11.4, page 138

1. 138 ft. **2.** 108 sq. in. **3.** 12 m **4.** 54 in.
5. 1271 sq. cm **6.** $10\frac{5}{8}$ **7.** 8 in.; 8 in.

Lesson 11.5, page 139

	a	b	c
1.	1.5 ft.	0.75 ft.	
2.		1.75 m	10.99 m
3.	6.5 in.		20.41 in.
4.	8.5 yd.	4.25 yd.	
5.		3.75 cm	23.55 cm
6.	30 in.		94.2 in.
7.	2.5 m	1.25 m	
8.		2.5 km	15.7 km
9.	10 ft.	5 ft.	
10.	90 cm		282.6 cm
11.		2 yd.	12.56 yd.
12.	3 mi.	1.5 mi.	

Lesson 11.6, page 140

	a	b	c
1.	50.2 sq. ft.	113 sq. m	530.7 sq. cm
2.	1017.4 sq. yd.	452.2 sq. km	153.9 sq. in.
3.	6 in.		28.3 sq. in.
4.		9 ft.	254.3 sq. ft.
5.		8.5 m	226.9 sq. m
6.	64 cm		3215.4 sq. cm
7.		15 km	706.5 sq. km
8.	12 yd.		113 sq. yd.

Lesson 11.7, page 141

	a	b	c
1.	52 sq. ft.	48 sq. m	24 sq. cm
2.	185 sq. yd.	9 sq. mi.	20 sq. in.
3.	25 sq. ft.	72 sq. in.	77 sq. cm

Lesson 11.8, page 142

	a	b	c
1.	62 sq. in.	48.7 sq. ft.	172 sq. yd.
2.	856 sq. cm	104 sq. m	248 sq. in.
3.	85.5 sq. ft.	2970 sq. mm	81.44 sq. cm

Lesson 11.9, page 143

	a	b	c
1.	18 cubic ft.	16 cubic m	135 cubic in.
2.	672 cubic cm	28 cubic yd.	672 cubic ft.
3.	27 cubic in.	10.5 cubic m	1035 cubic cm

Lesson 11.10, page 144

1. 7.85 in. **2.** 2289.06 sq. cm **3.** 76.5 sq. in.
4. 404 sq. m **5.** 30000 cubic cm **6.** 252 sq. in.

Lesson 11.11, page 145

	a	b	c
1.	1485 cubic in.	15 cubic m	22.5 cubic cm
2.	63 cubic ft.	3.75 cubic yd.	12.8 cubic in.
3.	3.9375 cubic m	15.456 cubic ft.	96.32 cubic cm

Lesson 11.12, page 146

	a	b	c
1.	376.8 sq. in.	1055.04 sq. ft.	5224.96 sq. mm
2.	37.68 sq. yd.	596.6 sq. cm	1004.8 sq. ft.
3.	173.328 sq. m	1099 sq. in.	2417.8 sq. cm

Lesson 11.13, page 147

	a	b	c
1.	16076.8 cubic in.	3538.78 cubic cm	747.7596 cubic ft.
2.	1582.56 cubic m	8440.32 cubic mm	87.92 cubic in.
3.	26660.013 cubic mm	2034.72 cubic yd.	4876.9224 cubic cm

Lesson 11.14, page 148

1. 13.5 cubic m **2.** 40 cubic cm **3.** 2 in.
4. 593.46 sq. cm; 1049.1525 cubic cm
5. 252.77 sq. in.; 307.72 cubic in.
6. 104.248 sq. m; 79.128 cubic m

Posttest, page 149

	a	b	c
1.	12 m	16 ft.	20 cm
2.	36 in.	20 yd.	55 mm
3.	81.64 m	56.52 cm	21.98 ft.
4.	63.585 sq. in.	75 sq. m	28 sq. yd.
5.	169 sq. cm	1296 sq. ft.	452.16 sq. mm

Posttest, page 150

6. 122 sq. yd. 72 cubic yd.
7. 45 sq. m 18 cubic m
8. 1976 sq. mm 5796 cubic mm
9. 93 sq. in. 45 cubic in.

	a	b	c
10.	3024 cubic in.	180 cubic cm	38.25 cubic m
11.	1.5 m	89.49 sq. m	56.52 cubic m
12.	4 yd.	113.04 sq. yd.	87.92 cubic yd.
13.	11 in.	3108.6 sq. in.	12917.96 cubic in.
14.	14 cm	439.6 sq. cm	461.58 cubic cm

Grade 7 Answers

Chapter 12

Pretest, page 151

	a	b
1.	$n - 5$	$b + 8$
2.	$n \div 6$	$2 \times n$
3.	$3 + n = 12$	$x - 6 = 19$
4.	$30 \div n = 3$	$5 \times n = 15$

	a	b	c
5.	6	9	12
6.	15	4	22
7.	14	12	16
8.	17	4	0
9.	5	6	7
10.	3	4	6
11.	36	42	14
12.	18	60	72

Pretest, page 152

	a	b	c
13.	5	24	20
14.	8	8	5
15.	−1	1	3
16.	−11	−1	−13
17.	−6	7	−6
18.	−5	9	−1
19.	−42	−12	10
20.	−20	16	−24
21.	−3	3	−3
22.	3	−5	−3
23.	243	64	64
24.	25	64	4096
25.	0.0625	0.33333	0.0016
26.	0.11111	0.16666	0.25

Lesson 12.1, page 153

1a. variable expression **1b.** equation **1c.** inequality
2a. numerical expression **2b.** inequality
2c. equation

	a	b
3.	$d + 3$	$8 \times w$
4.	$12 - 7$	$n + 2$
5.	$n \div 6$	$15 + 9$
6.	$5 + 6 = 11$	$12 \div s = 4$
7.	$t - 3 > 5$	$2 \times b > 4$
8.	$5 \times 3 = y$	$20 \div n = 5$

Lesson 12.2, page 154

	a	b
1.	commutative	associative
2.	identity	commutative
3.	associative	zero
4.	identity	commutative
5.	zero	associative
6.	$3 + (7 + y)$	642
7.	$z \times 15$	0
8.	$12a$	$(14 \times 3) \times p$
9.	0	$16 + 49$
10.	$d + 3$	$6 \times (4 \times n)$

Lesson 12.3, page 155

	a	b
1.	$a \times (4 + 3)$	$(b \times 6) + (b \times 12)$
2.	$(4 \times a) + (4 \times b)$	$3 \times (a + b)$
3.	$d \times (5 - 2)$	$(5 \times 8) + (5 \times p)$
4.	$(d \times 8) - (d \times h)$	$(12 \times s) - (12 \times 10)$
5.	$(r \times 16) + (r \times s)$	$35 \times (t + y)$
6.	$8 \times (a + b)$	$(r \times q) - (r \times s)$
7.	$6 \times (12 - w)$	$(p \times 15) + (p \times z)$
8.	$(15 \times y) + (15 \times 0)$	$d \times (d + b)$
9.	$a \times (2 + 3 + 4)$	$(p \times a) + (p \times b) + (p \times 4)$
10.	$a \times (b + c - d)$	$(8 \times a) + (8 \times b) + (8 \times c)$

Lesson 12.4, page 156

	a	b	c
1.	16	11	19
2.	17	33	2
3.	9	28	28
4.	36	3	7
5.	14	5	4
6.	1	4	2
7.	7	5	10
8.	18	5	45
9.	7	11	17
10.	6	3	5
11.	9	9	7
12.	6	12	8
13.	16	32	140
14.	11	43	17

Lesson 12.5, page 157

	a	b	c
1.	7	6	15
2.	14	2	22
3.	33	13	0
4.	23	0	15
5.	14	24	1
6.	6	6	24

7. $21 + n = 37$; 16
8. $n - 9 = 33$; 42
9. $2 + 5 + n = 25$; 18

Grade 7 Answers

Lesson 12.6, page 158

	a	b	c
1.	9	5	6
2.	12	27	15
3.	8	1	6
4.	50	36	48
5.	5	0	16
6.	19	28	63

7. $6 \times n = 12$ or $12 \div 6 = n$; 2
8. $48 \div n = 12$ or $48 \div 12 = n$; 4
9. $25 \times n = 150$ or $150 \div 25 = n$; 6

Lesson 12.7, page 159

	a	b	c	d
1.	8	5	−2	5
2.	−8	3	−10	10
3.	3	−9	−1	−23
4.	−15	1	−5	−11
5.	−16	−11	2	−5
6.	−15	−10	43	−15
7.	−9	1	−1	0
8.	0	−11	−4	−1
9.	0	−3	−10	11
10.	7	9	−16	4

Lesson 12.8, page 160

	a	b	c	d
1.	6	−24	−24	12
2.	3	−4	−2	−3
3.	−56	−30	24	−44
4.	−7	−2	−4	4
5.	−32	4	−88	70
6.	−27	−7	11	2
7.	40	−36	26	−81
8.	−3	−19	19	−7
9.	−17	−10	−42	35
10.	−1	−2	6	−9

Lesson 12.9, page 161

	a	b	c
1.	49	512	64
2.	100	6561	161051
3.	4913	15625	1296
4.	9261	65536	248832
5.	8^5; 32768	3^6; 729	2^4; 16
6.	7^2; 49	9^2; 81	16^2; 256
7.	6^5; 7776	4^6; 4096	3^4; 81
8.	10^2; 100	8^1; 8	7^3; 343
9.	5^5; 3125	10^7; 10000000	15^3; 3375
10.	2^5; 32	3^2; 9	6^3; 216

Lesson 12.10, page 162

	a	b	c
1.	$\frac{1}{3^2}$; 0.1111	$\frac{1}{6^3}$; 0.0046	$\frac{1}{8^2}$; 0.0156
2.	$\frac{1}{7^3}$; 0.0029	$\frac{1}{3^3}$; 0.0370	$\frac{1}{9^2}$; 0.0123
3.	$\frac{1}{4^3}$; 0.0156	$\frac{1}{5^2}$; 0.04	$\frac{1}{2^3}$; 0.125
4.	$\frac{1}{2^4}$; 0.0625	$\frac{1}{10^3}$; 0.001	$\frac{1}{1^4}$; 1
5.	0.00098	0.03125	0.00412
6.	0.00077	0.00006	0.01235
7.	0.01563	0.00292	0.125
8.	0.0625	0.01563	0.03704
9.	0.0625	0.04	0.00463
10.	0.00412	0.00391	0.125

Posttest, page 163

	a	b
1.	$n - 7$	$n + 8$
2.	$6 \times n$	$n \div 12$
3.	$4 \times n = 16$	$n + 9 = 11$
4.	$n - 3 = 20$	$25 \div b = 5$

	a	b	c
5.	7	5	21
6.	12	18	12
7.	5	8	11
8.	1	4	6
9.	9	5	5
10.	5	31	6
11.	33	54	16
12.	28	21	24

Posttest, page 164

	a	b	c
13.	6	15	16
14.	8	6	2
15.	−2	4	−7
16.	3	−3	−12
17.	−3	17	−10
18.	−3	15	−10
19.	−12	−18	16
20.	30	−63	6
21.	−2	−4	10
22.	−1	−17	−23
23.	16	243	216
24.	49	512	125
25.	0.03704	0.03125	0.0625
26.	0.33333	0.00292	0.25

Grade 7 Answers

Final Test

Page 165

	a	b	c	d
1.	$\frac{3}{40}$	$\frac{2}{7}$	$1\frac{27}{28}$	$3\frac{5}{24}$
2.	$\frac{11}{16}$	$2\frac{6}{7}$	$15\frac{1}{6}$	$\frac{29}{36}$
3.	$1\frac{5}{7}$	$\frac{6}{7}$	$1\frac{7}{8}$	$2\frac{7}{9}$
4.	$2\frac{8}{15}$	$1\frac{7}{27}$	$32\frac{1}{2}$	$1\frac{1}{6}$

5. $21; $371
6. $113.40; $833.40
7. $56.95; $1396.95
8. $85.50; $685.50

	a	b	c
9.	12	4	8
10.	24	32	36

Page 166

	a	b	c
11.	5720 yd.	63 in.	56 oz.
12.	$3\frac{1}{4}$ days	3 hr. 43 min.	14 pt.
13.	0.340 km	70 cm	1200 mg
14.	0.350 kL	1.246 kg	1.382 L

15. **Quiz Scores**

Stem	Leaves
0	8 9 9
1	0 1 2 3 4 5 6 7 7 8
2	0 1 2 2 2 3 3

Key: 0 | 8 = 8

16. **Quiz Scores**

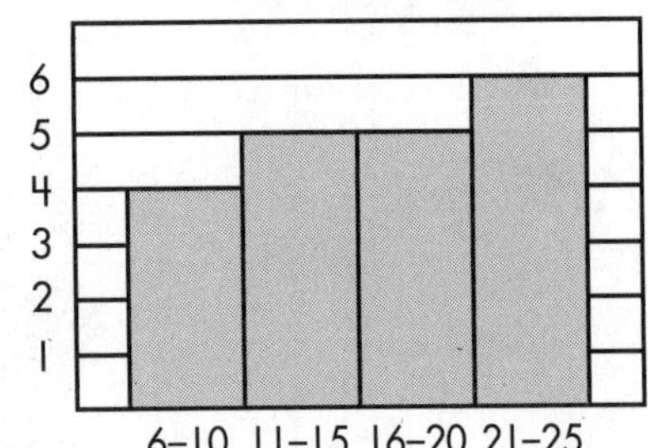

17. 16.1; 22
16.5; 15

18. 25% **19.** 23 **20.** 8 **21.** 30%

Page 167

	a	b	c
22.	20 yd.	17 m	28 in.
23.	126 sq. cm	324 sq. mm	176 sq. ft.
24.	50.24 cm	37.68 in.	113.04 yd.
	200.96 sq. cm	113.04 sq. in.	1017.36 sq. yd.
25.	812 sq. in.	2512 sq. ft.	182 sq. cm
26.	339.12 cubic in.	313.5 cubic cm	60 cubic m

Page 168

	a	b	c
27.	17	4	19
28.	17	18	8
29.	6	3	11
30.	25	40	60
31.	50	6	34
32.	−2	−5	−1
33.	−14	−3	26
34.	−12	−12	27
35.	−2	−2	7
36.	−10	−5	−10
37.	8	81	32
38.	0.03125	0.33333	0.25
39.	−1	0	−6
40.	13	4	7